S0-BSD-563

The Making of Modern German Christology

The Making of Modern German Christology

From the Enlightenment to Pannenberg

Alister E. McGrath

Basil Blackwell

First published 1986

Basil Blackwell Ltd
108 Cowley Road, Oxford OX4 1JF, UK

Basil Blackwell Inc.
432 South Park Avenue South, Suite 1505,
New York, NY 10016, USA

British Library Cataloguing in Publication Data

McGrath, Alister E.
The making of modern German Christology: from the Enlightenment to Pannenberg.
1. Jesus Christ—History of doctrines
2. Protestant churches—History 3. Theology, Doctrinal—History—Modern period, 1500–
I. Title
232'.0943 BT198

ISBN 0-631-14512-5

Library of Congress Cataloging in Publication Data

McGrath, Alister E., 1953–
The making of modern German Christology.

Bibliography: p.
Includes index.
1. Jesus Christ—History of doctrines. 2. Theology, Doctrinal—Germany—History. 3. Protestant churches—Germany—Doctrines—History. I. Title.
BT198.M399 1986 232 85-26710
ISBN 0-631-14512-5

Typeset by Finlandia Press, Gerrards Cross, Buckinghamshire
Printed in Great Britain by
The Bath Press, Avon

Contents

Acknowledgements

The present work is intended as an introduction to the themes, problems and personalities associated with the development of the Christology of modern German-speaking Protestantism. An undertaking of this nature owes much to many. I wish to acknowledge with particular gratitude the assistance generously rendered by Prof. Dr Gerhard Ebeling, Prof. Dr Eberhard Jüngel, Professor John Macquarrie, Prof. Dr Jürgen Moltmann, Mr Robert Morgan, Prof. Dr Wolfhart Pannenberg, Prof. Dr Gerhard Sauter and Prof. Dr Reinhard Slenczka. The substance of this book derives from a lecture course for Oxford University Faculty of Theology on 'The Problems of Christology from the Enlightenment to Pannenberg', and I am grateful to my students for their many invaluable comments and suggestions. My thanks are also due to the publishers, for their remarkable efficiency and enthusiasm. Finally, I wish to record once more my continuing appreciation of the staff and students of Wycliffe Hall, Oxford, for providing such an outstanding environment in which to study and to teach.

Introduction

The present work is intended to introduce to English speaking readers the main themes, problems and personalities associated with the development of the Christology of modern German-speaking Protestantism. It makes no claim to be exhaustive or totally comprehensive, but merely attempts to introduce a fascinating and important area of modern theology to those who would otherwise find themselves bewildered by its complexity, and unable to appreciate its full significance. Numerous excellent introductions of this type already exist in the German language:[1] the present work is not, however, based upon any of them, but represents an attempt to interpret, explain and evaluate the development of modern German Christology from outside the tradition upon which it is based.

At the heart of the Christian faith lies the question of the significance of Jesus Christ, and the subsequent intellectual struggle within the community of faith to articulate the significance of this event for those within and without the church, which continues to this day. Since the time of the Enlightenment, however, the traditional Christian understandings of the significance of Christ have been called into question through the rise of critical presuppositions and methods. The Enlightenment marked a decisive and irreversible change in the social, political and religious outlook of Western Europe. Modern theology may be said to have begun with the Enlightenment, in that that movement both raised the critical questions to which Christian theology has been forced to address itself, and, to a certain extent, dictated the means by which these questions might be answered. In view of the fact that the Enlightenment is now widely recognized as constituting the most significant development in the intellectual history of the Christian faith – far surpassing even the Reformation in this respect – it is proper to argue that it defines the *terminus a quo* from which any account of modern theology in general, and modern Christology in particular, must begin.[2]

The central Christological problem of the present day is not the ontological problem which dominated the patristic period,[3] but the question of the relationship between revelation and history.[4] The replacement of a predominantly metaphysical understanding of reality by an essentially historical understanding during the later Enlightenment necessitated a transformation of the traditional approaches to Christology, with consequences which are still the subject of intense debate within theological circles. The rise of critical historical thought brought to an end the era of metaphysical thought inherited from classical antiquity, which dominated Protestant theology until the late seventeenth century, and which still exercises considerable influence in England. No longer could the Christian revelation be regarded as something essentially distinct from nature and history: everything in history must be regarded as possessing the same historical nature and reality, and be open to critical investigation as an aspect of that history. The Christological task of transforming the *factum esse* of the past to the *fieri* of the present cannot now proceed without dealing with the problem of the 'ugly great ditch' (*garstige, breite Graben*) of history.[5] It must be emphasized that the new interest in the historical figure of Jesus did not arise from purely historical or scholarly motives, being an important aspect of the *Aufklärung* attempt to escape the limitations of dogma.[6] The attempt to discover the historical figure of Jesus of Nazareth who actually lived in first century Palestine through the means of the newly established historiographical methods was based upon the presupposition that this real historical figure had become obscured and distorted through the doctrinal presentations of him in the New Testament, the creeds and the Christian church. Schweitzer's words are to be taken seriously:

> A 'life of Jesus' can be written out of hate – and the greatest of their kind were written with hate: that of Reimarus, the Wolfenbüttel Fragmentist, and that of David Friedrich Strauss. It was not so much hate directed against the person of Jesus as against the supernatural nimbus with which he had come to be surrounded. They wished to represent him as a simple man, to remove the splendid robes which had been placed upon him, and clothe him once more with the rags in which he had wandered in Galilee.[7]

The Christological significance of the new historical positivism of the *Aufklärung* lay in the challenge which it posed to the metaphysical Christologies of Orthodoxy, and the restriction which it imposed upon the means by which this challenge might be met. The metaphysical foundations of theological supernaturalism were called into question through the rise of an historical understanding, and its associated critical historical method, which defined the arena within which the development of modern Christology would take place. As Ernst Troeltsch remarked, the very phrase 'purely historical' (*rein historisch*) implies a complete *Weltanschauung*, which embraced theology as much as it did every other aspect of existence. 'The historical method is a leaven which, once applied to biblical science and church history, alters everything until it finally explodes the entire structure of theological methods employed until the present.'[8] Whereas the theologians of Orthodoxy had been forced to come to terms with the Cartesian universalization of method,[9] their successors were forced to come to terms with the universal historicization of reality: either something is history, and open to critical historical investigation, or it does not exist: there is no alternative. What is of decisive importance in this respect is not so much the development of increasingly refined methods of historical enquiry by which reality might be investigated, but the radical historicization (*Historisierung*) of man himself, of his ways of thinking, and of reality as a whole. The alleged revelation of God to mankind must be regarded as having taken place within universal history, and thus be open to critical historical enquiry.[10] This challenge to traditional Christian understandings of the nature of revelation and the authority of the Bible was widely seen to be concentrated in and focused upon the question of the identity and significance of Jesus of Nazareth. Although this challenge was either ignored or dealt with in a characteristically undistinguished manner in English, and particularly Anglican, theological circles (Anglicans tending to follow Lightfoot in defending the doctrine of the Incarnation by maintaining the essential historicity of the gospels), it was met with some brilliance by their German counterparts. The development of German Protestant Christology in the last two centuries may thus be regarded as embodying and concentrating the critical questions which have exercised so decisive an influence over Christian theology in general during the period.

The present study is concerned with the main themes and personalities which have dominated the Christology of modern German-speaking Protestantism from the *Aufklärung* to the present day, with particular emphasis being placed upon the development of the doctrine since the end of the First World War. In effect, the development of the Christology of modern German-speaking Protestantism may be treated as a continuous narrative, the significance of any aspect of that development being determined by its context and consequences. The student who wishes to fully appreciate the contribution of modern writers on Christology, such as Wolfhart Pannenberg or Jürgen Moltmann, can only do so by becoming familiar with the problems of Christology, as perceived by the modern period, as well as the previously existing solutions to these problems (and their inevitable shortcomings), in order that the distinctiveness and significance of their contribution to this debate may be fully appreciated. It is hoped that this work will assist him in this process of understanding and evaluation. Although the present study is arranged primarily on the basis of strict chronology, it has proved possible to integrate much of the material thematically, which should assist the reader previously unfamiliar with the field.

The study opens with an analysis of the intellectual outlook of the Enlightenment of the eighteenth century in general, and the *Aufklärung* in particular, in order that the initial impact of the new critical historical approach to dogma in general, and the Christological dogma in particular, may be appreciated. These trends are illustrated with reference to Gotthold Ephraim Lessing. The origins of the *Leben-Jesu-Bewegung* are also shown to lie in this period of anti-dogmatism, and its initial forms are documented, with particular reference to Hermann Samuel Reimarus. The development of the cognitive crisis within the later *Aufklärung* sets the context for the assessment of the Christology of F. D. E. Schleiermacher.

In the second chapter, the Hegelian critique of Schleiermacher's *Vermittlungstheologie* is considered. After an analysis of the relationship of *Vorstellung* and *Begriff* within the context of Hegel's Christology, the criticism of Schleiermacher's mediating position by David Friedrich Strauss, Ferdinand Christian Baur and Ludwig Feuerbach in the fourth and fifth decades of the nineteenth century is considered. The third chapter deals with the rise of the 'liberal portrait of Christ' in the aftermath of the collapse of the Hegelian movement during the fifth and sixth decades of the century, with particular reference to Albrecht Ritschl and Adolf von Harnack. In the fourth chapter, the destruction of the foundations of this Christology in the final decades of the pre-war period is discussed, with particular reference to the apocalypticism of Johannes Weiss and Albert Schweitzer, the scepticism of William Wrede, the dogmatic critique of the *Leben-Jesu-Bewegung* of Martin

Kähler, and the radical critical historicism of Ernst Troeltsch.

In many respects, the First World War may be regarded as a turning-point in the development of the Christology of modern German-speaking Protestantism. The fifth chapter documents the development of the new theocentrism in Christology with particular reference to Karl Barth and Emil Brunner, and the sixth the rise of the 'kerygmatic' Christologies of Rudulf Bultmann, Gerhard Ebeling and Paul Tillich (who, although an *émigré* from National Socialist Germany, remained within its theological orbit). The Christological significance of the 'New Quest of the Historical Jesus' is explored in the seventh chapter, with particular reference to Ernst Käsemann, Günther Bornkamm and Wolfhart Pannenberg, while the eighth chapter deals with the new Christocentric 'theology of the cross' associated with Jürgen Moltmann and Eberhard Jüngel, perhaps one of the most exciting developments in modern theology. A final chapter concludes the study by considering the general trends underlying the development of the Christology of modern German-speaking Protestantism.

A major obstacle previously placed in the path of any serious attempt on the part of an English-speaking theologian to come to terms with modern German theology, despite its inherent brilliance and fascination, is now gradually disappearing. In the half-century since 1914, the equivalent of a theological iron curtain appears to have descended upon Europe, excluding ideas of German origin from the theological fora of the English-speaking world,[11] to their inevitable impoverishment. The origins of this isolation of these two theological traditions are complex, bound up with historical, social, political and cultural considerations which defy crude generalizations (such as the appeal to the different 'religious tempers' or 'national mentalities' to explain why England has never produced any theologians of consequence since William of Ockham). This trend has now been reversed, to the extent that a new generation of theologians is emerging within that world, unwilling to accept their predecessors' dismissal of such ideas. Although the problem of cultural distance remains, it is to be hoped that this development will lead to an enrichment of the theology of English-speaking Christendom, and an increasingly fruitful cross-fertilization of ideas.[12]

A more permanent obstacle, however, remains in the form of the German language itself. Many seminal works of German theology in general, and Christology in particular, have never been translated into English. Furthermore, there are serious difficulties associated with the very translation process itself. Well-established English translations (such as 'projection' for *Vergegenständigung*, or 'abolition' for *Aufhebung*) often serve only to conceal, rather than illuminate, the meaning of the German original. Furthermore, certain terms have come to have a technical significance (such as the Hegelian term *Vorstellung*), which is frequently overlooked or obscured by translators. All too many English-language studies of leading German theologians betray a purely superficial engagement with their ideas precisely because they are totally dependent upon mediocre translations which have not been checked against the original (this does not, of course, imply that the translations are necessarily *inaccurate*, although this is, in fact, occasionally the case: rather, we wish to emphasize the need to know precisely what technical German term or phrase is being translated, what allusions are being made, and so on). It must be emphasized that a knowledge of the German language is as essential to the study of German theology as a knowledge of Greek is to that of the New Testament. The present study, however, attempts to minimize the difficulties experienced by the student unfamiliar with the German language by introducing him to technical terms as they occur, and referring him to good English translations of German original works and reliable secondary studies in the English language, where these exist. It is hoped that the reader already familiar with German will not find such accommodations to his weaker brethren intolerable. Extensive reference is also made, where possible, to further studies which relate the matters discussed to other developments, and permit the reader to take his studies as deep as his requirements dictate. A bibliography of important primary and secondary works published in German or English is included.

Finally, it is necessary to apologize for the shortcomings which restrictions upon space have forced upon this study. Had space permitted, it would not have proved necessary to omit writers such as Dietrich Bonhoeffer; others, such as Wilhelm Herrmann and Friedrich Gogarten, deserve to be treated better than has proved possible here. Perhaps it may eventually prove possible to expand this work to remedy these deficiencies, of which the present writer is only too painfully aware. It is, however, hoped that the present work will serve to introduce a new generation of students to ideas and personalities which have dominated the development of modern Christology, and by doing so will increase the quality of a future generation of theologians, perhaps even to bring nearer the day when the present, fully merited theological hegemony of the German-speaking world will be ended.

NOTES

1 See Ernst-Heinz Amberg, *Christologie und Dogmatik: Untersuchung ihres Verhältnisses in der evangelischen Theologie der Gegenwart* (Göttingen, 1966); Wilhelm Dantine, *Jesus von Nazareth in der gegenwärtigen Diskussion* (Gütersloh, 1974); Hermann Dembowski, *Einführung in die Christologie* (Darmstadt, 1976), pp. 150–91; Gerhard Sauter, 'Fragestellungen der Christologie', *Verkündigung und Forschung* 11 (1966), pp. 37–68; *idem.*, 'Christologie in geschichtlicher Perspektive', *Verkündigung und Forschung* 21 (1976), pp. 2–31; *idem.*, 'Fragestellungen der Christologie II', *Verkündigung und Forschung* 23 (1978), pp. 21–41; Reinhard Slenczka, *Geschichtlichkeit und Personsein Jesu Christi: Studien zur christologischen Problematik der historischen Jesus-Frage* (Göttingen, 1967). A useful collection of relevant texts is assembled in *Die Frage nach dem historischen Jesus: Texte aus drei Jahrhunderten*, ed. Manfred Baumotte (Gütersloh, 1984).
2 The full recognition of this fact may be dated from the publication of Ernst Troeltsch's *Vernunft und Offenbarung bei Johann Gerhard und Melanchthon: Untersuchungen zur Geschichte der altprotestantischen Theologie* (Göttingen, 1891). Cf. his more mature statement of these insights in *Die Absolutheit des Christenthums* (Tübingen, 1902), p. 1, and the definitive statement in *Die Bedeutung des Protestantismus für die Entstehung der modernen Welt* (Munich/Berlin, 1911).
3 For an outstanding account of this early Christological development, see A. Grillmeier, *Christ in Christian Tradition: From the Apostolic Age to Chalcedon (451)* (London, 2nd edn, 1975).
4 This is well brought out by Slenczka, *Geschichtlichkeit und Personsein Jesu Christi*, pp. 33–46.
5 See M. Werner, 'Was bedeutet für uns die geschichtliche Persönlichkeit Jesu?', in *Der historische Jesus und der kerygmatische Christus*, ed. H. Ristow and K. Matthiae (Berlin, 2nd edn, 1961), pp. 614–46. The following essays in this most useful collection should also be consulted: Werner Georg Kümmel, 'Das Problem des geschichtlichen Jesus in der gegenwärtigen Forschungslage' (pp. 39–53); Ian Henderson, 'Der Historiker und der Theologe' (pp. 93–101).
6 See Joachim Jeremias, 'Der gegenwärtige Stand der Debatte um das Problem des historischen Jesus', in *Der historische Jesus und der kerygmatische Christus*, pp. 12–25.

7 Albert Schweitzer, *Geschichte der Leben-Jesu-Forschung* (2 vols: Munich/Hamburg, 3rd edn, 1966), vol. 1, p. 48; *The Quest of the Historical Jesus* (London, 3rd edn, 1954), pp. 4–5.

8 Ernst Troeltsch, *Gesammelte Schriften* (4 vols: Tübingen, 1912–25), vol. 2, p. 730. In view of the confusion between two related theologies, it is worth noting at this point the important observation of Gerhard Ebeling, *Wort und Glaube* (Tübingen, 1960), p. 48 'historisch-kritische Theologie ist nicht identisch mit liberaler Theologie'. See further chapter 4.

9 See our study of the development of theological method from the Reformation to the Enlightenment, in *The Science of Theology*, ed. P. D. L. Avis (London, 1986).

10 Two excellent studies available in English on this theme are: Alan Richardson, *History Sacred and Profane* (London, 1964); Van A. Harvey, *The Historian and the Believer: the Morality of Historical Knowledge and Christian Belief* (London, 1967).

11 For an excellent study of this chauvinist arrogance, still endemic within Anglicanism, see Stephen Sykes, *The Integrity of Anglicanism* (London, 1978), pp. 53–75; Robert Morgan, 'Non Angli sed Angeli: Some Anglican Reactions to German Gospel Criticism', in *New Studies in Theology I*, eds. Stephen Sykes and Derek Holmes (London, 1980), pp. 1-30.

12 The collection of essays assembled in *England and Germany: Studies in Theological Diplomacy*, ed. S. W. Sykes (Frankfurt, 1982), excellently exemplifies the opportunities such dialogue offers. Attempts to mediate English or American theological insights to Germany are rare: perhaps the most distinguished to date is Dietrich Ritschl, *Theologie in dem Neuen Welten* (Munich, 1981).

1

The Cognitive Crisis of the *Aufklärung*: From Reimarus to Schleiermacher

The Enlightenment marked a decisive and irreversible change in the political, social and religious outlook of Western Europe. Many of the fundamental ideas at the heart of this great movement of the eighteenth century transcended national boundaries. In particular, the German manifestation of the movement – the *Aufklärung* – was heavily influenced by currents of thought originating from England and France. However, it is impossible to treat the *Aufklärung* as a totally derivative phenomenon, in that it rapidly developed an original character and emphasis which permit it to be distinguished from its English and French counterparts.[1] In part, the similarities and differences between theological developments in England and Germany in the late eighteenth and nineteenth centuries reflect comparable similarities and differences between the course of the Enlightenment in the two countries. It is therefore appropriate to begin our analysis of the development of the Christology of modern German-speaking Protestantism by comparing the characteristics of the Enlightenment in each country.[2]

The onset of the Enlightenment in England was gradual, rather than sudden. The origins of the rationalist deism so characteristic of the English Enlightenment may be seen in the religious settlement of 1689, which encouraged both toleration of, and indifference to, religion. The revolution in the world of ideas accompanying the publication of Newton's *Principia Mathematica* (1689) and Locke's *Essay concerning Human Understanding* (1690) had a significant effect upon English religious attitudes, and may be regarded as laying the rational foundations for later deism. The *Aufklärung*, by contrast, developed with a suddenness which lends weight to those who see it as a revolution in German *Geistesgeschichte*.

The Thirty Years War ended in 1648, leaving Germany in a state of political, religious, economic and social depression. The religious character of this seemingly interminable conflict did much to engender a widespread dissatisfaction with theological confessionalism, particularly Protestant Orthodoxy. Nevertheless, German national feeling was closely allied to the national religious tradition, and it received a new vitality and popular appeal through the development of pietism, which was widely perceived as a theological alternative to the arid wastes of Aristotelian scholasticism, characteristic of later Orthodoxy. Unlike its English counterpart, in which pietism followed rationalism in the evangelical revivals of the later eighteenth century, the German *Aufklärung* arose in the wake of pietism, and appropriated much of its spirit. There is a growing recognition that pietism, with its individualism, its concern for the moral life, and emphasis upon *fides qua creditur* rather than *fides quae creditur*, was a precursor of the Enlightenment self-consciousness. The decline of Orthodoxy was thus not immediately followed by the onset of the Enlightenment, but by a significant modification of Orthodoxy which both delayed the *Aufklärung* and exercised considerable influence over its subsequent character. Nevertheless, it must not be supposed that Protestant Orthodoxy was without influence upon the character of the *Aufklärung*. Its strong and coherent doctrinal tradition had come to exercise a significant influence over German intellectual life, with the result that the theologians of the *Aufklärung* were forced to deal with specific matters of doctrine, where their English counterparts could content themselves with more general matters, such as the relation between faith and reason. Furthemore, unlike its French counterpart, the *Aufklärung* cannot be regarded as a specifically anti-religious or anti-Christian movement. Rather, the theologians of the *Aufklärung* were concerned to reformulate Christian doctrines upon the basis of premises more justifiable upon rational grounds, either by reducing them, reinterpreting them or eliminating them.

In the first phase of the *Aufklärung*, a serious confrontation between reason and faith was not necessarily envisaged. Wolffian rationalism may well have subordinated religion to philosophy, but it was not conceived as a challenge to it. In part, this was a consequence of Wolff's conviction that God is the ontological principle or being which determines what exists, and the structure of existence.[3] Thus theologians such as S. J. Baumgarten regarded reason and revelation to be in harmony, although conceding that, in effect, revelation is to be judged on the basis of reason. The hardening of the rationalism of the *Aufklärung* in the fifth and sixth decades of the eighteenth century was at least partly due to the increasing influence of English deism,[4] and increasing dissatisfaction with the Wolffian philosophy.[5] A new emphasis came to be placed upon man's rationality as the basis of his autonomy – an emphasis which inevitably led to a confrontation with Protestant Orthodoxy, which tended to regard man as dependent upon God for his salvation. This concept of a heteronomously determined existence was diametrically opposed to the emerging *Aufklärung* understanding of man's rationally grounded autonomy.[6] Truth is not something which can be regarded as mediated to man from outside (for example, on the basis of a recognized authority), but something which arises within man on account of its conformity with his rationality. It will therefore be evident that there was an inherent tendency within the *Aufklärung* to regard the concept of supernatural revelation with suspicion.

The ultimate foundation of the theology of the *Aufklärung* may be regarded as the doctrine that the natural faculty of human reason is qualitatively similar to (although quantitatively weaker than) the divine reason.[7] This doctrine is stated with particular clarity by Christian Wolff,[8] and may be regarded as the common heritage of the *Aufklärung*. The world of the *Aufklärung* was essentially a rational cosmos in which man, as a rational being, works towards his own moral perfection through conforming himself to the rational moral structures of the cosmos. Thus Johann Christian Gottsched argued that man's highest destiny was moral activity, and that the only practical guide by which such perfection might be attained was human reason.[9] The rationalism of the *Aufklärung* is probably best summarized in three propositions: (1) reality is rational; (2) man has the necessary epistemological capacities to uncover the rational *Ordnung* of reality; (3) man is capable of acting upon his cognition of reality in order to achieve his rational destiny by acting morally. Man's epistemological and moral autonomy is such that he may attain perfection unaided.

The theologians of the *Aufklärung* thus found themselves in immediate conflict with the Orthodox doctrine of original sin. Indeed, it may be argued that the primary theological thrust of the *Aufklärung* was directed against the Orthodox assertion that, on account of original sin, man's intellect was blinded so that he could not see into the divine mind, and his will perverted so that he could not function as an autonomous moral agent.[10] This critique of the Orthodox doctrine of original sin was, however, common to the English, French and German Enlightenments.[11] Where the *Aufklärung* differed from its English and French counterparts was in the theological sophistication with which the critique of this doctrine was mounted. Thus Gotthelf Samuel Steinbart opposed the doctrine of original sin, not merely because it posed a conceptual obstacle to moral perfection, but also because, on the basis of his analysis of the development of the doctrine, it appeared to him to have arisen through the influence of Manichaeism, and thus represented an anachronism with which reason could dispense.[12] As Loofs remarks, the development of the science of the history of dogma is a child of the *Aufklärung*.[13]

A further challenge to Orthodoxy was posed by the *Aufklärung* understanding of the nature of reality. Rational truth was regarded by the theologians of the *Aufklärung* as possessing qualities such as necessity, eternity and universality. It was regarded as axiomatic that such knowledge could not be had through an historical religion, in that history was not capable of conveying the necessary, unchanging and eternal core of rational reality. Historically mediated rational truth was regarded as a contradiction in terms. Underlying this conviction was Spinoza's dictum that knowledge of God 'should be derived from general ideas, in themselves certain and known, so that the truth of an historical narrative is very far from being a necessary requisite for our attaining our highest good'.[14] The most famous statement of this rationalist principle is due to Lessing: 'accidental truths of history (*zufällige Geschichtswahrheiten*) can never become the proof of necessary truths of reason (*notwendige Vernunftwahrheiten*)'.[15] Underlying this axiom is a static view of reality, in which the realm of historical experience is regarded as a totally relative realm of flux, in which nothing is absolute. In contrast, God must be regarded as belonging to the ideal world. As truths about God are timeless, and do not belong to the category of 'events', it is impossible to derive truths about God from historical events, such as those recorded in the gospels. This important conceptual distinction between 'event' and 'truth' laid the foundation for significant Christological development in the early nineteenth century, despite the challenge posed to rationalism by the rise of empiricism.

From the above sketch of the thought of the *Aufklärung*, it will be clear that it is better described as a *Weltanschauung* rather than a system of doctrines or methods. Indeed, the considerable difficulties attending the isolation and definition of the various strands of the movement reflect the fact that there is less coherence to the movement than is commonly realized.[16] Nevertheless, it is fair to characterize the *Weltanschauung* of the *Aufklärung* as moralist, naturalist and rationalist. It is now appropriate to ask what the consequences of this *Weltanschauung* were for the development of Christology during the period of the *Aufklärung*. Two leading characteristics of the Christology of the *Aufklärung* may be singled out for comment. First, Christ is primarily understood as a teacher in his lifetime, and as a supreme example of self-giving in his death. The 'exemplarist' or 'moral' theory of the Atonement – which, incidentally, has nothing to do with Peter Abailard – makes its first appearance in the Enlightenment.[17] Second, Christ is understood as a morally perfect man, embodying the fully realized potential of every rational individual. In other words, Christ possessed to a greater degree what every man has latent within him. Christ's function is thus moral, enabling man to realise his full potential through informing him that it is within his reach, and inspiring him to attain it.[18] Christianity is essentially ethical in character, concerned with the promotion of a 'supremely excellent and complete morality',[19] modelled on that embodied in the life of the 'founder of Christianity'. This approach may be regarded as characteristic of publications of the 'neologists' (such as Semler, Spalding, Töllner, Ernesti and Michaelis) in the period 1760-80. These writers attempted to evolve methods of internal and external criticism by which an historical re-evaluation of dogma might proceed, leading ultimately to the exclusion of doctrines which were considered to be irrational or morally indefensible. The excluded doctrines which were to prove relevant to Christology included the doctrines of original sin and vicarious satisfaction, although there was also growing scepticism concerning the supernaturalism of traditional language concerning the divinity of Christ. The later rationalist dogmaticians, such as Gabler, Ammon and de Wette, reinterpreted the concept of Christ's divinity in purely moral, or occasionally even aesthetical, terms. Nevertheless, it must be emphasized that the neologists retained the concept of divine revelation, which they generally interpreted in quasi-incarnational terms. Thus Steinbart, while employing a purely moralist concept of revelation, argues that the recognition of Christ as the 'Logos Incarnate' was essentially a recognition of that fact that spiritual truths may take tangible and historical forms.[20] The neologists thus retained the *concept* of divine revelation, while subjecting its *content* to historical criticism. It is therefore important to appreciate that there was division within the *Aufklärung* concerning whether the concept of divine revelation was historically defensible, and whether this historical revelation could be regarded as Christologically concentrated. There were those, such as Lessing, who regarded the neologists as espousing a shallow rationalism, an 'inconsistent and superficial compromise' between reason and revelation. There was, however, a more serious theological difficulty facing the theologians of the later *Aufklärung*. How could the persistent supernaturalism of Orthodox Christology be destroyed, when the New Testament itself appeared to legitimate such supernatural and transcendent understandings of Christ? The culmination of the rationalism of the *Aufklärung* is, in fact, to be sought in those who applied its *Weltanschauung* consistently – such as Hermann Samuel Reimarus.

During his sojourn at Hamburg, Lessing made the acquaintance of the family of Reimarus, and was presented with the late Professor of Oriental Languages' enormous unpublished *Schutzschrift für die vernünftigen Verehrer Gottes*.[21] Lessing published sections of this work over the period 1774-8, disingenuously suggesting that the author might be the noted deist Johann Lorenz Schmidt (who, having died in 1749, would not have been disadvantaged by any ensuing criticism). In the *Schutzschrift*, Reimarus applied the *Aufklärung* insights into the nature of truth and history with a consistency rarely hitherto seen. For Reimarus, the concept of revelation is untenable, in that the historical character of revelation is inconsistent with the universal and necessary character of rational truth. Furthermore, if truth necessary for man's salvation could only be obtained at, or after, a certain point in history, it necessarily follows that these truths are denied to all those who lived before this point. Thus historically mediated knowledge of God must be regarded as a contradiction.[22] Finally, even if an immediate revelation of God to an individual were conceivable, a distinction must be drawn between this immediate revelation and the historical report of it, as it is the latter upon which subsequent generations will be dependent. The mediation of revelation through history is called into question by the unreliability of human accounts of that revelation.[23] As such, the only arbiter of religious belief is reason. This, however, merely laid an epistemic foundation for the most significant assertion, made in the final published fragment, which inaugurated a new era in Christological reflection. This is the suggestion that a radical dichotomy exists, and has always existed, between the beliefs and intentions of Jesus and those of the apostolic church.

In the final fragment, *Von dem Zwecke Jesu und seiner Jünger* ('On the Intentions of Jesus and his Disciples'),[24] Reimarus argued that Jesus' ideas and language about God were those of a Jewish apocalyptic visionary, with a purely limited temporal reference and relevance. He accepted the late Jewish expectation of a Messiah who would deliver his people from the concrete historical situation of foreign domination (rather than from 'sin'), and believed that God would act to assist him in this task. His cry of dereliction on the cross expressed his final disillusionment, as he recognized the full extent of his delusions. The notion of a 'spiritual redemption' was invented by the disciples as a means of glossing over the difficulty posed for them by Jesus' death. Similarly, the resurrection story was a fraud initially perpetrated and subsequently perpetuated by the disciples. Those passages in the gospels which do not harmonize with this account of Jesus' fate are to be regarded as interpolations by the apostolic church, as the church developed doctrines unknown to Jesus himself (such as atonement for sin). It is therefore, in principle, possible to distinguish between the Jesus of history and the later beliefs of the apostolic church. The former was merely a confused, fanatical, and ultimately disillusioned, Jewish peasant, who knew nothing of doctrines such as those developed by his followers.

Although Reimarus found no followers at the time even among those who appreciated him most,[25] he raised questions of fundamental importance (even if his answers to them would initially be regarded with scepticism). Reimarus' assertion that Jesus did not intend to break away from Judaism raised the question of precisely what it was that *did* cause the bifurcation in the Judaeo-Christian tradition, thus implicitly posing a challenge to the traditional Christological exegesis of the Old Testament. Furthermore, the explicit distinction between the historical figure of Jesus and the interpretation imposed upon him by the apostolic church identified a problem which will recur frequently in the pages of this narrative – the relationship between the 'Jesus of history' and the 'Christ of faith'. Reimarus made the distinction for dogmatic reasons, being concerned to discredit the Orthodox portrait of Christ (*Christusbild*), and his solution to this problem was inept, resting upon unjustified a priori presuppositions. Nevertheless, the fact remains that it was in the aftermath of the publication of the *Fragments* that the questions which have dominated modern German Christology began to emerge.

Of these questions, the most significant was whether the gospel accounts of Jesus of Nazareth were accurate, and whether the demonstration of their factual truth or falsity could be regarded as establishing or destroying the traditional claims concerning his status. Following Reimarus, Lessing denied that human testimony to a past event was sufficient to make the event credible if it appeared to be at variance with contemporary direct experience, no matter how well documented the event may have been. Furthermore, even if there were reasons for supposing that a supernatural event had taken place in the history of Jesus, Lessing argued that it was impossible to deduce a doctrinal or metaphysical truth from a factual or historical event. It is this principle which underlies his celebrated dictum, alluded to above: 'The accidental truths of history can never become the proof of the necessary truths of reason.' For Lessing, there was an 'ugly great ditch' (*garstige, breite Graben*) between history and reason, which he personally was unable to cross. It was therefore, he argued, impossible to deduce Christ's metaphysical or doctrinal status from the New Testament accounts of his history. Lessing, like Kant, regarded it as conceptually impossible for any individual historical being to be the full revelation of eternal truth, and employed a concept of truth which made it impossible to validate any such putative claim on the basis of the New Testament material. In general, it may be said that the thought of the *Aufklärung* is anti-historical, in the sense that the Cartesian doubt about the possibility of historical knowledge led to historical truths being regarded as 'second-class knowledge'. This attitude was particularly striking in the French Enlightenment, the *philosophes* regarding historical research as unnecessary, in that philosophy was capable of uncovering the truth of human nature unaided. The most which history could do was to corroborate the truths which reason itself had discovered concerning human nature; it could not be permitted to establish them in the first place. Unless historical facts can be verified, and generalised under the form of immutable and universal scientific laws (such as those the 'new philosophy' had uncovered in the case of the motion of bodies), they were regarded as being of no philosophical significance. The claims of 'uniqueness' for at least some of the events recorded in the gospel narratives were sufficient, in the eyes of such *philosophes*, to discredit them.

The rationalism of the *Aufklärung* took several different forms, as we have indicated, with correspondingly different consequences for Christology. At one end of the spectrum was a fully developed rationalism, evident in Reimarus' *Fragments*, and which would be continued in later works such as Paulus' *Leben Jesu*, which totally rejected supernaturalism, and reinterpreted substantial portions of the gospel narratives accordingly.[26] At the other end were those, such as the neologists, whose understanding of the human spirit as both autonomous and historical was such that it was held to defy logical analysis, and thus to be beyond reduction to the purely natural level. Uniting these disparate elements, however, was the common *Aufklärung* presupposition of the autonomy of reason. The traditional distinction between scripture as *norma normans* and subsequent ecclesiastical tradition as *norma normata* was generally regarded as posing a threat to the immanent autonomy of the individual, which was held to reside exclusively in his capacity for ratiocination. The ultimate arbiter and criterion of truth is neither scripture nor tradition (though these may be treated with varying degrees of respect), but reason itself. Even where the concept of divine revelation was conceded, it was conceded solely upon the understanding that the content of that revelation should be subject to criticism (that is, to acceptance, modification, reduction or elimination) on the basis of the enlightened rational judgement of the individual. The origins of the 'Quest for the Historical Jesus' may be seen in the *Aufklärung* conviction that the gospels contained material concerning Jesus which was unacceptable (because it was immoral, or supernatural) and which thus required correction in the light of modern thought. The Christological consequence of this *Weltanschauung* was inevitably some form of Ebionitism, by which Jesus was understood as a teacher, a hero of humanity, a purely human phenomenon, whose concerns were primarily moral.

On the basis of the above analysis, it will be clear that the period of the *Aufklärung* raised three questions of considerable Christological import. First, the naturalism and rationalism of the movement raised questions concerning the traditional 'two natures' doctrine. It was widely held, upon logical and metaphysical grounds, that the doctrine was an absurdity which the 'Age of Reason' could eliminate in favour of a more reasonable moral or aesthetic interpretation of Christ's significance. The second difficulty arises from this. If Christ's significance is to be conceived in purely natural terms, how may his uniqueness be maintained? For the *Aufklärung* in general, Christ was a teacher of the good life, whose superiority over other such teachers was established, if it was conceded at all, upon the supremely moral character of his teachings. There seemed to be no way in which his uniqueness could be established without resorting to a discredited supernaturalism.[27] Third, there was growing scepticism concerning man's knowledge of Christ. How could faith be based upon accounts of Christ which were increasingly regarded as potentially unreliable factually, and which, on account of their historical character, could no longer be regarded as an adequate foundation for claims concerning Christ's status?

By 1790, the *Aufklärung* appeared to many to be at its zenith. What, if anything, could check its progress? Two developments within the world of ideas combined to bring the period of the *Aufklärung* to an end. The first was the gradual emergence of an awareness of limitations on the part of reason. The growing influence of empiricism, mediated primarily through British writers such as Hume, led to a growing recognition that knowledge about reality was grounded upon sensation.[28] This sensation, however, was grounded in empirical experience, which had to be treated as isolated units of temporal existence. In so far as knowledge is based upon sensation, man is thus denied access to universal and necessary knowledge. A crisis thus began to develop on account of the tension between the necessary truths of reason, and the contingent truths of experience.[29] The difficulty faced by the *Aufklärer* was how the application of a priori concepts of pure reason to an empirically given, and historically restricted, context could be justified. A serious and widely appreciated challenge was thus posed to the rationalist presuppositions of the *Aufklärung*, as may be seen from many writings of the period.[30] The most famous solution to this dilemma was Kant's *Kritik der reinen Vernunft* (1781), which exposed the inadequacies and weaknesses of the uncritical rationalism of the *Aufklärung*.

The second development was the rise of Romanticism, where the rediscovery of man's spirit (*Geist*) in the *Sturm und Drang* movement posed a powerful challenge to the cool rationality of the *Aufklärung*. Although the origins of the movement date from the 1760s, the movement underwent its most dramatic developments in the final decade of the eighteenth century. (The celebrated manifesto of German Romanticism, Wackenroder's *Herzensergiessungen eines kunstliebenden Klosterbruders* was published in 1797.) The new movement became particularly influential in Berlin, through the influence of the brothers Schlegel.[31] Under the influence of Novalis, the movement came to adopt two fundamental axioms concerning *das Gefühl* ('feeling' or 'sentiment'), the primordial act of the human spirit. First, the *locus* of *das Gefühl* is the individual self, the ego, as it becomes aware of its inward individuality. This may be regarded as a development of the later *Aufklärung* concept of the *Selbstdenker*, the individual who is aware of his subjectivity.[32] Second, the orientation of *das Gefühl* is towards the infinite and eternal, as contemplation of the finite leads to the 'magical idealism' of the infinite.[33] For Novalis (Friedrich von Hardenberg), the *Aufklärung* had declared imagination and *das Gefühl* to be 'heretical', in order that knowledge of 'higher worlds' might be suppressed by an appeal to philosophy.[34] This new intellectual climate made a new approach to Christology possible. This new approach is particularly associated with F. D. E. Schleiermacher, who rejected the previously prevailing tendency of the *Aufklärung* to identify religion with knowledge of morality in favour of its identification with *das Gefühl*. There is every indication that Schleiermacher, though not himself a Romantic, developed an approach to theology which struck a deep chord of sympathy within this new and influential school of thought.[35]

Schleiermacher's *Reden über die Religion* (1799) make a powerful appeal to the concept of *das Gefühl*.[36] It is difficult for the modern reader to understand the full significance of these speeches without a full appreciation of the cultural and historical situation to which they were originally addressed. Nevertheless, we have adequate testimony from contemporary writers to the challenge they posed to the rationalism of *Aufklärer* such as J. A. Eberhard.[37] As A. E. Biedermann later remarked, Schleiermacher's theology may be regarded as the subjection of man's deep religious feeling (*Gefühl*) to critical enquiry. Man's intellect (*Verstand*) is obliged to reflect upon his feeling, and interpret it to him.[38] By introspection, according to Schleiermacher, the polar structure (*Duplizität*) of self-consciousness is interpreted as consciousness of self and of another, coexisting. The scientific exposition of this theological programme is found in his *Glaubenslehre*,[39] unquestion ably one of the most significant works of systematic theology ever written. The Christological concentration of this work is evident from his definition of Christianity: 'Christianity is a monotheistic faith, belonging to the teleological type of religion (*eine der teleologischen Richtung der Frömmigkeit angehörige monotheistische Glaubensweise*), and is essentially distinguished from other such faiths by the fact that everything in it is related to the redemption accomplished by Jesus of Nazareth.'[40] For Schleiermacher, everything in a Christian dogmatics hinges upon the redemption of mankind in Christ. The *Glaubenslehre* is thus constructed around the antithesis of sin and grace – that is, around man's need for redemption, and the actuality of this redemption in Jesus Christ. In the *Glaubenslehre*, the discussion of this antithesis is preceded by an introductory section which deals with the concept of God-consciousness in general, which effectively establishes 'piety' (*Frömmigkeit*) as an irreducible abstraction. The essence of piety, the irreducible element in every religion, is to be sought in *das Gefühl*, rather than in intellectual beliefs or moral behaviour. This introduction is of particular importance in relation to the Kantian epistemology,[41] in that it develops the general Romantic concept of *das Gefühl* into the concept, peculiar to Schleiermacher, of *das Gefühl schlechthinniger Abhängigkeit* (the 'feeling of absolute dependence'),[42] upon which his dogmatic system is constructed. Part I deals with religious consciousness in general, while Part II deals with the specifically *Christian* understanding of religious self-consciousness. In effect, Part I may be seen as a critique of Kant's critical transcendental philosophy to accommodate Schleiermacher's conviction that it is religion alone which provides an adequate foundation for the union of the human spirit with its proper ground of being. Of particular significance is the assertion that dogmatics thus starts from an original revelation of God, rather than a rationally established idea.[43]

The origins of the leading features of the Christology of the *Glaubenslehre* may be sought in the dialogue *Die Weihnachtsfeier*, written in the final weeks of 1805.[44] In many respects, the dialogue appears to have been consciously modelled upon the Platonic dialogues which had so occupied Schleiermacher's attention from 1799. It is clear that the young Schleiermacher was convinced that the dialogic form was the most appropriate means of developing ideas, although it must be conceded that in this particular case the final product was less than might be hoped for. The participants in the dialogue are generally agreed to represent personalities with whom Schleiermacher was personally acquainted, and considerable attention has been directed towards establishing which of the participants most closely approximates to Schleiermacher's own position. In fact, with the exception of the fifth speech, the importance of the Christmas dialogue is largely a consequence of its *structure*, and particularly the considerations which determined it. Perhaps the most important of these considerations is Schleiermacher's insight that Jesus may only be approached through the experience of his benefits as mediated in the historical continuity of the community of faith. The family group gathered together on

Christmas eve to discuss the significance of Christ may be regarded as a symbol: the occasion of their reflection is the fact that they are preparing to celebrate the benefits which Christ has, in one way or another, bestowed upon them. Christ is thus reflected and refracted in the accounts of his historically and socially mediated *experience* upon their individual and corporate consciousness. The family group of the *Weihnachtsfeier* dialogue corresponds to the *Gemeinde* of the *Glaubenslehre*: in both cases, Christological reflection begins from the corporate and individual Christian consciousness.

This point is further developed in the discourse of Ernst,[45] perhaps the most orthodox member of the group, in response to the somewhat frivolous speech by Leonhardt. In this address, Ernst effectively argues from present religious experience to the existence of an historical founder of the Christian faith. Although his argument is difficult to follow (and the explanations added in the third edition do little to relieve those difficulties), it is clear that Ernst suggests that the idea of a redeemer is 'crystallized' by reflection upon the joy of Christmas and the simultaneous knowledge of the tensions within man's existence. The experience of a heightened sense of existence which underlies the Christmas joy of the Christian community can only be traced back to the historical appearance of the redeemer.

In many respects, the *Glaubenslehre* may be regarded as developing more systematically the themes of the discourses of this little dialogue. Although it is possible to suggest that the dialogue is merely a pure description of the Christian experience of the joy of Christmas, it is clear that the real importance of the dialogue lies in its critical reflection upon that experience. Christology is thus portrayed as reflection upon historically and socially mediated experience. More significantly, Christology must be regarded as based upon its object as it already exists in an historical context, rather than in isolation. It is thus significant that, from 1806 onwards, Schleiermacher was increasingly positive towards the *institutional* aspects of Christianity. By setting his dialogue in the context of a family group preparing to celebrate Christmas, Schleiermacher is able to emphasize that the thinker cannot divorce or abstract himself from his relation to Christ. Although one of the contributors to the dialogue (Leonhardt) raises the historical and critical difficulties noted by the *Aufklärung*, these are met (by Eduard and Ernst) by the appeal to the present experience of the community as an historical and social phenomenon. It is this appeal, although in a much more sophisticated form, which lies at the heart of the *Glaubenslehre*.

Schleiermacher's mature Christology, as encountered in the *Glaubenslehre*, is inferred from the present effect of Christ upon believers, arguing back from the observed effect to its sufficient cause. It is necessary to appreciate that Schleiermacher insists that the doctrines of the person and work of Christ are so intimately linked that it is impossible to isolate them: a statement about the person of Christ is simultaneously a statement about the work of Christ, and vice versa. It is therefore necessary to consider Schleiermacher's soteriology in parallel with his Christology. While conceding the existence of a God-consciousness in mankind, Schleiermacher exploits the Kantian principle of radical evil to argue that there is an inherent disposition within man towards sin, prior to any act of sin on man's part. For Schleiermacher, sin is essentially the disorder and impotence of the human God-consciousness.[46] Man's awareness of the shortcomings of his God-consciousness is interpreted by Schleiermacher as consciousness of sin, which in turn induces an awareness of the possibility of redemption.

Schleiermacher's Christology may be regarded as arising from the assertion that, although redemption is a real possibility for man, that redemption cannot be effected by man himself, on account of his distorted God-consciousness. If man is to be redeemed, he must be redeemed by one who stands outside the human condition of sin – in other words, one in whom the God-consciousness is dominant. The essence of redemption is that 'the God-consciousness already present in human nature, though feeble and repressed, becomes stimulated and made dominant by the entrance of the living influence of Christ'.[47] As the Redeemer (*Erlöser*), Christ is distinguished from all other men both in kind and degree through the uninterrupted and dominant power of his God-consciousness. Christ's uniqueness may be summarized thus: the archetype (*Urbild*) of the final perfection of God-consciousness is that which was historically manifested in Jesus of Nazareth.[48] Schleiermacher attributes to Jesus of Nazareth an absolutely powerful God-consciousness (*schlechthin kräftiges Gottesbewußtsein*), which is charged with an assimilative power capable of effecting the redemption of mankind. In making this assertion, Schleiermacher avoids the 'empirical' error of the *Aufklärung*, and the 'magical' error of Orthodoxy. The 'empirical' understanding of the person and work of Christ corresponds to the rationalism of the *Aufklärung*, which interpreted Christ primarily as a teacher or a prophet. Schleiermacher notes that this view 'attributes a redemptive activity on the part of Christ, but one which is held to consist only in bringing about an increasing perfection in us; and this cannot properly occur other wise than by teaching and example'. Similarly, Orthodoxy interpreted the work of Christ in a manner which supposed 'an influence not mediated by anything natural, yet attributed to a person'.[49] For Schleiermacher, this approach is incapable of doing justice to the historical existence of Jesus of Nazareth: if Christ were able to exert his influence in this supranaturalist manner, 'it would have been possible for him to work in just the same way at any time, and his real personal appearance in history would only have been a superfluous adjunct'. Underlying this criticism is the conviction that natural causal processes are abolished. For Schleiermacher, the divine status of Christ should not be understood in terms of an abrogation of natural causality, but rather as existing within the realm of natural causality.

Schleiermacher's soteriology proceeds upon the basis of the explicitly acknowledged presupposition that no causality other than that of nature itself may be permitted to operate. The essential difference between the Redeemer and the redeemed consists in the prototypal dominance of the God-consciousness in the Redeemer, into whose fellowship the believer may be admitted by a process substantially analogous to the formation of a human society around a charismatic leader, who unites them by his vision of their future state. This process of causality is essentially the same in each case, and does not involve the use of 'magical' causes, nor reduce the Redeemer's influence to the purely 'empirical' level. Although it might appear that Jesus' God-consciousness is, in fact, supernatural, Schleiermacher argues that it is a fundamentally human concept, representing the ideal of human existence. Whereas the theologians of the *Aufklärung* conceived man's goal rationally, in terms of moral perfection, Schleiermacher expressed it religiously, in terms of the domination of the God-consciousness. Schleiermacher's concept of the assimilative power of the Redeemer probably reflects his Romantic background, as this power is permitted to reside almost totally in the evocation of a deep emotional response within man himself – *das Gefühl* in its most profound sense.

Having established that Christ is capable of redeeming man through the establishment of a dominant God-consciousness by a natural causal sequence, and having established (apparently on a priori grounds) that man is incapable of redeeming himself, Schleiermacher proceeds to apply these insights to the four natural heresies of Christendom –

the Docetic and Ebionite interpretations of the person of Christ, and the Manichaean and Pelagian interpretations of man's soteriological resources.[50]

> Now, if the distinctive essence of Christianity consists in the fact that in it all religious emotions are related to the redemption wrought by Jesus of Nazareth, there will be two ways in which heresy can arise. That is to say: this fundamental formula will be retained in general. . . but *either* human nature will be so defined that a redemption in the strict sense of the term cannot be accomplished, *or* the Redeemer will be defined in such a way that he cannot accomplish redemption.[51]

If Christ is to be considered as the unique agent of God's reconciling work among mankind, it necessarily follows that certain affirmations be made concerning Christ and those whom he redeems. The answer to the fundamental question, Who is the Redeemer?, must be able to account both for the uniqueness of his office, and also for his ability to mediate between God and man. For Schleiermacher, the denial of the principle of redemption in Christ constitutes unbelief; the affirmation of this principle, while interpreting its terms in such a manner that an inconsistency results, constitutes heresy. If the superiority of Christ over mankind is emphasized, without a concomitant insistence upon his equality with man, his ability to redeem man is dissipated, in that he no longer possesses a point of contact with those whom he is to redeem. Similarly, if Christ's equality with men is emphasized, without a concomitant insistence upon his superiority, the Redeemer himself comes to require redemption, in that he shares the common sinful condition of mankind. This would either mean that redemption was impossible, or else that the Redeemer can only redeem to the same extent as other men – in which case, the uniqueness of his office is denied. In essence, the two positions outlined correspond to the Docetic and Ebionite or Nazarene heresies, although it may be pointed out that the frames of reference of the actual historical heresies are somewhat different from Schleiermacher's representation of them.[52] A proper tension must be maintained between Christ's divinity and humanity, so that the affirmation of the one does not amount to the denial of the other.

It will therefore be clear that Schleiermacher, by an analysis of the *Gesamtleben* ('collective life') of the Christian community, is able to infer that the community's consciousness of grace is a consequence of the influence of Jesus of Nazareth, mediated historically and socially through normal causal channels. In effect, Schleiermacher eliminates the distinction between 'natural' and 'supernatural', so that there is no longer any necessity for a non-natural or non-historical mediation of the divine. The mediation of the divine becomes both natural and historical, without losing its revelatory character and capacity on the one hand, or on the other degenerating to a form of reductionist rationalism which excludes the transcendent or objective by virtue of its a priori subjectivism. Just as the existence of God was for Kant a postulate of practical reason, so the dogma of Christ was for Schleiermacher a postulate of the collective Christian experience.[53] Dogmatics must attribute to Jesus the 'dignity' which his 'activity' demands. Although Schleiermacher does not appear to have intended to reinstate the Orthodox dogma of Christ in the face of the criticisms of the *Aufklärung*, he appears to have approached this goal in practice. The divine dignity of the Redeemer is not understood mythologically or supernaturally, but existentially. Indeed, one of the foundations of Schleiermacher's critique of the Christologies of the *Aufklärung* was that they presented Christ as the exemplar of a new religious principle, or the prophet of a new concept of God; for Schleiermacher, Christology should not be based upon a concept (*Vorstellung*), but upon an 'immediate existential relationship'.[54]

On the basis of this approach, Schleiermacher is able to meet the *Aufklärung* criticism of the Christological dogma in three ways. First, he is able to avoid the difficulties associated with the dogma of the two natures of Christ (difficulties which the *Aufklärung* had highlighted) by referring the dogma to an immediate existential relationship, as we saw above. Second, he is able to dismiss the suggestion that Christ was merely a teacher of the common religion of humanity, an educator rather than a redeemer. Christ's uniqueness resides in the irreducible religious character of his God-consciousness. Third, he is able to meet the growing critical scepticism concerning the gospel accounts of Christ by arguing that these accounts merely substantiate and verify what the Christian may obtain directly, through critical introspection. In many respects, therefore, it is possible to suggest that a new era in dogmatic theology, as in Christology, was inaugurated with the publication of the *Reden* in 1799. At the very least, Schleiermacher led the Christian consciousness back to confidence in its own content,[55] which, upon examination, was found to have profound Christological implications. Although it would not be correct to describe

Schleiermacher's theology as *Christocentric* in the strict sense of the term, it is certainly *Christomorphic*, in that the whole of his theology is 'shaped' by the interpretation, clarification and restructuring of the *datum* of Christian experience in the light of the person of Christ.

Although Schleiermacher cannot be said to have had followers, in the strict sense of the term, his influence transcended that of a mere school of thought. His critique of the rationalism of the *Aufklärung* opened the door for the new Christological developments of the nineteenth and twentieth centuries. Rather than establish a school, he inaugurated an era.[56] That era opened, however, with a sustained attack upon Schleiermacher's Christology upon three fronts. Such was the ferocity of the attack that Karl Marx, surveying the condition of German religious culture in 1844, concluded that the criticism of religion was essentially complete.[57] It is to this criticism that we now turn.

NOTES

1 For an excellent introduction, see E. Cassirer, *The Philosophy of the Enlightenment* (Boston, 1951). The witty essay of Karl Barth, 'Der Mensch im 18. Jahrhundert', in *Die protestantische Theologie im 19. Jahrhundert: Ihre Vorgeschichte und ihre Geschichte* (Zurich, 1952), pp. 16–59, is useful. For a general study of the development of theological method in the Enlightenment, see Alister E. McGrath, 'Reformation to Enlightenment', in *The Science of Theology*, ed. P. D. L. Avis (London, 1986). The myth that the fundamental principle of the Reformation was the right to exercise unrestricted private judgement appears to have been introduced by Lessing, in his polemic against the Lutheran Johann Melchior Goeze (1788): see H. Bornkamm, *Luther im Spiegel der deutschen Geistesgeschichte* (Heidelberg, 1955), pp. 14–15. Luther was frequently treated as a precursor of the *Aufklärung* in its polemic against Lutheran Orthodoxy.

2 See A. O. Dyson, 'Theological Legacies of the Enlightenment: England and Germany', in *England and Germany: Studies in Theological Diplomacy*, ed. S. W. Sykes (Frankfurt, 1982), pp. 45–62.

3 See A. Bissinger, *Die Struktur der Gotteserkenntnis: Studien zur Philosophie Christian Wolffs* (Bonn, 1970).

4 For example, through J. L. Schmidt's translation of Tindal's *Christianity as Old as Creation* (1741) and H. G. Schmidt's translation of Leland's *View of the Principal Deistical Writers* (1755-56).

5 See M. Wundt, *Die deutsche Schulphilosophie im Zeitalter der Aufklärung* (Hildesheim, 1964), p. 265. Wundt dates the period of breakdown of

Wolffianism as 1750–80. See also Paul Hazard, *La crise de la conscience européene (1680–1715)* (3 vols: Paris, 1935); id., *La pensée européene au XVIIIe siècle de Montesquieu à Lessing* (3 vols: Paris, 1946); G. Funke, *Die Aufklärung in ausgewählten Texten dargestellt* (Stuttgart, 1963), pp. 1–92; F. W. Kantzenbach, *Protestantisches Christenheit im Zeitalter des Rationalismus* (Gütersloh, 1965), especially pp. 22–30.

6 See Karl Friederich Bahrdt, *Ueber Preßfreyheit und deren Gränzen* (Züllichau, 1789), pp. 1–31.

7 See H. M. Wolff, *Weltanschauung der deutschen Aufklärung in geschichtlicher Entwicklung* (Berne, 1949), pp. 109–16.

8 Christian Wolff, *Vernunftige Gedancken von Gott, der Welt und der Seele des Menschen* (Frankfurt/Leipzig, 1729), p. 665. The ideas developed at this point are primarily due to the influence of Leibnitz.

9 See J. C. Gottsched, *Erste Gründe der gesamten Weltweisheit* (2 vols: Leipzig, 1733–44), vol. 1, p. 319. For an excellent study of the popular diffusion of the moralism of the *Aufklärung*, see Wolfgang Martens, *Die Botschaft der Tugend: Die Aufklärung im Spiegel der deutschen moralischen Wochenschriften* (Stuttgart, 1971).

10 See Karl Aner, *Die Theologie der Lessingzeit* (Halle/Saale, 1929), pp. 163–4; Wolff, *Weltanschauung der deutschen Aufklärung*, pp. 27–152.

11 See Cassirer, *Philosophy of the Enlightenment*, pp. 137–60.

12 G. S. Steinbart, *System der reinen Philosophie oder Glückseligkeitslehre des Christentums* (Züllichau, 1778), p. 146.

13 Friedrich Loofs, *Leitfaden zum Studium der Dogmengeschichte* (Halle, 4th edn, 1906), p. 1.

14 Spinoza, *Tractatus theologico-politicus* 4, in *Works*, trs. R. H. M. Elwes (2 vols: New York, 1951), vol. 1, p. 61.

15 'Über den Beweis des Geistes und der Kraft', in *Theologische Schriften*, ed. Leopold Zscharnack (4 vols: Berlin, 1929), vol. 4, p. 47; *Lessing's Theological Writings*, ed. H. Chadwick (London, 1956), p. 53 'Zufällige Geschichtswahrheiten können der Beweis von notwendigen Vernunftwahrheiten nie werden'. See further R. Hermann, 'Zu Lessings religionsphilosophischer und theologischer Problematik', *Zeitschrift für systematische Theologie* 22 (1953), pp. 127–48. On Lessing's debt to Spinoza, see R. Zimmermann, 'Leibnitz und Lessing', *Sitzungsberichte der Akademie der Wissenschaft zu Wien* 16 (1855), pp. 326–91. See further Wilm Peters, *Lessings Standort: Sinndeutung der Geschichte als Kern seines Denkens* (Heidelberg, 1972).

16 Thus Wolfgang Philipp goes against the majority opinion in distinguishing *three* phases of the *Aufklärung*, which he styles 'Physicotheology', 'Neology' and 'Rationalism': *Das Zeitalter der Aufklärung*, ed. W. Philipp (Bremen, 1963), pp. xiii-civ.

17 See Alister E. McGrath, 'The Moral Theory of the Atonement: An

Historical and Theological Critique', *Scottish Journal of Theology* 38 (1985), pp. 205–20.

18 See J. Bauer, *Salus Christiana: Die Rechtfertigungslehre in der Geschichte des christlichen Heilsverständnisses* (Gütersloh, 1968), pp. 111–79. For a valuable contemporary analysis, see F. C. Baur, *Vorlesungen über die christliche Dogmengeschichte* (3 vols: Leipzig, 1865–67), vol. 3, pp. 516–608. Baur's comments upon Kant (pp. 592–3) are particularly valuable.

19 Steinbart, *Glückseligkeitslehre*, p. 78.

20 Steinbart, *Glückseligkeitslehre*, pp. 78–93.

21 See D. F. Strauss, *Hermann Samuel Reimarus und seine Schutzschrift für die vernünftigen Verehrer Gottes* (Leipzig, 1862). The *Schutzschrift* was some 4,000 pages long, which goes some way towards justifying Lessing's decision to publish it in fragments.

22 See the fragment *Von Verschreiung der Vernunft auf den Kanzeln*; reprinted as *Ein Mehreres aus den Papieren des Ungenannten, die Offenbarung betreffend*, in G. E. Lessing, *Gesammelte Werke*, ed. Paul Rilla (10 vols: Berlin, 1954–58), vol. 7, pp. 673–85. Strictly speaking, Reimarus begins by arguing that God can reveal no more than that which is materially and formally universal, which man is capable of attaining by means of unaided reason. The conclusion that knowledge about God derived from history is not merely *superfluous*, but also *impossible*, is based upon the arguments which follow.

23 *Verschreiung der Vernunft*; ed. cit., p. 689 'Es ist also nicht mehr eine göttliche Offenbarung, sondern ein menschliches Zeugnis von einer göttlichen Offenbarung.' The implicit attack on the Orthodox teaching that the evangelists were preserved from error by supernatural inspiration will be evident.

24 For a synopsis, see Albert Schweitzer, *Geschichte der Leben-Jesu-Forschung* (2 vols: Munich/Hamburg, 3rd edn, 1966), vol. 1, pp. 56–68; *The Quest of the Historical Jesus: A Critical Study of its Progress from Reimarus to Wrede* (London, 3rd edn, 1954), pp. 13–26.

25 Hans Frei, *The Eclipse of Biblical Narrative: A Study in Eighteenth and Nineteenth Century Hermeneutics* (New Haven/London, 1977), p. 114.

26 See Schweitzer, *Geschichte der Leben-Jesu-Forschung*, vol. 1, pp. 88–96; *Quest of the Historical Jesus*, pp. 48–57. For the earlier phase of rationalism, see pp. 69–78 (English translation, pp. 27–37).

27 It may be pointed out that the 'ethical supernaturalism' of Friedrich Gottlieb Süskind – e.g., as found in *In welchem Sinne hat Jesus die Göttlichkeit seiner Religions- und Sittenlehre behauptet?* (Tübingen, 1802) – or of Ernst Gottlieb Bengel and his school – e.g., as expressed in his *Reden über Religion und Christenthum* (Tübingen, 1831) – does not constitute an exception to this rule. In both cases, the term 'supernatural' is used to convey something similar to Kant's concept of moral law, rather than the traditional ontological concept.

28 See E. Coreth, *Einführung in die Philosophie der Neuzeit: Rationalismus, Empirismus, Aufklärung* (Freiburg, 1972), especially pp. 136–50.

29 Cf. J. H. Randall Jr., *The Career of Philosophy* (2 vols: New York/London, 1970), vol. 2, pp. 50–127, who observes that the thinkers of the later *Aufklärung* were often 'tossed back and forth between the conflicting currents of rationalism and empiricism' (p. 77).

30 For example, in the case of the young Lessing: see F. J. Schmitz, *The Problem of Individualism and the Crisis in the Lives of Lessing and Hamann* (Berkeley, 1944), pp. 125–48. A similar crisis of confidence in reason is evident in the contemporary poem 'O Nacht' by the *Aufklärer* Karl Kasimir von Creuz:

> Wer leuchtet mir in dieser Dunkelheit?
> Wo is der Richter, der den groß Streit entscheidt,
> Und o wie ungewiß sind sterbliche Gedanken!
> Ja, die Vernunft hat mir zu sehr geheuchelt,
> Die Wissenschaft hat mir zu viel geschmeichelt:
> Die Wahrheit find ich nicht, die ich gesucht!
> Und größre Zweifel sind des Demonstrierens Frucht.

(We have used the version to be found in *Deutsche Dichtung im 18. Jahrhundert*, ed. A. Elschenbroich (Munich, 1960), p. 234).

31 For a general introduction, see F. Schultz, 'Romantik und romantiker als literarhistorische Terminologien und Begriffsbildungen', *Deutsche Vierteljahrsschrift für Literaturwissenschaft und Geistesgeschichte* 2 (1924), pp. 349–66. Arthur Lovejoy's comments on the various shades of meanings of the term 'Romanticism' should be borne in mind here: *Essays in the History of Ideas* (New York, 1960), pp. 228–53. On the movement in Berlin, see Josef Nadler, *Die Berliner Romantik 1800–1814* (Berlin, 1921).

32 Cf. Wundt's comment on the age of Lessing: 'Und so sucht man den letzten Grund alles Seins und Erkennens, wo man ihm neu nachfragt, im Menschen, im Ich oder Selbst' (Wundt, *Die deutsche Schulphilosophie*, p. 314). The recognition of this subjectivity, of course, contributed significantly to the cognitive crisis of the *Aufklärung*. The use of the concept of *Einfühlung* in biblical hermeneutics by Johann Gottfried Herder (1744–1803) is of considerable significance: see Frei, *Eclipse of Biblical Narrative*, pp. 183–201.

33 See G. Bonarius, *Zum magischen Realismus bei Keats und Novalis* (Giessen, 1950).

34 For example, see his remarkable historical essay on 'Christendom and Europe'; *Novalis Schriften* vol. 1, ed. P. Kluckhohn and R. Samuel (Darmstadt, 1960), pp. 507–24.

35 For an excellent discussion of Schleiermacher's complex relationship with

the Brothers Schlegel and Novalis, see J. Forstman, *A Romantic Triangle: Schleiermacher and Early German Romanticism* (Missoula, Mont., 1977). For an excellent introduction to Schleiermacher in English, see B. A. Gerrish, 'Friedrich Schleiermacher', in *Nineteenth Century Religious Thought*, ed. N. Smart, J. Clayton, P. Sherry and S. T. Katz (3 vols: Cambridge, 1985), vol. 1, pp. 123–56.

36 W. Schulze, 'Schleiermachers Theorie des Gefühls und ihre religiöse Bedeutung', *Zeitschrift für Theologie und Kirche* 53 (1956), pp. 75–103. For a more detailed discussion of the concept as it is found in the *Reden*, see F. W. Graf, 'Ursprüngliches Gefühl unmittelbarer Koinzidenz des Differenzen: Zur Modifikation des Religionsbegriffs in der verschiedenen Auflagen von Schleiermachers Reden über die Religion', *Zeitschrift für Theologie und Kirche* 75 (1978), pp. 147–86.

37 For example, Claus Harms, who remarked that the *Reden* 'killed rationalism for me': Martin Redeker, *Schleiermacher: Life and Thought* (Philadelphia, 1973), p. 34.

38 A. E. Biedermann, 'Schleiermacher', in *Ausgewählte Vorträge und Aufsätze*, ed. J. Kradolfer (Berlin, 1885), pp. 188–91; 197–8.

39 The title of the work to which Schleiermacher affectionately refers in this manner is *Der christliche Glaube* (1st edn, 1821–2; 2nd edn, 1830–1). We have used the fourth edition (2 vols: Berlin, 4th edn, 1842). The best English translation is that of H. R. Mackintosh and J. S. Stewart (Edinburgh, 1928); references are to these editions.

40 *Glaubenslehre*, §11; vol. 1, p. 67; *The Christian Faith*, p. 52. Readers of the English translation of Barth's *Protestantische Theologie im 19. Jahrhundert* will find references to a 'theological' religion in the useful section on Schleiermacher more intelligible if they substitute the correct word 'teleological'.

41 As pointed out by D. Offermann, *Schleiermachers Einleitung in die Glaubenslehre* (Berlin, 1969).

42 See F. Beisser, *Schleiermachers Lehre von Gott* (Göttingen, 1970), pp. 57–68; Offermann, *Einleitung in die Glaubenslehre*, pp. 47–65.

43 *Glaubenslehre*, §4, 4; vol. 1, pp. 20-2; *The Christian Faith*, pp. 16–18.

44 *Die Weihnachtsfeier: Ein Gespräch*, ed. Hermann Mulert (Philosophische Bibliothek 117: Leipzig, 1908). For an excellent account of the Christological significance of this dialogue, see Richard R. Niebuhr, *Schleiermacher on Christ and Religion* (London, 1965), pp. 21–71.

45 *Weihnachtsfeier*, ed. Mulert, pp. 116–20 (following the pagination of the first edition).

46 See G. Bader, 'Sünde und Bewußtsein der Sünde: Zu Schleiermachers Lehre von der Sünde', *Zeitschrift für Theologie und Kirche* 79 (1982), pp. 60–79.

47 *Glaubenslehre*, §106, 1; vol. 2, p. 162; *The Christian Faith*, p. 476.

48 See P. Seifert, *Die Theologie des jungen Schleiermacher* (Gütersloh, 1960), pp. 141–2.

49 *Glaubenslehre*, §100, 3; vol. 2, p. 100; *The Christian Faith*, p. 430. The reference to mathematics at the opening of this section (p. 98; English translation, p. 428) is more significant than might be imagined: see G. Tonelli, 'Der Streit über die mathematische Methode in der Philosophie in der ersten Hälfte des 18. Jahrhunderts und die Entstehung von Kants Schrift über die Deutlichkeit', *Archiv für Philosophie* 9 (1959), pp. 37–66.

50 *Glaubenslehre*, §22; vol. 1, pp. 124-9; *The Christian Faith*, pp. 97-101. See K.-M. Beckmann, *Der Begriff der Häresie bei Schleiermacher* (Munich, 1959), pp. 36–62.

51 *Glaubenslehre*, §22, 2; vol. 1, p. 125; *The Christian Faith*, p. 98.

52 See Beckmann, *Häresie bei Schleiermacher*, pp. 85–114. The Pelagian and Manichaean heresies are deduced in a similar manner, but do not concern us here.

53 See D. F. Strauss, *Charakteristiken und Kritiken* (Leipzig, 1844), p. 41.

54 See *Sendschreiben an Lücke*, ed. H. Mulert (Giessen, 1908), pp. 13–15.

55 See the famous statement of Alexander Schweizer, *Die protestantischen Centraldogma in ihrer Entwicklung innerhalb der reformierten Kirche* (2 vols: Zurich, 1854–56), vol. 2, p. 812. It was the same scholar, however, who pointed out that, at the purely logical level, Roman Catholics could deduce the sinlessness of Mary by a parallel argument (*Die Glaubenslehre der evangelisch-reformierten Kirche* (2 vols: Zurich, 1844–47), vol. 1, p. 94).

Much more serious, however, was the apparent disinclination of Schleiermacher to come to terms with the irreversible trend towards historicization initiated by the *Aufklärung*: see the highly critical comments of Albrecht Ritschl, *Schleiermachers Reden über die Religion* (Bonn, 1874), pp. 90–1; Otto Ritschl, *Schleiermachers Stellung zum Christentum in seiner Reden über die Religion* (Gotha, 1888), p. 31; Albert Schweitzer, *Geschichte der Leben-Jesu-Forschung*, vol. 1, pp. 100–5. Particularly critical is Ernst Troeltsch's review of Hermann Süskind, *Christentum und Geschichte bei Schleiermacher* (Tübingen, 1911), in *Theologische Literaturzeitung* 38 (1913), 21–4. This is ironical, in view of Schleiermacher's statement, 'Wer die Philosophie besitzen will, muß sie historisch verstehen' (Wilhelm Dilthey, *Leben Schleiermachers II*, ed. Martin Redeker (Berlin, 1966), p. 15).

56 Cf. Barth, *Protestantische Theologie im 19. Jahrhundert*, p. 379 'Nicht eine Schule stiftet er, sondern ein Zeitalter.' The words were originally used by Schleiermacher himself of Frederick the Great. Cf. the comments of R. A. Lipsius, 'Studien über Schleiermachers Dialektik', *Zeitschrift für wissenschaftliche Theologie* 12 (1869), p. 3.

57 *Marx and Engels on Religion*, ed. R. Niehbuhr (New York, 1964), p. 41.

2

The Hegelian Critique of Schleiermacher: Strauss, Baur and Feuerbach

The early nineteenth century witnessed the remarkable development of the complex phenomenon of German idealism, catalysed by Kant's critical idealism, whose complexity inhibits both succinct generalizations and detailed exposition.[1] The most significant form of idealism is that associated with Hegel, which exercised considerable influence over German Christology in the fourth and fifth decades of the nineteenth centuries. Hegel himself indicated the high importance of Christology, defining incarnation as the 'speculative mid-point (*Mittelpunkt*) of philosophy',[2] although it must be emphasised that he did not employ the language of classical Christology in its exposition. Hegel appears to establish the necessity, possibility and actuality of the 'incarnation' of God in a single individual on the basis of the anthropology of the divine-human union. The ideal unity of God and man is demonstrated through the appearance (*Erscheinung*) of God in the world in the flesh.[3] Hegel's distinction between *Vorstellung* ('representation') and *Begriff* ('concept') permitted the criticism of specific forms of religious expressions without undermining their philosophical content. On the basis of this *Vermittlungstheologie*, it was possible to assert that the eternal divine 'Idea' or 'Archetype' found full realization in the specific concrete instance of the historic human figure of Jesus of Nazareth, an idea developed with particular clarity by Philipp Konrad Marheineke. Although the followers of Hegel and Schleiermacher might have very different reasons for making this assertion, both grounded the doctrines of particular incarnation, historical revelation and positive religion upon it.

Hegel's Christology has been the subject of considerable attention recently, reflecting the renaissance in Hegel studies in general.[4] In his earlier period, Hegel's Christology was remarkably similar to that of the *Aufklärung*, Jesus being represented as an itinerant Kantian.[5] In his later writings, however, Hegel moved away from this position to his mature discussion of the *Vorstellung* of the incarnation. The Hegelian analysis of sensuous experience in general is characterized by the transition (*Übergang*) from 'representation' (*Vorstellung*)[6] to 'concept' (*Begriff*). Hegel understands *Vorstellung* to be the product of the analytical faculty of reason (*Verstand*) and the imaginative faculty of *Phantasie* to yield a perceptual image of experience. As such, *Vorstellung* is the mediating principle between *Anschauung* and *Denken*, between mere subjectivity and rational, or pure, objectivity. The philosophical mediation of truth is characterized by the constant oscillation between *Vorstellung* and *Begriff*, as one is compared with the other and refined accordingly (*ein Herüber- und Hinübergehen . . . von der Vorstellung zum Begriffe und von dem Begriffe zum Vorstellung*).[7] Hegel argues that such religious *Vorstellungen* are the first cognitive representations of the concept (*Begriff*) of God (that is, the Infinite). Religion initially comprises *Vorstellungen* of God which, although speculatively deficient, in that they combine 'finite' and 'infinite' elements, are capable of being resolved into the *Begriff* of God. It is therefore necessary to progress from the sensuously mediated images and experiences of *Vorstellung* to the *Begriff* of God.[8] Hegel's *ordo cognoscendi* is thus *Anschauungen* → *Vorstellungen* → *Gedanken* → *Begriff*, although Hegel emphasises that in the *ordo essendi*, the *Begriff* is prior to the *Vorstellungen* which embody it.

For Hegel, the incarnation is the supreme religious *Vorstellung* from which theological and philosophical speculation may begin. This *Vorstellung* is empirically and objectively grounded in the history of Jesus of Nazareth. Hegel assumes that the *Gedanke* of incarnation is common to all religions,[9] although the Christian *Vorstellung* of this *Gedanke* alone is absolutely adequate (*schlechthin gemäss*). Although *Vorstellungen* in all religions implicity, and with varying degrees of adequacy, bear witness to the incarnational truth of the human and divine natures, and to the reconciling action of God in the midst of human alienation, it is the Christian *Vorstellungen* which are supreme.[10] Christianity renders explicit what is only implicit in other religions. Thus the principle which Hegel understands the *Gedanke* of incarnation to express is that the Infinite Spirit (God) and the finite spirit (man) are not radically different or mutually incompatible.[11] The *Begriff* of God as the subsistent cause of all reality is revealed in the history of Jesus of Nazareth. The *Vorstellung* of the incarnation is thus inextricably linked with the external empirical event of the life of Jesus, although the process of reflection upon this event, by which the *Vorstellung* is transformed to the *Gedanke* and finally to the *Begriff*, necessarily entails increasing the epistemic distance between this history and the concept underlying it.

It will, however, be clear that there are certain questions raised by Hegel's discussion of the *Vorstellung* of the incarnation which require further consideration. Upon what grounds can the identification of the historical individual Jesus of Nazareth with the speculative principle of the incarnation be justified?[12] It will be evident that others in the course of history made similar claims: how may Jesus be distinguished from them? While Hegel concedes that others made similar claims, or that such claims were made on their behalf, he insists that these were but imperfect manifestations of the Infinite Spirit:

> The Idea . . . when it was ripe and the time was fulfilled, was able to attach itself only to Christ, and to realize itself only in him. The nature of Spirit is still imperfectly realized in the heroic deeds of Hercules. The history of Christ, however, belongs to the community, since it is absolutely adequate in relation to the Idea . . . It is the Spirit, the indwelling idea, which has witnessed to Christ's mission, and this is the verification for those who have believed and for us who possess the developed concept (*Begriff*).[13]

The weakness of this argument will be evident. Hegel actually employs an argument similar to the Lutheran *testimonium internum spiritus sancti* to justify his Christological commitment. By doing so, he effectively weakened the link between the *Vorstellung* and the *Begriff* of incarnation, so that it was possible for his successors to divorce what he had held together. If the grounds for holding together the history of Jesus of Nazareth and the concept of incarnation (understood in the Hegelian sense of the term) were defined solely in terms of a direct, immediate, inward certainty given by the Spirit, it would not prove difficult for a critic to challenge this somewhat weak Christological principle.

The breakdown of this mediating *modus vivendi* between philosophy and theology may be regarded as having taken place in the fourth and fifth decades of the century. Although there were Hegelians (such as Marheineke, Karl Daub and Karl Friederich Göschel) upon the right wing of the Hegelian school who were able and willing to integrate Hegel's speculative God-man with their orthodox Christology, there were others upon the left wing of the school who were not. It is the challenge posed to the Christology of Orthodoxy and of right wing Hegelianism by the work of David Friedrich Strauss, Ferdinand Christian Baur and Ludwig Feuerbach which we shall consider in the present chapter.[14]

In his early phase, Strauss showed considerable interest in the writings of Schleiermacher, which appear to have functioned as a catalyst for his conversion to Hegelianism.[15] Nevertheless, the Hegelianism which Strauss espoused was considerably different from that of Marheineke. For Hegel, the necessity and actuality of the incarnation could be justified rationally, thus permitting the *Begriff* of the realisation of the idea of divine-human unity to be harmonized with the *Vorstellung* of the incarnation of Christ. Strauss, however, pointed out that this left unanswered two crucial questions. First, must this idea necessarily be realized as *one specific individual*? Second, is speculative philosophy in any position to establish whether a given individual (such as Jesus of Nazareth) is, in fact, the historical realization of this idea? For Strauss, it seemed that the answer to the second of these questions lay in the negative – despite the protestations of right wing Hegelians. The only way of establishing whether a specific individual was, in fact, the historical realization of the idea of divine-human unity was through critical historical enquiry: the historical facts of the gospel narratives and their religious significance were not necessarily related. In order to establish the significance of Jesus of Nazareth, an empirical enquiry into the gospel narratives, independent of the presuppositions of speculative philosophy, was essential. Although this historical enquiry would not be capable of casting any light on the question of whether this idea necessarily found historical embodiment, it would be capable of establishing whether *any specific individual* – and it is clear that Strauss has Jesus of Nazareth in mind – was that historical embodiment.

The remarkable impact of Strauss's *Leben Jesu* appears to have been due as much to cultural as to theological considerations,[16] in that it was widely perceived to be a challenge to the reactionary society of Restoration Germany. However, the work posed a serious challenge to contemporary Christology for three reasons.

First, Strauss insisted that the Christian proclamation had to be treated as philosophical in nature, and hence that it could not be regarded as having any essential or necessary connection with any historical event, or series of events, such as the existence of a God-man in general, or the assertion that this God-man was the historic figure of Jesus of Nazareth. In other words, the truth of dogmatic claims was not dependent upon, and could not be verified with reference to, the gospel accounts of Jesus of Nazareth. This conclusion follows from Strauss's Hegelian presuppositions.

Second, the investigation of the gospel accounts of Jesus of Nazareth must be regarded as an historical, rather than a theological, undertaking. Historico-critical exegesis alone may be permitted to establish the historical veracity of the gospel accounts: indeed, if the truth claims of Christianity are based upon the historical veracity of these accounts, the truth claims must be based upon the independent findings of historical science. As such, history is prior to dogma.

Third, the gospel writers must be regarded as sharing the mythical *Weltanschauung* of their cultural situation. Strauss thus distances himself from Reimarus's suggestion that the evangelists distorted their accounts of Jesus of Nazareth, whether unconsciously or deliberately, and argues that mythical language is the natural mode of expression of a primitive group culture which had yet to rise to the level of abstract conceptualization. For Reimarus, the gospel writers were either telling the truth or lying (for whatever reason), his own researches having convinced him that they were lying. Strauss's distinctive contribution to the debate was to introduce the category of *Mythos* ('Myth'), a reflection of the gospel writers' social conditioning and cultural outlook, rather than a challenge to their integrity.[17] Whereas both rationalist and supernaturalist accepted the gospel accounts as factual accounts of the history of Jesus of Nazareth (the former regarding miracles as misunderstandings of natural events, the latter as literal accounts of divine intervention), Strauss argued that the gospel accounts are heavily impregnated with mythical elements. Strauss understands 'myth' to be an expression of the religious imagination, located at the level of *Vorstellung* rather than *Begriff*. Indeed, Strauss is able to develop an Hegelian interpretation of myth as a primitive stage in the self-development of 'spirit' through its own history. In the third and fourth editions of the *Leben Jesu*, Strauss distinguished three levels of myth:

Evangelical myth is a narrative relating directly or indirectly to Jesus, which may be considered not as the expression of a fact (*Tatsache*), but as the impression of an idea of his earliest followers ... *Pure myth* in the gospel has two sources... the Messianic ideas and expectations existing according to their several forms in the Jewish mind before Jesus, and independently of him; the other is that particular impression which was left by the personal character, actions and fate of Jesus, and which served to modify the Messianic idea of his people. *Historical myth* (*Mythus an der Geschichte*) has for its background a definite individual fact which has been seized upon by religious enthusiasm, and surrounded with mythical conceptions deriving from the idea of the Christ.[18]

The supernaturalists, according to Strauss, remained loyal to the gospel text, and as a result demanded belief in the incredible; the naturalists distorted the text beyond credible limits in an attempt to posit a natural event which might underlie the gospel account. For Strauss, the explanation lay in myth, whose presence in a gospel pericope was a positive criterion of its unhistoricity. Although Strauss does not deny that an historical event may lie behind myth, myths themselves are not to be regarded as historical formulations.[19] Thus Strauss argued that, although the presence of myth may be detected in practically every aspect of the gospel accounts of the history of Jesus of Nazareth, genuinely historical events may be supposed to underlie this history. Thus it may be stated that Jesus actually lived, that he had disciples, that he regarded himself as the Messiah, and that he was crucified. Furthermore, Strauss concedes that the gospel accounts of Jesus' discourses are substantially correct. Nevertheless, for reasons which we noted above, this factual kernel at the heart of the mythical husk was of no significance. Furthermore, at every point which might be deemed theologically significant by Orthodox criteria (such as many details of the passion accounts, and the accounts of the resurrection and ascension), Strauss detected extensive mythical elements, thus indicating the unhistorical nature of these narratives. Thus, for example, he argues that because the idea of 'resurrection' includes the obviously supernatural idea of the return to life of a dead man, a rational observer is forced to conclude that 'either Jesus was not really dead, or he did not really rise again'.[20] In effect, Strauss destroyed both the foundations of the supernaturalist citadel and the compromises of rationalism, and forced those who followed him to deal with the New Testament foundations of Christology in a new manner.

Strauss was thus able to eliminate the need to explain gospel passages such as the resurrection account on either supernatural or natural grounds: the account is ultimately an expression of the cultural consciousness of a primitive people. There was simply no possibility of mediation between historico-critical investigation and Christian faith. As such, faith must either collapse, or else must be reinterpreted by dissociating the dogmatic principle of incarnation from the claim that this idea had been fully embodied in a concrete historical individual, Jesus of Nazareth. In effect, Strauss argued that the *Vorstellung* and *Begriff* of incarnation (that is, the unity of the divine and human spirit) could be kept strictly separate, and that the latter could replace the former, fulfilling the same religious need in a more adequate manner.[21] For Strauss, conceptual thinking is as existentially satisfying as, and considerably more precise than, symbolic or mythical forms of the religious imagination. This must be regarded as a significant departure from Hegel's insistence upon the necessity of the foundation of philosophy upon religious experience: the religious image (*Vorstellung*) gives rise to the speculative concept (*Begriff*), and the *Begriff* articulates the true meaning of the *Vorstellung*.[22] In effect, Strauss's programme amounts to a severing of the Hegelian link between speculative thought and the religious imagination and historical experience, detaching theology from religious consciousness. Through his introduction of the category of 'myth', Strauss believed he had a means of destroying religious symbols, which rendered unnecessary the more difficult task of reinterpreting them. On the basis of this assumption, Strauss developed a form of monistic pantheism which had little, if any, connection with the historical figure of Jesus of Nazareth, who he regarded as having little significance for modern man. This tendency alarmed many of those who were otherwise sympathetic to his aims, such as Ferdinand Christian Baur.

Baur had been deeply impressed by Schleiermacher's *Glaubenslehre* as a young man, which he regarded as ending the old and sterile debate between rationalism and supernaturalism.[23] However, Baur considered that Schleiermacher appeared to be unable to accomodate the historical and ecclesiastical dimensions of Christianity within the context of his *Glaubenslehre*, which appeared to be dominated by the philosophical and the idealistic. Nowhere, he argues, does Schleiermacher explain how he moves from the general consciousness of redemption to a specific historical individual as the ground of that consciousness. In fact, Schleiermacher appears to make the archetypal Christ (that is, the Christological interpretation of the subjective experience of redemption) prior to the historical Jesus, so that the person and work of Christ may only be treated as derivative functions of the religious consciousness. Baur therefore developed a penetrating critique of the Christology of Schleiermacher's *Glaubenslehre* on the basis of its perceived failure to mediate between the archetypal Christ and the historical Jesus. Unless theology begins with the historical Jesus, in terms of a critical analysis of the gospel accounts (in which alone he may be encountered), he will never be found. Baur is particularly critical of the manner in which Schleiermacher infers his Christology from religious consciousness. The experience of pious consciousness within the Christian community is treated as the effect of the influence of a single individual, whose identity may be inferred by arguing backwards from effect to cause. For Baur, this is illegitimate: to understand a historical process, it is necessary to begin with the cause, and thence to follow through its effects. In the case of Schleiermacher's argument, there is no *historical* necessity that the cause of religious consciousness is a *single* individual, nor that it be the *specific* historical individual Jesus of Nazareth. Baur's conclusion may be stated as follows: in terms of the nature of Schleiermacher's argument from the ideal or archetypal Christ to the historical Jesus, he fails to demonstrate the possibility of an authentically historical Jesus; in terms of the direction of the argument (the inference of the cause from the effect), he fails to demonstrate the necessity of an historical Jesus. Baur himself argued that the foundations of Christology must be regarded as historico-critical, and had already established the techniques which he felt were necessary for this undertaking. During the period at which he taught classics at the Blaubeuren seminary (1817–26), he had become familiar with the new source-critical methods discussed in B. G. Niehbuhr's *Römische Geschichte* (1811–12), and had developed an interest in ancient religion through reading G. F. Creuzer's *Symbolik und Mythologie der alten Völker* (2nd edn, 1819–23). The need for a conceptual philosophy and critical history in dealing with the Christian tradition was clearly identified in his own *Symbolik und Mythologie* (1824–25), although it would be a decade before Baur committed himself to Hegelianism[24] as the appropriate philosophy to revive history from its 'eternally dead and dumb' state. The catalyst for this development was the publication of Strauss's *Leben Jesu*.

As noted above, Strauss drew the conclusion that the historical Jesus has at best only an accidental connection with the ideal or archetypal Christ, thus effectively denying the significance of the historical individual Jesus of Nazareth for Christian faith. Furthermore, Strauss's radical criticism of the relationship between *Vorstellung* and *Begriff* effectively eliminated any means by which the historical Jesus could be employed as a means of verifying the interpretation which the Christian community had placed upon him. Baur's task was therefore to distinguish between the critical-historical and speculative philosophical viewpoints, without destroying their inherent interconnection.

For Baur, Strauss engaged in historical criticism solely in order to destroy the Christian tradition: it is for this reason that he characterized Strauss's *Glaubenslehre* as the 'most striking example' of the rationalism of the eighteenth century.[25] For Strauss, 'the true criticism of dogma is its history';[26] for Baur, the strongly anti-dogmatic approach to the history of dogma was more concerned with the destruction of dogma than the investigation of its history. For Baur, the key to a correct understanding of the significance of Jesus of Nazareth lay in a critical study of Christian origins.[27]

The most significant and immediate casualty of this approach was the Fourth Gospel, regarded as an historical source by Schleiermacher. For Schleiermacher, the Fourth Gospel was the most nearly continuous, complete and historically reliable portrait of Jesus, giving insights into his personality, and a thoroughly spiritual and religious interpretation of his identity and mission, tinged only to a slight degree with apocalyptic messianic supernaturalism. The traditional interpretation of the *Vorstellung* of the incarnation, to name but one significant theologoumenon, was derived practically in its totality from the Fourth Gospel. The historicity of that gospel had been called into question, although on somewhat weak grounds, by Strauss: it was, however, through the massive critical studies of Baur that its peculiar character was first established on critical grounds. In an important study of 1837, Baur attempted to compare the relation of Socrates to Platonism with the relation of Jesus to Christianity,[28] in order to cast light upon the origins of Christianity, emphasizing in so doing the dependence of Christianity upon the person of its founder. In that study, he treated the Fourth Gospel as a relatively reliable historical source, primarily concerned with Christ's higher nature and immediate divinity. By 1847, however, Baur had concluded that the narratives and discourses of the Fourth Gospel were so controlled by an idealizing *Weltanschauung* that they could not be regarded as historical.[29] The Fourth Gospel was thus a source for the theology of the early church (how early being a matter of debate), rather than a source for the history of Jesus of Nazareth. Baur argued that the rejection of the historicity of the Fourth

Gospel was tantamount to the rejection of the dogma of the incarnation of the Logos,[30] and thus proceeded to construct a purely historical Jesus on the basis of a purely historical method.[31] For Baur, it was possible and necessary to go behind the Christ of faith, on the presupposition (*contra* Strauss) that there existed an inextricable connection between the two (although, it should be added, Baur was not prepared to accept the *identity* or *coincidence* of the Jesus of history and the Christ of faith, *contra* Orthodoxy). It is in this respect that Baur's divergence from Hegel is perhaps at its clearest. For Hegel, Christianity was primarily about a concept (*Begriff*), so that it was not necessary to go behind the Christ of faith to consider the 'historically factual objective reality' underlying faith; for Baur, Christianity was primarily about a *person*.[32] Thus his account of the historical figure of Jesus of Nazareth is of decisive significance for his Christology, as well as for his theology in general. It is, however, possible to seriously misunderstand Baur's attitude to Hegel. Baur does not suggest that Hegel severed all essential or internal connections between the Christ of faith and the Jesus of history, but merely draws attention to the inadequate manner in which he formulates their relationship. For Baur, the 'the unity of the divine and human nature first became concrete truth and self-conscious knowledge in Christ, and was expressed and taught by him as truth'.[33] By making this significant assertion, Baur is able to provide an integral connection between the historical and the ideal, which he found lacking in Hegel. Having made this step, Baur is then able to avoid the historically unjustifiable compromise of Schleiermacher, and the philosophically untenable and ungrounded assertion of Marheineke and Daub, all of whom resorted to *identifying* the archetypal Christ with the historical figure of Jesus of Nazareth.[34] Baur insisted that the two are integrally and inextricably interrelated, and that the latter is absolutely indispensable to faith. However, despite a careful analysis of Baur's writings, we are forced to the conclusion that Baur's antithesis between the Jesus of history and the Christ of faith represents an unresolved dualism, bestowed to his successors within the Tübingen school for further critical investigation. Nevertheless, we are not primarily concerned with the ambiguities of Baur's Christology, but with the significance of his historical approach to Christology, which has such important consequences for Schleiermacher's Christology in general, and the theological method of the *Glaubenslehre* in general. It is clear that Baur's historical critique of Schleiermacher's causal argument concerning the relationship between the archetypal Christ and historical Jesus, and supremely his rejection of the use of the Fourth Gospel as a source for the history of Jesus of Nazareth, have devastating consequences for Schleiermacher's *Christusbild*. A perhaps still more significant criticism was, however, yet to come, again arising from Hegelian idealism – the anti-theology of Ludwig Feuerbach.

The matrix within which Feuerbach's thought emerged is the philosophical radicalism of the so-called 'Young Hegelians', a somewhat diffuse group of thinkers prominent in Berlin in the 1830s and 1840s.[35] Although initially a defender of Hegel against his critics, by 1839 he had come to share many of their misgivings concerning him.[36] Many of the insights which are incorporated into the substance of *Das Wesen des Christenthums* (1841) may be shown to date from this earlier period.[37] The publication of this work caused a sensation, evoking the admiration of thinkers such as Strauss and Engels, and is rightly regarded as a milestone in the development of religious criticism in the nineteenth century.[38] In view of the importance of this work in relation to Schleiermacher,[39] we propose to consider it in some detail.

In the foreword to the first edition of *Das Wesen des Christenthums*, Feuerbach states that the 'purpose of this work is to show that the supernatural mysteries of religion are based upon quite simple natural truths'.[40] The leading idea of the work is deceptively simple: man has created the gods, who embody his own idealized conception of his aspirations, needs and fears. Nevertheless, to suggest that Feuerbach merely reduces the divine to the natural (as, for example, one might reduce divine activity to a natural phenomenon) is to seriously misunderstand him, and to inhibit appreciation of his full significance. The permanent significance of the work lies not in its repetition of the reduced theology of Xenophanes or Lucretius, but in its detailed analysis of the means by which religious concepts arise within the human consciousness. The thesis that man creates the gods in his own image is but the conclusion of a radical and penetrating critique of concept formation in religion, based on the Hegelian concepts of 'self-alienation' and 'self-objectification'.

The Hegelian analysis of consciousness requires that there be a formal relation of subject to object. The concept of 'consciousness' cannot be isolated as an abstract idea, in that it is necessarily linked with an object: to be 'conscious' is to be *conscious of something*, so that there is a latent differentiation within consciousness between its subject and object. When Hegel introduces the phenomenological concept of the 'other Being of consciousness' (*das Anderssein des Bewusstsein*), he intends us to understand the process by which man's consciousness identifies its object, thus transferring the object from its 'abstract' to its 'concretized' form. Whatever the object may be in itself, it is an object *in consciousness* only to the extent that it is an object for some conscious subject. The process by which the conscious subject identifies the object of that consciousness is defined as 'objectification' (*Vergegenständigung*) or 'externalization' (*Entaüsserung*). It is this process of 'objectification' which is taken up by Feuerbach, and developed in an anti-theological direction: it is therefore necessary to point out that George Eliot has seriously impeded the proper understanding of Feuerbach on this point by translating *Vergegenständigung* as 'projection', thus obscuring the Hegelian background to his thought. For Feuerbach, the process of the self-objectification of human consciousness requires that the 'other Being' (*Anderssein*) of consciousness must be *like* the conscious subject, but *distinct from it*. In other words, to develop Feuerbach's point, the 'other Being' must be a *You*, rather than an *I*, but identical in species (*Gattung*) to the subject.[41] For Feuerbach, the culmination of a dialectical phenomenology is *man's self-knowledge as a species being*.

With this point in mind, we are in a position to develop Feuerbach's 'anthropotheism'. Man's consciousness of feelings, such as fear or love, leads to his objectification and externalization of these feelings. Although he is not mistaken in the attribution of such predicates to external objects, he may be mistaken in relation to the object to which he attributes them. It is possible to treat natural objects (such as trees) or fantasy objects (such as ghosts) as if they were human, so that they serve as surrogates of humanity in the attribution of feelings such as love or fear. In other words, they are examples of the *real but mistaken* objectification of human feelings. The predicates which are thus objectified are *properly conceived, but misapplied*: properly speaking, they can only be applied to the human species, and not to non-human or imaginary human objects. By objectifying such human emotions in inappropriate manners, the subject has simply made a species or category mistake, applying predicates which properly belong to man (considered as *Gattung*) to inappropriate objects. As God cannot be included in the human *Gattung*, such emotions cannot be objectified in relation to him. Divine predicates are thus recognized to be human predicates, precisely because the processes of *Entäusserung* and

Vergegenständigung cannot be applied to God. Whereas Hegel understood the subject of the dialectic of self-differentiation to be the Absolute Idea (in order to rationalize the manner of its unfolding), Feuerbach understood it to be man as species being.[42] With this shift in the point of reference of the dialectical process, a universal pantheism effectively became an atheism:

Consciousness of God is man's self-consciousness; knowledge of God is man's self-knowledge. By his God you know the man, and conversely, by the man, you know his God. The two are one. What God is to a man, that too is his spirit, his soul; and what his spirit, his soul, are to a man, that is his God. God is the revealed and explicit inner self of man . . . The historical progress of religion consists therefore in this: that what an earlier religion took to be objective, is later recognized to be subjective; what formerly was taken to be God, and worshipped as such, is now recognized to be something *human*. What was earlier religion is later taken to be idolatry: man is seen to have adored his own nature. Man objectified himself, but failed to recognize himself as this object. The later religion takes this step; every advance in religion is therefore a deepening in self-knowledge.[43]

It is obvious that Feuerbach tends to use the terms 'Christianity' and 'religion' interchangeably throughout *Das Wesen des Christenthums*, thus glossing over the fact that his theory has some difficulty in accounting for non-theistic religions. Nevertheless, it is clear that his reduction of Christian theology to anthropology is of considerable significance in relation to the solution to the Christological dilemma developed by Schleiermacher.

The most important *epistemological* analysis in *Das Wesen des Christenthums* is that concerned with the role of feeling in the process of religious concept formation, and has important consequences for the *Gefühl*-centred philosophies of Jacobi and Schleiermacher. For Feuerbach, Christian theology has tended to interpret the externalized image of 'feeling' or self-consciousness as a wholly other, absolute essence, whereas it is in fact *das selbstfühlende Gefühl*, a species feeling which cannot be objectified in any manner save in the form of the human species. The instrument by which the improper objectification of *das selbstfühlende Gefühl* takes place is the religious imagination.[44] In other words, imagination (*Phantasie*) is the instrument of human consciousness which interprets feelings as a concrete sensory representation – and in doing so, is prone to make species or category errors. For Feuerbach, every act of *das religiöse Gefühl* is nothing more than an expression or an embodiment of the feeling that man has for his own sensible nature. As such, man is liable to mistakenly objectify *das Gefühl* as God: 'If feeling is the essential instrumentality or organ of religion, then God's nature is nothing other than an expression of the nature of feeling . . . The divine essence, which is comprehended by feeling, is actually nothing other than the essence of feeling, enraptured and delighted with itself – nothing but self-intoxicated, self-contented feeling.'[45] For Schleiermacher, the nature of the pious self-consciousness was such that the existence of the Redeemer could be inferred from it; for Feuerbach, this species self-consciousness was nothing more and nothing less than man's awareness of himself. Whereas Baur had challenged Schleiermacher's argument from consciousness to its origins in terms of its logic, Feuerbach effectively reduced it to the inevitable delusion of self-objectification and self-externalization.[46] Man merely objectifies himself in religion. Although those who might care to defend Schleiermacher in the face of this critique could conceivably appeal to the fact that Schleiermacher appeals to the *corporate*, rather than the *individual*, self-consciousness, Feuerbach has already cut the ground from under this objection by his insistence that the dialectical process has as its subject man's self-knowledge as a *species* being. Thus for Feuerbach, the incarnation enshrines the insight that God is human, and enables man to value his own humanity as he would otherwise value deity. 'Religion is the reflection, the mirroring of human nature in itself.'[47] What is most emphatically *not* permissible, according to Feuerbach, is the argument from man's feeling or self-consciousness to the existence of a different species, distinct from man. 'God-consciousness' is merely man's awareness of himself, and not a distinct category of human experience, a milestone in man's journey from primitive to modern understandings of himself. Although Feuerbach does not make this point, it may be stated that, on the basis of his analysis of human concept-formation, the 'dominant God-consciousness' which Schleiermacher ascribes to Jesus of Nazareth can only be regarded as a deluded self-consciousness.[48] Where Schleiermacher speaks of God, he is merely making unconscious anthropological statements. Even if Feuerbach did not totally reduce theology to anthropology, he at least succeeded in making it an anthropological epiphenomenon, with devastating effects for any theology which began with man's feelings, and inferred the existence of external or objective realities from them. Feuerbach's critique of religion may indeed lose much of its force when dealing with non-theistic religions, or theologies (such as that of Karl Barth) which claim to deal with an divine encounter with man from outside him;[49] when applied to a theistic construction or interpretation of man's emotional or psychological states, however, it is in its element. Has man *really* spoken about God or Christ? Or has he simply projected his longings and fears onto an imaginary transcendent plane, or onto a distant historical figure about whom we know so little? The growing conviction that Christology must be objectively grounded in the history of Jesus of Nazareth is at least due in part to Feuerbach's critique of religion. The very idea of 'God' was, according to Feuerbach, an illusion which men could at least in principle avoid, and, with sufficient progress in self-knowledge, could discard altogether. It is, of course, a small – and perhaps an inevitable – step to proceed from this assumption to the Marxist view that religious feeling is itself the product of an alienated social existence. Thus for Marx, 'the basis of irreligious criticism is: Man makes religion, religion does not make man.'[50] Whereas Feuerbach regarded religion as one stage in man's evolution, Marx regarded it as a response to a socio-economic structure: if the structure was altered, a corresponding change in religion could be expected, perhaps to the point of its total elimination. It is this presupposition which underlies the most famous of Marx's 'Theses on Feuerbach': 'The philosophers have only interpreted the world, in various ways; the point, however, is to change it.'[51]

It will be helpful if we summarize the developments which took place in the decade after Schleiermacher's death in 1834 which posed so effective a challenge to his solution to the Christological problem.

(1) The historicity of the Fourth Gospel was called into question, so that it could no longer be treated as a source for the history of Jesus of Nazareth, but only as a source for the history of the early church. This development is associated initially with Strauss, and was subsequently championed by Baur. Schleiermacher's *Christusbild* was constructed on the assumption of the historicity of the Fourth Gospel: for Schleiermacher, the markedly spiritual content of the gospel indicated that its author was a witness to the events it portrayed. From this point onward, the question of the historical Jesus had to be discussed solely with reference to the Synoptic Gospels.

(2) Within the Synoptic Gospels themselves, the researches of Strauss had called into question the historical character of a substantial number of passages, generally in contexts of significance for Orthodox theology (such as the account of the resurrection), on account

of their including 'mythical' material. Whereas it had been generally assumed up to this point that the gospel records were true accounts of the history of Jesus of Nazareth (the difference between supernaturalists and naturalists lying primarily in the manner in which miracles were interpreted), Strauss argued that they incorporated a substantial quantity of non-historical material. On the basis of this conclusion, he effectively restricted the source material for the history of Jesus of Nazareth to a small section of material, which he himself deemed insignificant.

(3) The rise in historical thinking particularly associated with the Tübingen school led to an emphasis being placed upon the methodological priority of the *origins of Christianity* over its present-day manifestations. In other words, the question of the significance of Jesus of Nazareth, and particularly his relation to the 'archetypal Christ', had to be answered by seeking that significance in his history, and not by inferring such significance from the present-day pious consciousness of the community of faith.

(4) Feuerbach's critique of religion called into question the propriety of inferring the existence or nature of 'God' from religious feeling, in that this feeling could only be interpreted *anthropologically*, and not theologically. The possibility that the putative relation between the 'archetypal Christ' and the Jesus of history was purely illusory, resulting from the erroneous objectification and externalization of man's aspirations, could no longer be ignored. The unsatisfactory foundation which Schleiermacher established for this relation was thus cruelly exposed, its inadequacy obvious to all.

As we noted in the previous chapter, Schleiermacher must be regarded as founding an era, rather than a school. The opening of that era witnessed the near-total destructive criticism of his Christocentric *Glaubenslehre*, and raised the question of whether this was, in fact, the way forward. Although Schleiermacher's original Christological method now appeared to be seriously inadequate, it was not totally beyond salvage. In the following chapter, we shall indicate how a new *Christusbild* arose from the ashes of the old.

NOTES

1 On Hegel's critique of Kant, see Ingtraud Görland, *Die Kantkritik des jungen Hegel* (Frankfurt, 1966).

2 *Vorlesungen über die Philosophie der Religion*; *Werke* (18 vols: Berlin, 1832-45), vol. 11, p. 146.
3 See Peter C. Hodgson, 'Hegel', in *Nineteenth Century Religious Thought in the West*, ed. Ninian Smart, John Clayton, Patrick Sherry and Steven T. Katz (3 vols: Cambridge, 1985), vol. 1, pp. 81–121; pp. 102–5.
4 See Hans Küng, *Menschwerdung Gottes: Eine Einführung in Hegels theologisches Denken als Prolegomena zu einer künftigen Christologie* (Freiburg, 1970); James Yerkes, *The Christology of Hegel* (Albany, NY, 1983). For a critical appraisal of Küng's important work, see Joseph Fitzer, 'Hegel and the Incarnation: A Response to Hans Küng', *Journal of Religion* 52 (1972), pp. 240–67. Yerkes's study is one of the finest studies of Hegel's thought ever to have been published.
5 See Yerkes, *Christology of Hegel*, pp. 7–49, for an excellent discussion of the Christology of the *Jugendschriften*.
6 It is, in fact, very difficult to translate *Vorstellung* into English in such a way that the full complexity of Hegel's thought may be adequately captured: see Malcolm Clark, *Logic and System: A Study of the Transition from Vorstellung to Thought in the Philosophy of Hegel* (The Hague, 1970) – an unusually lucid exposition of a very difficult idea. In general, English translators have confused the issue by using a variety of English words to translate the same German term – see the very poor translation of the *Phänomenologie des Geistes* by J. B. Baillie: *Phenomenology of Mind* (New York, 2nd edn, 1949).
7 *Vorlesungen über die Philosophie der Religion*; *Werke*, vol. 11, p. 26. Cf. Clark, *Logic and System*, pp. 24–6. For a critical evaluation of Hegel's dialectic at this particular point, see Michael Rosen, *Hegel's Dialectic and Its Criticism* (Cambridge, 1985), pp. 55–91, especially pp. 57–63.
8 *Vorlesungen über die Philosophie der Religion*; *Werke*, vol. 11, p. 26.
9 Ibid., p. 77. Cf. the important study of Reinhard Leuze, *Die ausserchristlichen Religionen bei Hegel* (Göttingen, 1975).
10 *Vorlesungen über die Philosophie der Religion*; *Werke*, vol. 12, pp. 320–1.
11 It is on the basis of such suggestions that Hegel has been regarded as a pantheist. Hegel was prepared to concede this, provided the world was understood as *Allgötterei* (i.e., as divine in its unifying foundation), rather than *Allesgötterei* (i.e., divine in its totality): see *Vorlesungen über die Philosophie der Religion*; *Werke*, vol. 11, pp. 390–1.
12 See Yerkes, *Christology of Hegel*, pp. 114–47.
13 *Vorlesungen über die Philosophie der Religion*; *Werke* vol. 12, pp. 320–1.
14 It may, of course, be pointed out that a perhaps more effective challenge to Hegel was posed by the Danish philosopher Søren Kierkegaard: see Hayo Gerdes, *Das Christusbild Sören Kierkegaards: Vergleichen mit der Christologie Hegels und Schleiermachers* (Düsseldorf, 1960); Stephen Crites, *In the Twilight of Christendom: Hegel vs. Kierkegaard on Faith and History*

(Chambersburg, Pa., 1972); N. Thulstrup, *Kierkegaard's Relation to Hegel* (Princeton, 1980). However, the full force of this critique would not be experienced within the German theological consciousness until the twentieth century, and belongs to a later point in the present study. The development of Hegelianism over the period 1805–41 is complex. The best study of this development currently available is John E. Toews, *Hegelianism: The Path Towards Dialectical Humanism 1805–1841* (Cambridge, 1985), pp. 71–369. The reader will find himself greatly assisted, particularly in relation to Strauss and Feuerbach, by a familiarity with this analysis.

15 See J. F. Sandberger, *David Friedrich Strauss als theologische Hegelianer* (Göttingen, 1972) for an excellent analysis of Strauss's understanding of the relationship between *Vorstellung* and *Begriff*. For two useful studies of Strauss in English, see P. C. Hodgson's introduction to *The Life of Jesus Critically Examined* (London, 1972), pp. xv–xlvii; Hans Frei, 'David Friedrich Strauss', in *Nineteenth Century Religious Thought in the West*, vol. 1, pp. 215–60.

16 See M. C. Massey, 'The Literature of Young Germany and D. F. Strauss's *Life of Jesus*', *Journal of Religion* 59 (1979), pp. 298–323. A list of the works written in response to Strauss may be found in Albert Schweitzer, *Geschichte der Leben-Jesu-Forschung* (2 vols: Munich/Hamburg, 3rd edn, 1966), vol. 2, pp. 632–5 (not in the English translation). For an evaluation of the English reaction to this work, see Robert Morgan, 'Non Angli sed Angeli: Some Anglican Reactions to German Gospel Criticism', in *New Studies in Theology 1*, eds. S. Sykes and D. Holmes (London, 1980), pp. 1–30.

17 See C. Hartlich and W. Sachs, *Der Ursprung des Mythosbegriffes in der modernen Bibelwissenschaft* (Tübingen, 1952), where Strauss's work is set in a broader context, including the work of J. G. Eichorn, J. P. Gabler and J. G. Herder. See also the more recent study of D. Lange, *Historischer Jesus oder mythischer Christus: Untersuchungen zu dem Gegensatz zwischen Friedrich Schleiermacher und David Friedrich Strauss* (Gütersloh, 1975), where the significance of Schleiermacher is fully brought out.

18 *Das Leben Jesu, kritisch bearbeitet* (2 vols: Tübingen, 3rd edn, 1838), vol. 1, pp. 113–14; *The Life of Jesus Critically Examined*, ed. P. C. Hodgson, pp. 86–7.

19 *Leben Jesu*, vol. 1, pp. 119–24; *The Life of Jesus*, pp. 89–92.

20 *Leben Jesu*, vol. 2, pp. 676–9; citation, p. 679; *The Life of Jesus*, pp. 735–6; citation p. 736.

21 This is made particularly clear in Strauss's discussion of the manner in which the theologian may reconcile his opinions with those of the church: *The Life of Jesus*, p. 783. This section is not to be found in the third edition: see Hodgson, *The Life of Jesus*, pp. 797–8 for a discussion of the point.

The basic principle was developed in the unpublished *Vorlesungen über Logik und Metaphysik* (1832).

22 This point has already been discussed at sufficient length: on the general point, see Clark, *Logic and System*, passim.

23 See Heinz Liebing, 'Ferdinand Christian Baurs Kritik an Schleiermachers Glaubenslehre', *Zeitschrift für Theologie und Kirche* 54 (1957), pp. 225–43 for an excellent analysis of Baur's attitude to Schleiermacher. Two excellent studies of Baur currently available in English are: P. C. Hodgson, *The Formation of Historical Theology: A Study of Ferdinand Christian Baur* (New York, 1966); Robert Morgan, 'Ferdinand Christian Baur', in *Nineteenth Century Religious Thought in the West*, vol. 1, pp. 261-89.

24 The question of precisely what form of Hegelianism Baur adopted is important: see Hodgson, *Formation of Historical Theology*, pp.54–73; Sandberger, *Strauss als theologische Hegelianer*, p. 152.

25 See Hodgson, *Formation of Historical Theology*, pp. 73–86.

26 F. D. Strauss, *Die christliche Glaubenslehre in ihrer geschichtlichen Entwickelung* (2 vols: Tübingen, 1840-41), vol. 1, p. 71. Cf. Albert Schweitzer, *Geschichte der Leben-Jesu-Forschung*, vol. 1, p. 47; *The Quest of the Historical Jesus* (London, 3rd edn, 1954), p. 4: 'The historical investigation of the life of Jesus did not take its rise from a purely historical interest; it turned to the Jesus of history as an ally in the struggle for liberation from dogma'.

27 The origins of the Tübingen school are usually traced to the aftermath of the publication of Strauss's *Leben Jesu*, and Baur's reaction to it: see the somewhat hostile study of Horton Harris, *The Tübingen School* (Oxford, 1975), pp. 2–3.

28 F. C. Baur, 'Das christlich des Platonismus oder Sokrates und Christus', *Tübinger Zeitschrift für Theologie* 10 (1837), pp. 1–154.

29 For example, F. C. Baur, 'Über die Composition und den Charakter des johanneïschen Evangeliums', *Theologische Jahrbücher* 3 (1844), pp. 1–191; 397–475; 615–700. The fundamental point emphasized by Baur is that these narratives and discourses are all made subservient to the theme of the incarnation of the divine Logos.

30 As Morgan points out, ('Ferdinand Christian Baur', pp. 267–8), this was not actually correct, although this was not fully appreciated at the time.

31 For an outstanding analysis of this historical method, see Hodgson, *Formation of Historical Theology*, pp. 90–201.

32 At this point, Baur parts company with Strauss, as well as Hegel. The essential point which underlies Baur's concern with the person of Jesus of Nazareth is his fear that speculative theology might become based upon the a priori deductions of scholastic metaphysics. Morgan has helpfully pointed out the similarities between the Strauss-Baur and the Bultmann-Käsemann debates: Morgan, 'Ferdinand Christian Baur', pp. 280–1.

33 *Die christliche Gnosis* (Tübingen, 1835), p. 717 'Die nothwendige Voraussezung (sic) ist in jedem Falle, daß. . .die Einheit der göttlichen und menschlichen Natur, in Christus zuerst zur concreten Wahrheit, zum selbstbewußten Wissen wurde, und von ihm als Wahrheit ausgesprochen und gelehrt wurde.' At this point, it is necessary to question Hodgson's otherwise reliable judgements: cf. *Formation of Historical Theology*, p. 62, where this passage is seriously mistranslated, and Baur's attitude to Hegel is misunderstood, apparently on the basis of this mistranslation.

34 *Die christliche Gnosis*, pp. 639–40; 734–5.

35 See Karl Löwith, *Von Hegel zu Nietzsche* (Stuttgart, 4th edn, 1958); W. I. Brazall, *The Young Hegelians* (New Haven, 1970). The definitive study of the development of Feuerbach's thought to 1843 is Max Wartofsky, *Feuerbach* (Cambridge, 1982).

36 See Wartofsky, *Feuerbach*, pp. 135–95, for an outstanding analysis in English. See further K. Grün, *Ludwig Feuerbachs philosophische Charakterentwicklung* (2 vols: Leipzig/Heidelberg, 1974), which brings together much personal material for the period 1820–72.

37 For example, see Wartofsky, *Feuerbach*, pp. 205–6.

38 For a critical (and sometimes not so critical) appreciation of this work, see Michael von Gagern, *Ludwig Feuerbach: Philosophie- und Religionskritik* (Munich/Salzburg, 1970); Marcel Xhaufflaire, *Feuerbach et la théologie de la sécularisation* (Paris, 1972); E. Schneider, *Die Theologie und Feuerbachs Religionskritik: Die Reaktion des 19. Jahrhunderts auf Ludwig Feuerbachs Religionskritik* (Göttingen, 1972). The suggestion that it was not *Das Wesen des Christenthums* but the philosophical works of 1843 which turned Karl Marx into a fervent Feuerbachian may be treated with some scepticism: see H. Arvon, 'Engels' Feuerbach kritisch beleuchtet', in *Atheismus in der Diskussion*, ed. H. Lübbe and H. M. Sass (Munich/Mainz, 1975), pp. 109–19. Note especially the critical comments of Sass and Schuffenhauer in the subsequent discussion.

39 Curiously, Wartofsky's otherwise brilliant analysis of Feuerbach fails to bring out his significance in this respect: see James Bradley, 'Across the River and Beyond the Trees: Feuerbach's Relevance to Modern Thought', in *New Studies in Theology 1*, ed. S. Sykes and D. Holmes (London, 1980), pp. 139–61.

40 Feuerbach, *Das Wesen des Christenthums*, ed. W. Schuffenhauer (2 vols: Berlin, 1956), vol. 1, p. 4. George Eliot translated the second edition into English, with such infelicity that it should not be used as a critical source for Feuerbach. Unfortunately, a better translation is not forthcoming.

41 It is significant that Martin Buber appeals to Feuerbach in his articulation of his dialogical personalism: M. Buber, 'Das Problem des Menschen',

Werke (3 vols: Munich/Heidelberg, 1962-64), vol. 1, pp. 309–47, especially pp. 339–43.

42 For an excellent account of the development of Feuerbach's *Gattungsbegriff*, see Wartofsky, *Feuerbach*, pp. 220–6.

43 *Das Wesen des Christenthums*, ed. Schuffenhauer, vol. 1, pp. 51–2.

44 See Wartofsky, *Feuerbach*, pp. 215–20.

45 *Das Wesen des Christenthums*, ed. Schuffenhauer, vol. 1, p. 46.

46 We confess ourselves puzzled by the study of R. R. Williams, *Schleiermacher the Theologian: The Construction of the Doctrine of God* (Philadelphia, 1978), which seems (for example, pp. 165–7) to misunderstand *both* Schleiermacher *and* Feuerbach in order to refute the latter.

47 *Das Wesen des Christenthums*, ed. Schuffenhauer, vol. 1, p. 118. Cf. p. 122, where Feuerbach states that the image of God is the 'mirror of man'.

48 For Feuerbach's reduction of the *Vorstellung* of the incarnation, see Wartofsky, *Feuerbach*, pp. 226–8.

49 See John Glasse, 'Barth on Feuerbach', *Harvard Theological Review* 57 (1964), pp. 69–96; M. H. Vogel, 'The Barth-Feuerbach Confrontation', *Harvard Theological Review* 59 (1966), pp. 27–52.

50 *Marx and Engels on Religion*, ed. R. Niebuhr (New York, 1964), p. 41.

51 *Marx and Engels on Religion*, p. 72.

3

The Liberal Picture of Christ: from Ritschl to Harnack

The second half of the nineteenth century witnessed a growing reaction against the Idealism of the earlier part of the century, and a growing conviction that Christology was of decisive importance within the context of Christian dogmatics. Thus Isaak August Dorner, writing in 1856, stated that the Christological dogma had come to the fore as a consequence of the critical questions with which German theology was faced in the wake of the subjectivity of the *Aufklärung*.[1] In part, this may be seen as a reflection of Schleiermacher's call for a Christocentric principle – that everything in theology should be directly related to the redemption accomplished in Jesus of Nazareth. In his celebrated later work, *System der christlichen Glaubenslehre*, Dorner stated the importance of the Christological dogma as follows:

> It must be said that, in the present century, our dogma has again, in its exegetical, historical and dogmatic aspects, come to the fore, and been affected by more profound change than at any time since the first centuries. The most vital concern is to gain a true and living view and knowledge of the person of Christ.[2]

On the basis of his massive researches into the development of the Christological dogma,[3] Dorner concluded that a third major epoch in that development began around the year 1800, on the basis of assumptions unknown to the first eighteen hundred years of church history.

In its earlier phase, that epoch had been dependent upon Idealist assumptions which were increasingly abandoned during the second half of the nineteenth century. Thus Alois Emanuel Biedermann, whilst retaining the Hegelian concept of *Vorstellung*, insisted that the constitutive element in religion was not *Vorstellung* itself (for that would be to reduce religion to a theoretical relation to God), but the 'whole personal relation of the individual to God, which is carried out in a unified manner in man's thinking, feeling and willing'.[4] Biedermann exemplifies the reaction against Hegelianism by insisting that the 'Christ-principle' (*Christusprinzip*) was understood metaphysically or anthropologically, rather than as an expression of piety:

> The error of all previous speculative Christologies, which correctly understand the essential content of the dogma to be an idea newly emerging in human history in his person, rather than a personal definition of the single person Jesus, has been that they did not define this idea as specifically religious, whose content immediately constituted the essence of the religious personality of Jesus (*die religiöse Persönlichkeit Jesu*), and from this historically constituted the essence of Christian piety. Rather, they understood the content of this idea as a universal metaphysical truth concerning the abstract relation of the absolute and the finite (universally cosmically) or of the divine and the human (anthropologically).[5]

Like Dorner, Biedermann was highly critical of the neo-Lutheran kenotic Christologies of Gottfried Thomasius and W. F. Gess, which called the basis of this principle into question, without supplying a viable alternative in its place.[6]

It is not clear precisely what factors led to the remarkable and general decline of Hegelianism in the fifth decade of the century. It is certainly true that there were serious tensions within the Hegelian school itself, which inevitably weakened it. Perhaps more significant, however, were the remarkable advances being made in the natural sciences at the time, which led many to conclude that advancement in knowledge was more likely to come about through the meticulous observation and analysis of natural phenomena.[7]

The challenge posed to the Hegelian *Naturphilosophie* by *Naturwissenschaft* dates from the opening of the nineteenth century, and may be illustrated with reference to the incident which is often regarded as a turning point in the battle between idealism and empiricism. In his *Dissertatio philosophica de orbitis planetarum* (1801), Hegel had argued, on the basis of idealist presuppositions, that the number of planets was necessarily restricted to seven, and that no planet existed between Mars and Jupiter. On 1 January 1801, as the new century dawned, J. E. Bode discovered the planetoid Ceres, and established that its orbit fell between that of Mars and Jupiter. Although Schelling's *Naturphilosophie* exercised considerable influence in the field of botany until the second half of the century, when Wilhelm Hofmeister displaced it with an empirically grounded plant morphology, the successes of the 'exact sciences' – of which the discovery of Ceres, and subsequently of Neptune, were typical – led to a widespread reaction against idealism. The somewhat elusive Hegelian thesis of the manifestation of the Absolute and Infinite in the finite and relative conditions of human history appeared chimerical in the light of the concrete, empirical and verifiable knowledge deriving from the natural sciences. The origins of liberal theology may be seen in this growing disillusionment with Hegelian idealism, which left an ideological vacuum at a critical phase in German intellectual history. It was within this vacuum that the highly influential liberal theology of Albrecht Ritschl developed.[8]

For Ritschl, the nature and function of religion are inherently pragmatic, with a strong ethical bias reflecting his conviction that Christianity is primarily concerned with action in relation to God and to man. Ritschl appears to be in agreement with Schleiermacher, that the facts of Christian experience constitute the proper starting point for theological reflection, but insists that the 'experience' in question is the consequence of objective data, open to critical empirical investigation. The empiricism which has been detected in Ritschl's *Weltanschauung*[9] may reflect the fact that the University of Göttingen, to which Ritschl was called as a professor in 1864, was by then regarded as a leading centre of scientific research and speculation. By 1870, Ritschl had concluded that the starting point for theological speculation was the 'moral effects of the life, passion, death and resurrection of Christ towards the founding of the church.'[10] Christian theology is, for Ritschl, a discipline which is carried out within the sphere of the Christian church, and presupposes the committment of the theologian to certain soteriological principles (the 'idea of the forgiveness of sins, justification and reconciliation'), which 'had been called into existence by Jesus as the founder of the Christian church, and maintained by the apostles as its earliest representatives'.[11] However, this idea was taken up in the consciousness of the Christian community, and its peculiar theological status derives from its perceived significance within that community:

The material of the theological doctrines of forgiveness of sin, justification and reconciliation is to be sought not so much directly in the words of Christ, as in the correlative representations of the original consciousness of the community. The faith of the community that it stands to God in a relation essentially conditioned by the forgiveness of sins is the immediate object of theological cognition. So far, however, as this benefit is traced back to the personal action and passion of Christ, his proved intention to adopt such means makes the mediation of the community more intelligible.[12]

It is, in effect, axiomatic for Ritschl that there is no *direct* or *immediate* relationship between the believer and God, in that the presence of God or Jesus Christ is always mediated through the community of faith.[13] But in what sense is Christ 'present' in the community of faith?

The supernatural interpretation of this concept of the presence of Christ is rigorously excluded by Ritschl. The 'presence of Christ' is to be understood as the spatio-temporal extension of the ideas and principles represented in his person within the community of faith, the 'tradition of Christ propagated in the church'.[14] This 'tradition' is essentially empirical and historical, referring to a general ethical and religious principle or idea first embodied in the historical Jesus. This idea was then taken up and propagated by the community of faith:

Christ comes to act upon the individual believer on the one hand through the historical recollection of him which is possible in the church, on the other hand as the permanent author of all the influences and impulses which are due to other men, and like in nature to himself. . . To believe in Christ implies that we accept the value of the divine love, which is manifest in his work, for our reconciliation with God, with that trust which, directed to him, subordinates itself to God as his and our Father.[15]

As a consequence, Christ occupies a unique position towards all those within the community of faith, expressed in a religious judgement concerning his status. Those who 'believe in Christ' (in Ritschl's sense of the phrase) participate in the Kingdom of God, and are therefore reconciled to God, participating in the same qualitative relationship to God as the founder of their religion. In terms of its material content, the calling (*Beruf*) of Christ was 'the establishment of the universal ethical fellowship of mankind (*die Gründung der universellen sittlichen Gemeinschaft der Menschen*) as the objective in the world which rises above all conditions included in the notion of the world'.[16]

Although Ritschl is critical of the Christologies of the *Aufklärung*, it is very difficult to avoid the conclusion that he regards Christ as an archetypally significant and unsurpassable individual, whose significance cannot be articulated in any categories other than those of humanity in general. This point becomes particularly clear from Ritschl's discussion of two questions: in what sense, if any, is Christ 'unique', and in what manner did this putative 'uniqueness' arise? Ritschl's replies to these questions are widely regarded as unsatisfactory. Christ's 'uniqueness' is primarily to be articulated in terms of his being *the founder of the Christian community*, thus possessing temporal priority over those who followed him. Ritschl argues that, although it is conceivable that another individual could arise, equal in his religious and ethical status to Christ, 'he would stand in historical dependence upon Christ, and would therefore be distinguishable from him.'[17] The concession, however, is significant, in that it indicates that Christ's 'uniqueness' is understood *historically* rather than *ontologically*, a *primus inter pares* whose primacy arises through the historical accident of his being the unique founder of the Christian church. To use Brunner's terms, discussed in chapter 5, Christ is *Einzigartig*, rather than *Einmalig*. The fact that the community of faith is historically dependent upon the person of its founder is a remarkably weak defence of his uniqueness, and prompts even the most uncritical reader of Ritschl's *Hauptwerk* to ask whether this 'uniqueness' cannot be grounded in terms of Christ's relationship to God, and whether this 'uniqueness' can be determined by objective scientific investigation, or is only a subjective value-judgement (*Werthurtheil*) made by faith.

For Ritschl, this is an improper question, as Christ's *person* must be determined from his *work* – in other words, from his historic function of establishing the Kingdom of God. The basic *datum* upon which Christology is based is the historical priority of Christ over believers in establishing and ruling the Kingdom of God:

> One must avoid all attempts to go behind this datum, that is to determine in detail how it has come into being and empirically how it has come to be what it is. These attempts are superfluous because they are ineffectual; and it is dangerous to give oneself to these attempts since they are superfluous.[18]

It is difficult to avoid the conclusion that Ritschl considers Jesus to be nothing more than the historical point of departure for a self-sufficient idea. The 'divinity' of Christ is thus not true in any objective sense of the term, as had been suggested by the theologians of

Orthodoxy, but is a value-judgement evoked by, and conveyed in, the proclamation of the community of faith. Although Jesus may be viewed as a man objectively, faith recognizes him as having the religious value of God. Nevertheless, Ritschl's discussion of the manner by which this 'divinity' is recognized is, as we have indicated, unsatisfactory. It is, in fact, difficult to avoid the conclusion that Ritschl understood Christ to have introduced into history certain ideas, such as that of the 'Kingdom of God' (which ultimately derive from God, and hence may be regarded as 'divine' in a restricted sense of the term)[19] – but, in doing so, appears to have made himself vulnerable to the results of the increasingly dominant critical historical method.[20] Ritschl's heavy dependence upon the Fourth Gospel at points of importance[21] was also open to critical challenge, particularly from the Tübingen school to which he had once belonged. However, as his later followers, such as Wilhelm Herrmann, demonstrated, it was possible to adopt a negatively critical attitude towards the New Testament without destroying the powerful personal influence which the perfection of Christ's personality, reflected in the gospels, had upon the sincere believer.[22] The tradition concerning Jesus is merely the medium through which the historical reality of the man Jesus is conveyed to the believer, and is not in itself a constitutive factor of Christian experience. For Herrmann, faith is essentially concerned with finding God in one's own spiritual life, through encountering another who inspires certainty and trust. This takes place through the encounter of the individual with the 'tradition about Jesus in the books of the New Testament', which portrays the person of Jesus with such force that it becomes the ground of faith. Herrmann thus draws his celebrated distinction between the *ground of faith* (Jesus) and the *content of faith* (Christ). The existence of the man Jesus of Nazareth is an undoubted reality,[23] adequate in itself as the basis of personal faith. The starting point of Christian faith, and hence also of Christian theology, must be with the historical Jesus with whom the believer is confronted in the gospel narratives, whose inner life (rather than the metaphysical dogmas about his person) becomes the revelation of God. In effect, the later Ritschlian school adopted an ethical idealism, with Jesus as the historical fact embodying and exemplifying that ideal.[24]

The most influential presentation of the liberal picture of Christ appeared in the year 1900, even as its foundations were near to collapse through the erosion of criticisms such as those we shall consider in the following chapter. Adolf von Harnack's *Das Wesen des Christentums* originally took the form of a series of open lectures to students of all the faculties at the University of Berlin.[25] Although not intended for publication, the lectures were taken down in shorthand by one of the students present, to become a publishing sensation. Its portrait of Christ is widely regarded as the definitive culmination of the liberal school in nineteenth century Germany, and it is necessary to appreciate the critical historical insights underlying the work if its full significance is to be apprehended.

Harnack's *History of Dogma* was intended to demonstrate the unacceptable manner in which dogma originated and developed, in order to bring about its more rapid elimination, while at the same time enabling the historian to identify the essential features of the Christian faith in its historic forms.[26] For Harnack, the origins of dogma were to be sought in the 'activity of the Hellenic spirit upon the gospel soil',[27] as the early church attempted to make the gospel comprehensible to the Hellenistic world within which its early expansion took place:

> The gospel entered into the world, not as a doctrine, but as a joyful message and as a power of the Spirit of God, originally in the forms of Judaism. It stripped off these forms with amazing rapidity, and united and amalgamated itself with Greek science, the Roman Empire and ancient culture, developing, as a counterpoise to this, renunciation of the world and the striving after supernatural life, after deification. All this was summed up in the old dogma and in dogmatic Christianity.[28]

Harnack thus replaced the traditional dogmatic criterion of the *doctrines* of Christianity with the historical criterion of the *nature* of Christianity, by which the fundamental principles (*Grundzüge*) of the gospel might be established and verified through a critical historical analysis which isolated the distinctive essence (*das Wesen*) of Christianity from the temporary historical forms in which it manifested itself. In many respects, Harnack may be regarded as bringing the historical theology of *Aufklärer* such as Johann Salomo Semler to a state of near-perfection.[29]

The Christological significance of this approach to the 'essence' of Christianity is clear from Harnack's historical studies. 'Dogma must be purified by history.'[30] For Harnack, the Christological dogma is the dogma *par excellence*, whose origins may be exposed through critical historical analysis.[31] The Chalcedonian definition of the two natures of Christ is seen as the culmination of secular, and supremely Hellenistic, influences upon the gospel. For Harnack, the process leading up to the Chalcedonian Christological dogma was an *historical* process, by which the early church maintained its identity in the face of the Roman Empire and Hellenistic culture – but this *historical* development may be reversed now that such threats have vanished. Indeed, to maintain them in the absence of such a threat represents a intellectual capitulation to authoritarianism, alien to the spirit of Christianity. As early as March 1875, Harnack had defined his life's programme as the initial criticism and subsequent reversal of the 'philosophical evaporation of our Saviour' (*philosophische Verflüchtigung unseres Heilandes*) through historical investigation.[32] The Ritschlian school in general was intensely suspicious of the intrusion of metaphysics into theology: Harnack in particular was convinced that the history of dogma was *Krankheitsgeschichte*,[33] the story of the gradual adulteration of the original Palestinian gospel through the infiltration of Greek philosophy and Roman law, in order that the gospel might survive in its new (but now irrelevant) cultural situation:

> The gospel did not enter into the world as a positive statutory religion, and cannot therefore have its classic manifestation in any form of its intellectual or social types, not even in the first. It is therefore the duty of the historian of the first century of the church, as well as that of those which follow, not to be content with fixing the changes of the Christian religion, but to examine how far the new forms were capable of defending, propagating, and impressing the gospel itself. It would probably have perished if the forms of primitive Christianity had been scrupulously maintained in the church; but now primitive Christianity has perished in order that the gospel might be preserved.[34]

The 'kernel of the matter' thus received new and transitory historical forms, with which it became encrusted, and from which it must ultimately be disentangled. It is this programme of identifying and isolating the kernel from the husk which Harnack expounded to great effect in *Das Wesen des Christentums*.

In this important work, Harnack states explicitly that he proposed to analyse the question of what Christianity fundamentally is *historically*, thus excluding apologetic or philosophical responses.[35] Noting the multiplicity of historical forms which Christianity has taken during its development, and the radical departure of the later from the primitive forms, Harnack concludes: 'There are only two possibilities here: either the gospel is in all respects identical with its first form, in which case it came with its time and has departed with it; or else it contains something which is of permanent validity, in historically changing forms. The latter is the correct view.'[36] It is thus the task of the historian, having established the historical phenomena, to apprehend what is essential in these phenomena, and distinguish the kernel from the husk.[37] For Harnack, the gospel 'has only one goal – that the living God might be found, and that every individual should find him as *his* God, and thus gain strength and joy and peace.'[38] How this aim was achieved in the course of history is of secondary importance. The irreducible element in the gospel has, in the course of history, become overlaid with *unnecessary* (although not therefore necessarily *incorrect*) hypotheses arising primarily from the influence of speculative Hellenistic philosophy: the 'Logos Christology', the dogma of the 'Incarnation' and the concept of salvation as 'deification' are all cited as examples of the Hellenization of the gospel during the first three centuries of its existence.[39] Indeed, Harnack foreshadows Whitehead's celebrated remark, 'Christianity is a religion seeking a metaphysic', when he asserts that the gospel presupposes no philosophy of nature, no specific metaphysical outlook, and is 'doctrine' only to the extent that it proclaims the reality of God the Father.[40] But how does the historical figure of Jesus of Nazareth enter into Harnack's historical analysis of the essence of Christianity?

In view of the numerous, and influential, misunderstandings of Harnack's Christology,[41] it is necessary to consider this question in some detail. For Harnack, the gospels are evangelistic, rather than historical documents, insufficient for a biography of Jesus, although giving information upon three important points: 'In the first place, they offer us a plain picture of the preaching of Jesus, both of its main features and of its individual application; in the second place, they describe how his life issued in the service of his vocation; in the third place, they describe to us the impression which he made upon his disciples, and which they transmitted.'[42] Although Harnack identifies the main elements of Jesus' teaching, and analyses these elements in some detail,[43] he does *not* reduce the gospel to the teaching of Jesus, or absolutize it in this form. Harnack was too sophisticated an historian to suppose that the earliest recorded form of the gospel could be treated as its sole legitimate expression, or to overlook the historical impact which the gospel initially made, as a result of which certain aspects of Jesus' teaching were passed over. For Harnack, 'the gospel, as Jesus proclaimed it, has to do with the Father alone, and not with the

Son.'[44] Nevertheless, this version of the gospel cannot be permitted to be considered as normative or constitutive; it is merely one of many historical forms which the gospel has taken. As Harnack emphasizes, 'within two generations of his death Jesus Christ was already spoken of in the highest possible terms humanly possible',[45] so that the Son *was subsequently* an element of the gospel proclamation. Harnack's important distinction between the 'Easter message' and the 'Easter faith' is significant in this respect.[46]

Those who suggest that the gospel may therefore, according to Harnack, be identified with the teachings of Jesus are imputing an historical naïveté to him which he simply did not possess. For Harnack, Jesus' teaching was of enormous significance, but, like every historical manifestation of the gospel in its history, it contained elements which were peripheral rather than necessary, husk rather than kernel. The subsequent development of Christianity in the apostolic era revealed a significantly different understanding of the total teaching of Jesus, and the relation between his life and death, which is no less important an aspect of the historical manifestation of the gospel. It is for this reason that Harnack asserts that the gospel, *as the New Testament proclaims it*, contains two elements: (1) the preaching of Jesus, and (2) the proclamation of Jesus as the Christ who died and rose again for the sake of sin and who gives assurance of forgiveness and eternal life.[47] On the basis of his historical approach to the development of Christianity, Harnack is able to build up a series of profiles: the gospel *as proclaimed by Jesus himself*; the gospel *as proclaimed by Paul*; the gospel *as proclaimed by Augustine*; the gospel *as proclaimed by Luther*; and so forth – and *none* of these may be identified with the essence of the gospel itself. For Harnack, it is impossible for the historian to *define* Christianity; indeed, Harnack never portrays the 'essence' of Christianity as an historical phenomenon – his proper task is to document its historical forms, none of which may be absolutized or treated as normative. Jesus' significance therefore ultimately lies elsewhere than in his being the teacher of the 'higher righteousness'.

Harnack summarizes his understanding of the permanent significance of Christ as follows: 'Jesus does not belong to the gospel as one of its elements, but *was the personal realisation and power of the gospel, and we still perceive him as such*.'[48] Although it is clear that Harnack has the highest possible estimation of Christ, he insists that the irreducible element of the gospel concerns man's relationship to *God the Father*. Such a faith in God the Father is linked to Jesus Christ *historically*, not *theologically*. The peculiar significance of Christ in relation to Christianity resides in the power of his religious personality:

> Whoever receives the gospel, and tries to recognize the one who brought it to us, will testify that here the divine appeared as purely as it can appear on earth, and that Jesus was himself the power of the gospel for his followers. What they experienced and recognized in him, however, they have proclaimed, and this proclamation is still a living force.[49]

It will therefore be clear that Harnack's Christology rests upon assumptions which he justifies inferentially, with reference to their historical development, of which two are particularly important. First, the 'Logos Christology' and 'incarnational' modes of thought are identified as arising from extra-biblical and secular Hellenistic philosophical intrusions into Christian thought. Second, the connection between the gospel of 'eternal life in the midst of time, by the strength of and under the eyes of God' and Jesus of Nazareth is demonstrated to be *historical* rather than *theological*.

Harnack's importance to our study lies not in his Christology itself, but in the means he employed to derive it. By adopting the methodologically legitimate procedure of permitting the history of Christianity itself to define the questions to be answered, Harnack believed he would be capable of developing an 'undogmatic' Christology.[50] In a reminiscence of his student days in 1894, Theophil Wurm reported that Harnack suggested the following structure for a work of dogmatic theology:

> Part I: The teachings of Jesus and their apostolic interpretation.
> Part II: Mysteries.

To this second part Harnack assigned everything usually included in a work on dogmatic theology.[51] The 'liberal portrait of Christ' may not have reduced Christ to a German professor,[52] but it effectively prohibited any normative pronouncements concerning his significance, and simultaneously seemed to legitimate an astonishingly wide range of Christological opinions. Even as late as 1925, Harnack himself suggested that the irreducible Christological affirmation was that Jesus was the 'mirror of God's fatherly heart'.[53] Perhaps his critics might have suggested that the only reflection to be seen in that mirror was that of a liberal Protestant face.[54] By then, however, the historical approach to Christology had been undermined to such an extent that it attracted little notice. We now turn to the final decade of the nineteenth century, to consider the rise of the ideas which would eventually destroy even the most genial liberal portrait of Christ.

NOTES

1 I. A. Dorner, 'Die deutsche Theologie und ihre dogmatischen und ethischen Aufgaben in der Gegenwart', reprinted in *Gesammelte Schriften aus dem Gebiet der systematische Theologie, Exegese und Geschichte* (Berlin, 1883), pp. 1–47.
2 *System der christlichen Glaubenslehre* (2 vols: Berlin, 1879–81) §98, 1; vol. 2, p. 357.
3 *Entwicklungsgeschichte der Lehre von der Person Christi* (Stuttgart, 2nd edn, 1846–56).
4 A. E. Biedermann, *Ausgewählte Vorträge und Aufsätze*, ed. J. Kradolfer (Berlin, 1885), p. 413. For his earlier critique of Hegelianism, see his *Unsere junghegelsche Weltanschauung oder der sogenannte neueste Pantheismus* (Zurich, 1849).
5 A. E. Biedermann, *Christliche Dogmatik* (2 vols: Zurich, 2nd edn, 1884–5), vol. 2, §793. For a pertinent observation of the consequences of this approach to the relation of the Jesus of history and the Christ of faith, see W. Pannenberg, *Grundzüge der Christologie* (Gütersloh, 6th edn, 1982), p. 42.
6 Biedermann, *Christliche Dogmatik*, vol. 2, §§405–7. Cf. I. A. Dorner, 'Über die richtige Fassung des dogmatischen Begriffs der Unveränderlichkeit Gottes', in *Gesammelte Schriften*, pp. 188–377. The chief kenotic works are Gottfried Thomasius, *Christi Person und Werk: Darstellung der evangelisch-lutherischen Dogmatik vom Mittelpunkte der Christologie aus* (2 vols: Erlangen, 1853–61), and the more radical work of W. F. Gess, *Die Lehre von der Person Christi, entwickelt aus dem Selbstbewußtsein Christi und aus dem Zeugniß der Apostel* (Basle, 1856). The reader wishing to follow the original German controversy should consult Ernst Günther, *Die Entwicklung der Lehre von der Person Christi im 19. Jahrhundert* (Tübingen, 1911), pp. 165–200. For its later English dimension, see D. G. Dawe, 'A Fresh Look at the Kenotic Christology', *Scottish Journal of Theology* 15 (1962), pp. 337–49.
7 See the excellent study of Karl Löwith, *Von Hegel zu Nietzsche* (Stuttgart, 4th edn, 1958).
8 This gap appears to have been filled by Otto Liebmann's *Kant und die Epigonen* (1865), which paved the way for the neo-Kantian revival later

in the century. However, a careful analysis of Ritschl's writings suggests not merely that he was not neo-Kantian, but that he had no real interest in metaphysics at all: see the important study of Paul Wrzecionko, *Die philosophischen Wurzeln der Theologie Albrecht Ritschls: Beitrag zum Problem des Verhältnisses von Theologie und Philosophie im 19. Jahrhundert* (Berlin, 1964). The older study of Leonhard Stählin, *Kant, Lotze and Ritschl: A Critical Examination* (Edinburgh, 1889) is still useful.

The older *Naturphilosophie* may be summed up in Schelling's maxim 'In der Natur strebt alles kontinuierlich vorwärts': F. W. J. Schelling, *Von der Weltseele* (Hamburg, 1809), p. 3. On Hofmeister, see K. von Goebel, *Wilhelm Hofmeister* (London, 1926). Hegel's *Dissertatio* may be found in volume sixteen of the Berlin edition of his works.

9 See D. L. Deegan, 'Critical Empiricism in the Theology of Albrecht Ritschl', *Scottish Journal of Theology* 18 (1965), pp. 40–56. Two excellent studies of Ritschl available in English are D. L. Mueller, *An Introduction to the Theology of Albrecht Ritschl* (Philadelphia, 1959); James Richmond, *Ritschl: A Reappraisal* (London, 1978).

10 Albrecht Ritschl, *Die christliche Lehre von der Rechtfertigung und Versöhnung* (3 vols: Bonn, 1870–74); vol. 1, p. 1. In this first volume of his three-volumed work, Ritschl surveys the development of these doctrines, before presenting his positive exposition of them in the third. The general conclusions of that final volume are, however, already to be found in the preface to the first (§1, pp. 1–9). In the present study, the third edition of 1888-9 will be used: for the differences between the various editions of the third volume, see C. Fabricius, *Die Entwicklung in Albrecht Ritschls Theologie von 1874 bis 1889 nach der verschiedenen Auflagen seiner Hauptwerke dargestellt und beurteilt* (Tübingen, 1909).

11 *Rechtfertigung und Versöhnung*, vol. 3, §1; p. 1; *The Christian Doctrine of Justification and Reconciliation* (Edinburgh, 1900), vol. 3, p. 1.

12 *Rechtfertigung und Versöhnung*, vol. 3, §1; p. 3; *Justification and Reconciliation*, vol. 3, p. 3.

13 This is well brought out by Gösta Hök, *Die elliptische Theologie Albrecht Ritschls* (Uppsala, 1942), pp. 6-8. Ritschl's intense hostility towards Pietism undoubtedly underlies this assertion.

14 *Rechtfertigung und Versöhnung*, vol. 3, §60, p. 559; *Justification and Reconciliation*, vol. 3, p. 592 '. . .die in der Kirche fortgepflanzten Ueberlieferung von Christus'.

15 *Rechtfertigung und Versöhnung*, vol. 3, §60, p. 558; *Justification and Reconciliation*, vol. 3, p. 591.

16 *Rechtfertigung und Versöhnung*, vol. 3, §48, p. 423; *Justification and Reconciliation*, vol. 3, p. 449.

17 *Rechtfertigung und Versöhnung*, vol. 3, §49, p. 438; *Justification and Reconciliation*, vol. 3, p. 465 'Daraus folgt, daß Christus als der geschlichtliche

Urheber dieser Gemeinschaft der Menschen mit Gott und unter einander nothwendig der Einzige in seiner Art ist. Denn wenn ein Zweiter nachgewiesen werden könnte, welcher materiell ihm gleich wäre an Gnade und Treue, an weltbeherrschender Geduld, wie an Umfang der Absicht und des Erfolges, so würde er doch in geschichtlicher Abhängigkeit von Christus stehen, ihm also formell ungleich sein.' Cf. pp. 441–2 (English translation, p. 469). The idea of Jesus as the founder of the Kingdom of God may be found in his earlier works: *Die Entstehung der altkatholischen Kirche* (Bonn, 2nd edn, 1857), pp. 27–51.

18 This famous citation is taken from his 1881 essay *Theologie und Metaphysik: Zur Verständigung und Abwehr* (Bonn, 1881). For the intense critical reaction to this work, see Otto Ritschl, *Albrecht Ritschls Leben* (2 vols: Freiburg/Leipzig, 1892-6), vol. 2, pp. 385–404. The English translation may be found in *Albrecht Ritschl: Three Essays*, ed. P. Hefner (Philadelphia, 1972), p. 178. Cf. *Rechtfertigung und Versöhnung*, vol. 3, §48, pp. 426–7; *Justification and Reconciliation*, vol. 3, pp. 451–2 for a similar rejection of any attempt to ground Christ's 'uniqueness' in other terms.

19 For an excellent discussion of Ritschl's concept of the 'Kingdom of God', see Richmond, *Ritschl*, pp. 220–65. For a more general survey, with useful references to the later liberal school, see T. Bohlin, 'Die Reich-Gottes-Idee im letzten halben Jahrhundert', *Zeitschrift für Theologie und Kirche* 10 (1929), pp. 1–27.

20 D. L. Deegan argues that Ritschl avoids both the error of understanding Jesus *apart from* the faith of the community and of *opposing* the Jesus of history to the Christ of faith: 'Albrecht Ritschl on the Historical Jesus'. While this is true, it hardly meets the charge that Ritschl's historical analysis is open to critical challenge at crucial points.

21 For example, his use of John 4.34 and other Johannine texts to demonstrate the complete identity of will, purpose and function between Christ and God (*Rechtfertigung und Versöhnung*, vol. 3, §48, pp. 424–5; *Justification and Reconciliation*, vol. 3, pp. 449–50). Cf. the use made of John 1.14 (*Rechtfertigung und Versöhnung*, vol. 3, §45, p. 382; *Justification and Reconciliation*, vol. 3, pp. 404–5). For a comment upon Ritschl's uncritical approach, see W. G. Kümmel, *Das Neue Testament: Geschichte der Erforschung seiner Probleme* (Munich, 1958), p. 201. In contrast, Harnack treats the Fourth Gospel as unhistorical 'in the ordinary meaning of the word', so that 'it can hardly make any claim to be considered an authority for Jesus' history'.

22 For example, see Wilhelm Herrmann, *The Communion of the Christian with God* (London, 1895), pp. 1–17; 57–78.

23 *Communion of the Christian with God*, p. 52.

24 This trend may be detected as early as 1879, with the publication of Herrmann's *Die Religion im Verhältnis zum Welterkennen und zur Sittlichkeit.*

25 See the important study of F. M. Bartos, 'Cesta Adolfa Harnacka za pod statou krestanstvi Theologická priloha', *Krest'anska Revue* (Praha) 27 (1960), pp. 265–70.

26 A. von Harnack, *Outlines of the History of Dogma* (Boston, 1957), pp. 7–8. This work illustrates the deep gulf which developed during the nineteenth century between 'scientific' (i.e. historical) theology, and 'ecclesiastical' (i.e. dogmatic) theology. For a contemporary assessment of this division, see the important study of C. A. Bernoulli, *Die wissenschaftliche und die kirchliche Methode in der Theologie* (Tübingen, 1897).

27 *Outlines of the History of Dogma*, p. 5. For a useful general introduction to Harnack in English, see G. W. Glick, *The Reality of Christianity: A Study of Adolf von Harnack as Historian and Theologian* (New York/London, 1967); for an excellent study of his theology of history, see H. M. Rumscheidt, *Revelation and Theology: An Analysis of the Barth-Harnack Correspondence of 1923* (Cambridge, 1972), pp. 68–119.

28 A. von Harnack, *History of Dogma* (7 vols: Edinburgh, 1894-9), vol. 7, p. 272. For an excellent study, see K. H. Neufeld, *Adolf von Harnack: Theologie als Suche nach der Kirche* (Paderborn, 1977).

29 On the development of *Dogmengeschichte* prior to Harnack, see K. G. Steck, 'Dogma und Dogmengeschichte in der Theologie des 19. Jahrhunderts', in *Das Erbe des 19. Jahrhunderts*, ed. W. Schneemelcher (Berlin, 1960), pp. 21–66.

30 For this maxim in its proper context, see the full text of the memorandum of 27 November 1888, in Agnes von Zahn-Harnack, *Adolf von Harnack* (Berlin, 2nd edn, 1951), pp. 130–1. The maxim is constructed in opposition to Cardinal Manning's suggestion that history should be overcome by dogma. Later, of course, Ernst Troeltsch would insist that 'history can be overcome by history': *Der Historismus und seine Probleme*, in *Gesammelte Schriften* (4 vols: Tübingen, 1912-25), vol. 3, p. 772.

31 See Neufeld, *Adolf von Harnack*, pp. 66–86; 102–29. The earlier study of Alois Grillmeier, 'Hellenisierung-Judaisierung des Christentums als Deuteprinzipien der Geschichte des kirchlichen Dogmas', *Scholastik* 33 (1958), pp. 321–55; 528–58, is of significance in this connection.

32 For the text of the letter in which this programme is stated, see Neufeld, *Adolf von Harnack*, p. 109.

33 See Grillmeier, 'Hellenisierung-Judaisierung des Christentums', p. 322; Neufeld, *Adolf von Harnack*, p. 66.

34 Harnack, *History of Dogma*, vol. 1, p. 75.

35 A. von Harnack, *Das Wesen des Christentums* (Leipzig, 1906) p. 4; *What is Christianity?* (New York, 1955), p. 6 (This English translation is inaccurate, and the reader is advised to check it against the original German before drawing any weighty conclusions on its basis).

36 *Das Wesen des Christentums*, pp. 8–9; *What is Christianity?*, pp. 13–14.

37 *Das Wesen des Christentums*, pp. 7; 112–13; *What is Christianity?*, pp. 12; 179–80.

38 *Das Wesen des Christentums*, p. 120; *What is Christianity?*, p. 191. The important comments upon the adaptability and timelessness of the gospel on pp. 94–5 (English translation, pp. 149–50) should be noted.

39 *Das Wesen des Christentums*, pp. 126–8; 144–6; *What is Christianity?*, pp. 202–5; 232–3.

40 *Das Wesen des Christentums*, pp. 92–3; *What is Christianity?*, pp. 146–8.

41 For example, the oft-quoted (and seldom criticised!) comments of George Tyrrell, *Christianity at the Cross-Roads* (London, 1963), pp. 46–9.

42 *Das Wesen des Christentums*, p. 20; *What is Christianity?*, p. 31.

43 *Das Wesen des Christentums*, pp. 33–47; *What is Christianity?*, pp. 51–78. Harnack identifies three circles of thought in Jesus' teaching, each of which contains the whole proclamation of the gospel: the coming of the Kingdom of God; the fatherhood of God and the infinite value of the human soul; the higher righteousness and the commandment of love.

44 *Das Wesen des Christentums*, p. 91; *What is Christianity?*, p. 144 'Nicht der Sohn, sondern allein der Vater gehört in das Evangelium, wie es Jesus verkündigt hat, hinein.' Note that Harnack is *not* saying that the *gospel* has nothing to do with the Son, but that the gospel, *as proclaimed by Jesus*, excludes such self-reference. Cf. *History of Dogma*, vol. 1, pp. 58–76.

45 *Das Wesen des Christentums*, p. 97. Cf. pp. 96–103; *What is Christianity?*, p. 154. Cf. pp. 152–64.

46 *Das Wesen des Christentums*, pp. 101–3; *What is Christianity?*, pp. 160–3.

47 *History of Dogma*, vol. 1, pp. 76–89.

48 *Das Wesen des Christentums*, pp. 91-2; *What is Christianity?*, p. 145.

49 *Das Wesen des Christentums*, p. 92; *What is Christianity?*, p. 146. The German original is very contorted.

50 For example, see the comments of P. T. Forsyth, *The Person and Place of Jesus Christ* (London, 4th edn, 1930), pp. 3–31.

51 Theophil Wurm, 'Harnack und Schlatter', *Theologische Blätter* 9 (1931), pp. 272–4; p. 273.

52 Tyrrell, *Christianity at the Cross-Roads*, p. 47.

53 Zahn-Harnack, *Adolf von Harnack*, p. 161.

54 Tyrrell, *Christianity at the Cross-Roads*, p. 49 'The Christ that Harnack sees, looking back through nineteen centuries of Catholic darkness, is only the reflection of a Liberal Protestant face, seen at the bottom of a deep well.'

4

The Collapse of the Liberal Christology: from Weiss to Troeltsch

The rise of the Ritschlian school in the final quarter of the nineteenth century led to a new interest in the religious personality of Jesus, and hence to a new interest in the question of the nature of the New Testament sources upon which the life of the historical Jesus could be constructed. The intense interest in the synoptic problem was thus partly a consequence of the perceived dogmatic need to establish facts concerning the historical Jesus, in order to bring out the unique nature of his religous personality. It was widely believed that the new literary approach to the New Testament in general, and the synoptic gospels in particular, would permit scholars to establish a 'firmly drawn and life-like portrait which, with a few bold strokes, should bring out clearly the originality, the force, the personality of Jesus'.[1] It was this enterprise which has been poetically described as the 'Quest of the Historical Jesus'.[2] The assumption underlying the 'life of Jesus movement' in the later nineteenth century was that the remarkable personality of Jesus would provide a solidly historical foundation for faith. The firm ground of historical truth upon which Christian faith depended was not supernatural or anti-rational, but merely the personality of Jesus, a fact of history open to scientific investigation. The impression which he made upon his contemporaries could be reproduced in his followers of every age. The first century legendary embellishments to the gospel stories could thus be discarded, as could the anachronistic dogmatic formulations of a later age concerning him. The remarkable number of 'lives of Jesus' produced in the later nineteenth century in England, America and France, as well as Germany itself, is an adequate testimony to the popular appeal of the ideas underlying the 'life of Jesus' movement. Through it, the religious personality of the 'far-off mystic of the Galilean hills' (to use Lord Morley's famous phrase) could be brought into the present, uncluttered by irrelevancies, in order to form the basis of faith for the coming generation.

It was, of course, inevitable that the portrayals of the religious personality of Jesus were radically subjective, so that the rediscovered Jesus of history turned out to be merely the embodiment of an ideal figure by the progressive standards of the nineteenth century. George Tyrell's comments merit repetition here:

> They wanted to bring Jesus into the nineteenth century as the incarnation of its ideal of divine righteousness, i.e. of all the highest principles and aspirations that ensure the healthy progress of civilisation. They wanted to acquit him of that exclusive and earth-scorning otherworldliness, which had led men to look on his religion as the foe of progress and energy, and which came from confusing the accidental form with the essential substance of his gospel.[3]

More seriously, there was a widespread tendency to assume that 'Jesus of Nazareth as he actually was' coincided with 'Jesus of Nazareth as he may be reconstructed by means of the objective historical method'. The assumption that lay beneath the liberal picture of Christ was that the 'Jesus of history who lived in first century Palestine' could be defined in terms of dates, places, events, sequences, causes and effects – in other words, on the basis of a very superficial view of history which fails to take account of the deeper levels of historical actuality, as it is now understood.[4] Indeed, it is possible to argue that the fundamental defect in the liberal picture of Christ, underlying both the criticisms we have just made, was a failure to recognize the historicity of the historian's own situation, so that the historically relative was misunderstood as the historically absolute. The relativity of historical research was not immediately obvious to the nineteenth century 'life of Jesus' movement, whose adherents regarded themselves as practitioners of the objective historical method, rather than as an historically conditioned phenomenon in themselves.

The most sustained challenge to the 'life of Jesus' movement developed during the final decade of the nineteenth century, and may be argued to date from the foundation of the *kleine Göttinger Fakultät* in 1890,[5] later to become known as the 'history of religions school' (*religionsgeschichtliche Schule*),[6] at this stage characterized primarily by its corporate hostility towards the Göttingen master, Albrecht Ritschl. An important series of studies from within this school, as well as several from outside it, called the foundations of the liberal 'quest of the historical Jesus' into question. Broadly speaking, four main criticisms of the *Christusbild* of liberal Protestantism emerged in the period 1890-1911: (1) The *apocalyptic* critique (Weiss, Schweitzer), which maintained that the strongly eschatological bias of Jesus' proclamation of the Kingdom of God called the essentially Kantian liberal interpretation of the concept into question. (2) The *sceptical* critique (Wrede), which called into question the reliability of our knowledge of Jesus in the first place. (3) The *dogmatic* critique (Kähler), which challenged the theological significance of the reconstruction of the historical Jesus. (4) The *historical* critique (Troeltsch), which called into question the understanding of history underlying the 'quest'. In the present chapter, we shall consider these four criticisms of the liberal picture of Christ, and assess their theological significance.

In 1892, Johannes Weiss published *Die Predigt Jesu vom Reich Gottes*, a work of a mere 67 pages, occasioning a crisis within liberal Protestantism in doing so.[7] The idea of the 'Kingdom of God' was understood by the Ritschlians to mean the exercise of the moral life in society, or a supreme ethical ideal.[8] In other words, it was conceived primarily as something subjective, inward or spiritual, rather than in spatio-temporal terms. For Weiss himself, Ritschl's concept of the Kingdom of God was essentially continuous with that of the *Aufklärung*,[9] primarily a moral concept without eschatological overtones. The rediscovery of the eschatology of the preaching of Jesus called not merely this understanding of the Kingdom of God, but also the liberal *Christusbild* in general, into question.

As noted in an earlier chapter, Hermann Samuel Reimarus had suggested that Jesus was essentially an apocalyptic visionary whose ideas had been radically modified in a non-political direction by his disciples. This idea found little favour at the time, although it was taken up sporadically in the century following its appearance.[10] In 1891, two monographs appeared from the presses of E. J. Brill in Leiden on the subject of the eschatological character of Jesus' preaching.[11] As Weiss indicates, the publication of these books provided the necessary stimulus for him to publish his own,[12] in which the radical difference between the biblical and Ritschlian concept of the Kingdom of God was first exposed.

Weiss records that he was disturbed at an early phase of his career by the 'clear perception that Ritschl's idea of the Kingdom of God and the corresponding idea in the preaching of Jesus were two very different things'.[13] Weiss therefore undertook investigation of two distinct, although clearly related, questions, of which the first is historical and the second theological in nature. First, what did Jesus teach concerning the Kingdom of God? Second, what is the relationship between this understanding of the Kingdom of God and that of the church subsequently? Although it is clear that Weiss's interest lies primarily with the first question, the significance of the second could hardly be overlooked.[14] For Weiss, Jesus understood the Kingdom of God in characteristically apocalyptic and eschatological terms. The career of Jesus, and especially his teaching, may be explained on the basis of late Jewish apocalyptic, with its expectation of the imminent end of the world and its hope of the coming of the Messiah, the Son of Man, who would transform the world and inaugurate the Kingdom of God. The Kingdom of God is thus radically other worldly and belonged to the future:

> The interpretation of the Kingdom of God as an innerworldly ethical idea is a vestige of a Kantian ideal, and does not stand up before a more precise historical examination . . . The Kingdom of God, as Jesus thought of it, is never something subjective, inward or spiritual, but always the objective messianic Kingdom, which is usually portrayed as a territory into which one enters, a land in which one has a share, or a treasure which comes down from heaven.[15]

For Jesus, the Kingdom of God was an event, to be brought about by God himself in the imminent future. Jesus cannot be thought of as having *initiated* the Kingdom of God: his preaching was essentially the proclamation of a penitential ethic by which his followers might be prepared for the impending advent of the Kingdom. The 'new righteousness' which Jesus required of his disciples must be understood *eschatologically*, as the condition for entrance into the coming Kingdom of God, rather than as an end in itself. The Kingdom of God is thus the motive for ethics, rather than its embodiment.[16] Weiss states this as follows:

> The Kingdom of God, as Jesus conceived it, is a radically otherworldly entity which stands in diametric opposition to this world. This is to say that there can be no talk of an innerworldly development of the Kingdom of God in the mind of Jesus! On the basis of this observation, it seems to follow that

the dogmatic religious-ethical application of this idea in more recent theology (an application which has stripped away the original eschatological-apocalyptical meaning of the idea) is unjustified.[17]

The Kingdom of God, as Jesus conceived it, thus does not come about as the result of a long period of human development within the world, on the basis of insights first enunciated by Jesus, but comes as a catastrophe from heaven. The demands which it made of man were so radical and absolute that it overthrew, rather than confirmed, human understandings of civilisation and morality. It might therefore be thought that Weiss abandoned Ritschlianism. In fact, Weiss remained attached to the Ritschlian theology, despite his radical critique of its religious-ethical foundations.[18] Where Herrmann regarded Jesus as the object of trust, Weiss regarded him as an example to be imitated. However, the little book brought one era to an end, and began another.[19] The destructive effect of his *Predigt Jesu* was reinforced considerably through the appearance of Albert Schweitzer's *Das Messianitäts- und Leidensgeheimnis* in 1901.

As we noted, Weiss remained Ritschlian in outlook even after the publication of the second edition of his *Predigt Jesu* (1900). He was able to maintain this apparently impossible position by insisting that the apocalyptic element was absent from certain parts of Jesus' preaching, thus permitting these non-eschatological elements to have a permanent significance where the eschatological elements did not.[20] Thus the command to 'love God and one's neighbour' was non-eschatological, and constituted the *Kern und Stern* of Jesus' preaching. For Schweitzer, however, the whole character of Jesus' ministry was conditioned and determined by his apocalyptic outlook.[21] It is this idea which has become familiar to the English-speaking world as 'thoroughgoing eschatology',[22] although the more obvious English equivalent 'consistent eschatology' perhaps conveys the sense of the German *konsequente Eschatologie* more readily. Where Weiss regarded Jesus as merely thinking and talking eschatologically, Schweitzer extended this analysis to his actions as well. The result of this consistent eschatological interpretation of the person and message of Jesus of Nazareth was a portrait of Christ as a remote and strange figure, with dark anxieties and fears, an apocalyptic and wholly unworldly figure, whose hopes and expectations finally came to nothing. Far from being an incidental and dispensable 'husk' which could be discarded in order to establish the true 'kernel' of Jesus' teaching concerning the universal fatherhood of God, eschatology was an essential, dominant and inalienable characteristic of his *Weltanschauung*. Jesus thus appears to us as a strange figure from an alien first-century Jewish apocalyptic milieu, so that, in Schweitzer's famous words, 'he comes to us as one unknown'.[23] Although Weiss and Schweitzer alike appear to have evaded the dogmatic consequences of their eschatological approach to the historical Jesus, it was inevitable that historical consistency would triumph over dogma. It was thus necessary to attempt to develop some means of approaching the history of Jesus of Nazareth, for, as Julius Kaftan observed, 'if Johannes Weiss is right, and the conception of the Kingdom of God is an eschatological one, it is then impossible to make use of this concept in dogmatics.'[24] The reaction of English theologians to the rediscovery of the 'apocalyptic' Jesus is indicative of its serious and far-reaching Christological consequences.[25]

On the same day as Schweitzer's *Das Messianitäts- und Leidensgeheimnis* was published at Tübingen, Wrede's *Das Messiasgeheimnis in den Evangelien* appeared at Göttingen. Although the significance of the work was not fully appreciated until immediately after the First World War,[26] the challenge posed to liberal Christology could not be ignored. Within the liberal school, it was widely believed that the resolution of the *literary* question concerning the gospels, which had led to the conclusion that Mark was the oldest of the synoptic gospels, was also the resolution of the question concerning the most reliable source material for the construction of a 'life of Jesus'. The pioneer study of Wilke and the later study of Holtzmann had established the literary priority of Mark.[27] There was thus a widespread interest in the *Christusbild* of the Second Gospel, which was held to be a reliable source for details of Jesus' ministry and insights into his religious personality. The concept of a growing recognition on the part of Jesus that he was indeed the Messiah was fundamental to many representatives of the 'life of Jesus' movement. The 'developing Messianic consciousness' hypothesis was heavily dependent upon Mark for both its chronology and its factual basis. Furthermore, even Schweitzer himself assumed the basic accuracy of Mark's historical sequence: his critique of the older 'Quest of the Historical Jesus' was essentially that it had failed to take the apocalyptic element in Jesus' thought sufficiently seriously. At no point does he suggest that the whole enterprise of producing a 'developmental life of Jesus' was, by its very nature, impossible. The significance of Wrede's *Messiasgeheimnis* lies chiefly in the fact that he demonstrated that the old developmental view of the life of Jesus cannot be sustained on the basis of Mark's gospel. Wrede was able to demonstrate that Mark was not writing with the objectivity of the interests of the modern theologian, but rather as a theologian of the *Messiasgeheimnis* (which could be translated 'messianic *mystery*', as well as the customary 'messianic *secret*'). According to Wrede, Mark was painting a theological picture in the guise of history, imposing his theology upon the material which he had at his disposal. The Second Gospel was thus not objectively historical, but was actually a creative theological reinterpretation of history.

The gospel writers in general, according to Wrede, thus had to be understood in the social context of the communities in which they lived and wrote, and which both shaped and modified the materials they used.[28] Although one of Wrede's chief conclusions was that the so-called 'messianic secret' was not part of the history of Jesus, but arose within the community of faith (indeed, it may be suggested that, far from being a conclusion drawn from a study of Mark, it was a presupposition with which he approached it!), it was the general approach Wrede adopted which proved the more devastating for the liberal portrait of Christ: the synoptic gospels could at best be considered as *secondary* sources for the life of Jesus, being primary sources only for the views of the evangelists and the communities they represented.

Wrede's contribution to the destruction of the liberal picture of Christ is, in fact, considerably greater than Schweitzer's, although this point has been obscured by the uncritical English evaluation of Schweitzer's study of the development of the 'quest of the historical Jesus'.[29] Wrede identified three radical and fatal errors underlying the liberal *Christusbild*.[30] First, although the liberal theologians appealed to later modifications of an earlier tradition when faced with unpalatable features of the synoptic accounts of Jesus (such as miracles, or obvious contradictions between sources), they failed to apply this principle *consistently*. In other words, they failed to realize that the later belief of the community had exercised a normative influence over the evangelist at *every* stage of his work. Second, the motives of the evangelists were not taken into account. The liberal theologians tended simply to exclude those portions of the narratives they found unacceptable, and contented themselves with what remained. By doing so, they failed to take seriously the fact that the evangelist himself had a positive statement to make, and substituted for this something quite distinct. The first priority should be to approach the gospel narratives on their own terms, to establish what the evangelist wished to convey to his readers, and thence to make this the foundation of critical historiography. Third, the psychological approach to the gospel narratives tends to confuse what is conceivable with what actually took place, being based upon an inadequate foundation. In effect, liberal theologians tended to find in the gospels precisely what they were seeking, on the basis of a 'sort of psychological guesswork' which appeared to value emotive descriptions more than strict accuracy and certainty of knowledge.

Although it is possible to argue that Wrede actually bases his analysis of Mark upon his a priori reconstruction of the nature of the beliefs of primitive Christianity, it is impossible to deny the cumulative force of his critique of the methodology underlying the liberal 'quest of the historical Jesus'. Particularly significant in this respect is the all too frequently overlooked divergence of opinion between Schweitzer and Wrede on the *dogmatic content* of the Marcan tradition. For Wrede, the *Messiasgeheimnis* exemplified the unhistorical character of the tradition in general; for Schweitzer, the dogmatic element was genuinely historical, and might be explained on the basis of Jesus's eschatological milieu.[31] For Schweitzer, the only ways forward were his own consistent eschatology, and the so-called 'Wredestrasse' – consistent scepticism. *Tertium non datur* – there was no alternative. Schweitzer does not, however, appear to have recognized the significance of a little essay published in 1892, originally delivered as a lecture to the Wuppertal pastoral conference, expanded in 1896, and which indicated a third possible way, whose exploration would prove to be one of the most fertile and significant areas of twentieth-century Christology.

Martin Kähler's *Der sogenannten historische Jesus und der geschichtliche, biblische Christus*, a mere 45 pages in length, may be regarded as an attempt to establish an 'invulnerable area' (*sturmfreies Gebiet*) of faith in the midst of the crisis which he correctly perceived to be developing in the final decade of the century. How can Jesus Christ be the authentic basis and content of Christian faith, when historical science can never establish certain knowledge concerning the historical Jesus? How can faith be based upon an historical event without being vulnerable to the charge of historical relativism? It was precisely these questions which Kähler addressed in this famous work. Before considering his response, it is appropriate to consider a difficulty encountered in translating its title. An important distinction is drawn between two senses of 'historical', which cannot be adequately reproduced in English. The term *historisch* is used to refer to Jesus as the object of critical historical investigation, whereas the term *geschichtlich* is used to refer to Jesus as the object of faith. Of the various suggested English equivalents for the word-pair *historisch-geschichtlich*, two may be noted. *Historisch* may be translated as 'objective-historical', and *geschichtlich* as 'existential-historical': this brings out this distinction between the objective empirical facts of history, and their perceived significance for the individual.[32] Alternatively, *historisch* may be translated 'historical', and *geschichtlich* as 'historic': this emphasizes the distinction between an event *in* history and an event which *makes* history.[33] To avoid confusion, we propose to translate both German terms as 'historical' and indicate which of the two German terms is being translated thus.

Kähler has been seriously neglected within the English-speaking world, largely through the absence of translations of his principal works. Thus his celebrated *Die Wissenschaft der christlichen Lehre* is often cited as the greatest single volume dogmatic work to appear in the period between Schleiermacher and Barth. Kähler was increasingly alarmed by the subjectivism of his contemporaries, such as Schleiermacher, J. C. K. von Hofmann, Ritschl and Herrmann,[34] and attempted to rectify this in a number of important works published in the period 1892–1917. Kähler, it may be emphasized, was a dogmatic theologian, rather than a New Testament scholar, whose interest in the New Testament was primarily a consequence of his dogmatic interest in the question of the grounds of faith. It is for this reason that his approach differs so sharply from that of Wrede and Schweitzer, even if their conclusions at times coincide. Kähler effectively challenges the Christology of the *Aufklärung* and liberal school (or 'Jesuology', as he styles their Ebionitism) on the grounds of its implicit (and apparently unacknowledged) dogmatic presuppositions. *Der historische Jesus* of 1892 was intended as a critique of the theological foundations of the 'life of Jesus' movement.

Kähler identified two objectives in this work: first, to criticise and reject the errors of the 'life of Jesus' movement; and second, to establish the validity of an alternative approach, this latter being by far the more important. For Kähler:

> the historical Jesus of modern writers conceals the living Christ from us. The Jesus of the 'life of Jesus' movement is merely a modern example of

a brain-child of the human imagination (*eine moderne Abart von Erzeugnissen menschlicher erfindlicher Kunst*), no better than the notorious dogmatic Christ of Byzantine Christology. They are both equally far removed from the real Christ. In this respect, historicism is just as arbitrary, just as humanly arrogant, just as speculative and 'faithlessly gnostic', as that dogmatism which was itself considered modern in its own day.[35]

Kähler concedes immediately that the 'life of Jesus' movement was completely correct in so far as it contrasted the biblical witness to Christ with an abstract dogmatism. He nevertheless insists upon its futility, a view summarized in his well-known statement to the effect that the entire life of Jesus movement is a blind alley. His reasons for making this assertion are complex, and foreshadow those of Wrede (and thus evoked charges of 'morbid scepticism' from his critics).

The most fundamental reason is that Christ must be regarded as a 'supra-historical' (*übergeschichtlich*)[36] rather than an 'historical' (*geschichtlich*) figure, so that the critical historical method cannot be applied in his case. The critical historical method could not deal with the supra-historical (and hence supra-human) characteristics of Jesus, and hence was obliged to ignore or deny them. In effect, the critical historical method could only lead to an Arian or Ebionite Christology, on account of its latent dogmatic presuppositions. This point, made frequently throughout the essay, is developed with particular force in relation to the psychological interpretation of the personality of Jesus, and the related question concerning the use of the principle of analogy in the critical historical method. Kähler notes that the psychological interpretation of the personality of Jesus is dependent upon the (unrecognized) presupposition that the distinction between ourselves and Jesus is one of degree (*Grade*) rather than kind (*Art*), which Kähler suggests must be challenged on dogmatic grounds.[37] More significantly, Kähler challenged the principle of analogy in the interpretation of the New Testament portrayal of Christ in general (which inevitably led to Jesus being treated as analogous to modern man, and hence to a reduced or degree Christology).[38] In fact, precisely this point underlies his later criticisms of Harnack's *Das Wesen des Christentums*, which he argues reduced piety from worship of God to worship of a hero.

Second, Kähler argued that 'we do not possess any sources for a life of Jesus which an historian could accept as reliable and adequate.'[39] This is not to say that the sources are unreliable and inadequate *for the purposes of faith*. Kähler is rather concerned to emphasize that the gospels are not the accounts of disinterested, impartial observers, but rather accounts of the faith of believers, which cannot be isolated, either in form or content, from that faith: the gospel accounts 'are not the reports of alert impartial observers, but are throughout the testimonies and confessions (*Zeugnisse und Bekenntnisse*) of believers in Christ'.[40] In that 'it is only through these accounts that we are able to come into contact with him', it will be clear that the 'biblical portrait of Christ' is of decisive importance for faith. What is important for Kähler is not who Christ *was*, but what he presently *does* for believers. The 'Jesus of history' lacks the soteriological significance of the 'Christ of faith'. The thorny problems of Christology may therefore be left behind in order to develop soterology, 'the knowledge of faith concerning the person of the saviour'.[41] In effect, Kähler argues that the 'life of Jesus' movement has done little more than create a fictitious and pseudo-scientific Christ, devoid of existential significance. For Kähler, 'the real Christ is the preached Christ (*der wirkliche Christus ist der gepredigte Christus*)'. Christian faith is not based upon this *historische Jesus*, but upon the existentially significant and faith-evoking figure of the *geschichtliche Christus*. As Kähler emphasizes, the New Testament proclamation of Christ does not presuppose or necessitate a distinction between 'the memory of the days of his flesh and the confession of his eternal significance (*Erinnerung an die Tage seines Fleisches und Bekenntnis zu seiner ewigen Deutung*)', with a result that the New Testament itself contains an irreducible dogmatic element, which cannot be eliminated without gross historical distortion.[42] It is for this reason that Kähler feels able to assert that, even in those circles in which 'apostolic dogma' is depreciated, 'one finds a dim reflection of that dogma, namely the knowledge of a certain incomparable evaluation of Jesus within the church, and the mediation of his portrait for attention and approval.'[43] The *biblische, geschichtliche Christus* is thus the *total* Christ, rather than the fictitious and soteriologically evacuated *historische Jesus*.

By accepting the distinction between the 'Jesus of history' and the 'Christ of faith', Kähler is thus able to argue that, as a matter of fact, Christian faith is based upon the latter, rather than the former. The 'life of Jesus' movement has thus little significance for faith, in that the 'historical Christ' (*geschichtliche Christus*) cannot be reduced to a mere biography or intellectual analysis of the 'historical Jesus' (*historische Jesus*). For Kähler, the historical method cannot objectively demonstrate (or, indeed, negate) the revelation upon which faith stands – and as such, has little significance for faith. The saving significance of the historical figure of Jesus of Nazareth is encapsulated in the biblical portrait of Christ, which is immeasurably richer, and which alone evokes and sustains faith. It is this biblical portrait of Christ as saviour which, for Kähler, constitutes the invulnerable foundation of faith.

Kähler was, of course, heavily criticised by his contemporaries. In the same year as the publication of Kähler's essay, Wilhelm Herrmann argued that Kähler's approach made it utterly impossible to ascertain whether the 'historical Christ' (*geschichtliche Christus*) – supposedly the basis of faith – was not, in fact, merely a product of faith rather than an historical actuality.[44] In the following year, Otto Ritschl argued that Kähler had misunderstood and unnecessarily depreciated the results of the application of the critical historical method.[45] Nevertheless, Kähler's dogmatic point concerning the priority of the 'biblical, historical (*geschichtlich*) Christ' over the 'historical (*historisch*) Jesus' did not go unnoticed, and was destined to exercise considerable influence over later discussion of the relationship between faith and revelation, particularly in the writings of the dialectical theologians.

The publication of Schweitzer's *Geschichte der Leben-Jesu-Forschung* in 1906 may be regarded as the final and most cruel exposure of the inadequacy of the pseudo-historical theology of liberal Protestantism. Although the book was, in many respects, unoriginal, it succeeded in highlighting the deficiencies of the 'Life of Jesus' movement in a manner whose coherence had never been seen before.[46] With great force and persuasiveness, Schweitzer relentlessly posed the three great questions of 'Either-Or' which the 'Life of Jesus' movement could not ignore: 'The first was posed by Strauss: either *purely historical* or *purely supernatural*; the second was fought out by the Tübingen school and Holtzmann: either *synoptic* or *Johannine*; and now the third: either *eschatological* or *non-eschatological*.'[47] In every case, Schweitzer himself effectively demonstrated the necessity to adopt the first of the two positions: it was necessary to adopt a purely historical approach to the synoptic gospels, recognising the full weight which had to be given to their eschatological cast and presuppositions. The full recognition of the eschatological character of the historical *Christusbild* of the synoptic gospels inevitably led to the rejection of the decidedly non-eschatological, Kantian *Christusbild* of liberal Protestantism. Writing in 1962, Ernst Käsemann assessed the theological impact of the rediscovery of primitive Christian apocalyptic as follows:

The history of theology in the last two generations demonstrates that the rediscovery of primitive Christian apocalyptic, and the recognition of its significance for the entire New Testament (especially due to Kabisch, Johannes Weiss and Albert Schweitzer), was a shock to its discoverers and their contemporaries beyond our imagination. Weiss promptly fell back upon the liberal *Christusbild*, Schweitzer bravely drew the consequences from his theses about the historical Jesus (untenable theses, as it happened), and the remainder paid enthusiastic attention to the fields of religious history, cultic piety and mysticism. Barth's *Römerbrief* brought 'consistent eschatology' out of its shadowy existence, and made it the dominant programme of the exposition of the New Testament (although in a variety of interpretations) in Germany.[48]

Karl Barth's enthusiastic proclamation of the eschatological *Christusbild* in his *Römerbrief* is perhaps most memorably stated as follows: 'A Christianity which is not totally and utterly eschatology, has nothing whatsoever to do with Christ (*Christentum, das nicht ganz und gar und restlos Eschatologie ist, hat mit Christus ganz und gar und restlos nichts zu tun*).'[49] Schweitzer, by bringing together the results of the critical study of the life of Jesus, erected a monument to the 'Life of Jesus' movement which proved to be its gravestone, precisely because the full coherence of the case against the movement was now obvious. Schweitzer did not, in fact, add to the history which he so carefully documented – he simply brought it to an end by demonstrating its inner tensions and contradictions. Schweitzer did not need to employ extensive dogmatic arguments (such as those of Kähler) in reaching his conclusions: the case was established simply on the basis of the history of the *Leben-Jesu-Forschung* itself. It also, however, drew widespread attention to the critical questions of modern Christology. One of those questions, relating to the historical approach to the person of Christ, was particularly closely scrutinized in the years before the First World War by the 'history of religions' school.

The most consistent and radical application of *das religionsgeschichtliche Denken* to Christian dogmatics in general, and to Christology in particular, is associated with Ernst Troeltsch.[50] To many, Troeltsch appeared to have completely undermined the foundations of constructive theology, his radical application of the historical method leading to the radical dissolution of dogmatics.[51] It is therefore necessary to understand how the historical method, exploited to such effect by writers such as Harnack, could come to be turned against them.

Writing in 1911, Troeltsch stated that he regarded his teacher

Albrecht Ritschl as having correctly identified the programme by which the Christian tradition could be accomodated to the modern situation. This programme consisted of the correlation of the dogmatic tradition of Protestantism with the demands of the modern situation.[52] For Troeltsch, Ritschl's mistakes were to be located in his analysis of these two elements, rather than in his essential programme itself. In his doctoral dissertation on the relationship between reason and revelation in Philip Melanchthon and Johann Gerhard, Troeltsch emphasized the discontinuity between modern theology and that of the period of the Reformation (exemplified by Melanchthon) or of Orthodoxy (exemplified by Gerhard).[53] Troeltsch thus corrected Ritschl's historical analysis, effectively concluding that the Ritschlian theology could not be justified with reference to the dogmatic tradition of Protestantism.

The origins of this break with the Ritschlian school may be seen in the aftermath of the publication in 1897 of Gustav Ecke's study of the Ritschlian school.[54] In this study, Ecke documented the division between the right and left wings of the school (regarding Harnack, Herrmann, Loofs and Kattenbusch as representatives of the former, and Bousset, Gunkel, Troeltsch, Weiss and Wrede as representatives of the latter). In July of the following year, Troeltsch responded both to the book itself, and to reviews by Harnack and Kattenbusch (the latter of which had been particularly critical of Troeltsch's 'modern' tendency to deny the supernatural).[55] Troeltsch, speaking as a representative of the 'younger generation' of Ritschlians, argued that the original successes of the Ritschlian theology was a direct consequence of the cultural situation in the 1850s, in the aftermath of the collapse of the Hegelian speculative systems which had dominated the first half of the century. Ritschl's anti-speculative and empirically grounded theology was thus ideally placed to exploit the cultural situation of the period, and thus to base itself upon such ideas as the absoluteness of Christianity or supernaturalism. In the meantime, however, culture had not remained unchanged: intellectual interest, in the universities and elsewhere, had shifted away from speculative philosophy to historical analysis, thus highlighting the deficiencies of the older Ritschlian analysis.

The general lines of Troeltsch's mature historical approach to Christianity can be seen in his 1898 article on the relation between history and metaphysics.[56] In this essay, Troeltsch suggested that the fundamental difference between himself and the Ritschlians was that the latter based themselves upon a discredited supernaturalism, whereas he based himself upon a consistent historicism. The general trend within the Ritschlian school, which grounded theology in the unique historical revelation in Jesus Christ, is, according to Troeltsch, an instance of the now discredited dogmatic method, exemplifying the persistent tendency of the Ritschlians to deal with specific individal problems raised by the critical historical method, without coming to terms with the underlying presuppositions of that method. For Troeltsch, the critical historical method itself is the 'much more fundamental ground upon which the disintegration of the Christian complex of ideas actually originates'. It is this method itself which is a 'leaven which, once applied to biblical science and church history, alters everything until it finally explodes the entire structure of theological methods employed until the present'. It is this development of a *Theologie des Historismus*[57] which is now recognized to be Troeltsch's distinctive contribution to modern German theology.[58]

For Troeltsch, 'dogmatic' or 'supernaturalist' understandings of the nature of Christianity had been discredited by the rise of the critical historical method. If one is to think historically, one is committed to the principles and presuppositions of the historical method, in that it is impossible to 'think without and against this method'.[59] For this reason, Troeltsch holds that it is impossible to make exclusive claims concerning Christianity: all religions must be regarded as historical phenomena, characterized by the intermingling of the human and the divine spirit.[60] As such, the same methods may be applied to the study of Christianity as to the study of other religions, or other historical phenomena in general. If Christianity is unique, 'this uniqueness lies in the content of its object, not in special methods of study or demonstration',[61] and should therefore be open to critical investigation by purely secular historical methods, unfettered by supernaturalist assumptions or subjective value-judgements.[62] In his 1900 essay on historical method, Troeltsch thus argued that the critical historical method is characterized by three fundamental and interrelated principles. The *principle of criticism* recognized that historical judgements are matters of probability, rather than truth or falsity, and are thus open to correction and refinement. The absolute historical judgements of Christianity concerning Jesus of Nazareth are thus unrealistic. The *principle of analogy* states that such historical judgements are based upon the presupposition that the events of the past are similar to the events of the present. As such, supernatural elements must be rigorously excluded from any interpretation of the historical figure of Jesus of Nazareth. The *principle of correlation* recognized that historical phenomena are interrelated in such a manner that events must be interpreted in terms of their antecedents and consequences. As such, the historically conditioned character of the history of Jesus of Nazareth must be conceded. For Troeltsch, these three principles combined to preclude any traditional Orthodox *Christusbild* based upon historical analysis, including that of the Ritschlian school.

This approach, characteristic of *das religionsgeschichtliche Denken*, figures prominently in his *Die Absolutheit des Christentums und die Religiongeschichte* (1902).[63] In this work, Troeltsch emphatically rejected the Ritschlian idea, underlying the liberal *Christusbild*, that Christianity represented the culmination of man's religious development, so that it could claim to represent the embodiment of religion itself. All religions, he insisted, naïvely advance claims for absoluteness which cannot be effectively refuted without unacceptable dogmatic presuppositions. The suggestion that religion was merely an aspect of culture was not excluded, although Troeltsch appears reluctant to deduce the absolute cultural relativism of religion. It is, however, significant that Troeltsch elsewhere frequently cites with approval Rousseau's maxim, that religion is *une affaire de geographie*. Although the full significance of Troeltsch's approach to Christianity for Christology was evident to some by this time, the full force of his views was not generally appreciated until 1909–10.

In 1909, the Karlsruhe controversialist Arthur Drews published *Die Christusmythe*, and set off a furious controversy by doing so.[64] While this controversy is not without interest, our attention is claimed by the important essay on the historical existence (*Geschichtlichkeit*) of Jesus, published by Troeltsch as a contribution to this remarkably vigorous debate.[65] In this work, Troeltsch argued that the liberal portraits of Christ, as presented by Ritschl and Herrmann, were nothing more than *Mischformem* or 'hybrids', which unsuccessfully attempted to mediate between the historicization of reality and the old supernaturalism of Orthodoxy. This is not to say that Troeltsch rejected the possibility of such mediation, in that he readily conceded that a purely historical and pedagogical interpretation of the meaning of the person of Jesus is devoid of warmth.[66] Rather, he located the correct mediating position in the cultic life of the Christian community, for which the *Christusbild* is a focal point.[67] The Christian community lives by constant recollection of the memory of its head, Christ. This

Christocentrism may well be to religion what geocentrism is to cosmology,[68] but the fact remains that it was perceived to meet a social need. In this, Troeltsch may be regarded as developing the theological programme of Schleiermacher:[69] for the latter, Christ's significance within the community of faith was to be explained religiously; for Troeltsch, it was to be explained sociologically and psychologically. The centrality of Christ within the Christian community may thus be justified upon grounds of socio-psychological utility, which may be defended against Orthodoxy and the *Aufklärung* alike. The Schleiermacher-Ritschl-Harnack tradition grasped the significance of Jesus' person as the formative factor in the creation of the Christian community, but tended, according to Troeltsch, to accommodate their Christological claims to the accepted modes of dogmatic expression: for Troeltsch, those claims were to be articulated in terms of general social phenomena. The necessity of the actual historical existence of Jesus for the Christian community may be maintained, according to Troeltsch, on the assumption that the *Christuskult* requires foundation in historical actuality (*die Wurzelung in geschichtlichen Tatsächlichkeit*).[70] It will, however, be clear that Troeltsch's mediating Christology is constructed upon principles of social psychology quite unacceptable to the followers of Herrmann or Harnack – and, indeed, to the subsequent leading protagonists of dialectical theology.[71]

It will therefore be clear that by the year 1911, the liberal mediating Christology of the Ritschl-Herrmann-Harnack tradition was widely regarded as discredited. Although there remained those who were convinced that it remained viable, there was a growing recognition of its pseudo-historical foundations and latent dogmatic presuppositions. It was not entirely clear in what direction Christology could now develop: the apocalyptic approach to the gospel *Christusbild* yielded a strange and distant figure, ill-suited to the perceived needs of Christian piety and worship; the *religionsgeschichtlich* approach appeared to many to destroy, rather than merely recast, the traditional Christian understanding of the person of Christ; the consistent sceptical approach appeared to reduce Christology to silence, lest it overstate itself. As it happened, the new direction in which Christology would develop was largely determined by an historical event, rather than scholarly reflection upon the nature of the historical process of which it was unquestionably a part. On 1 August 1914, the First World War broke out.

NOTES

1 Wilhelm Bousset; cited Albert Schweitzer, *Geschichte der Leben-Jesu-Forschung* (2 vols: Munich/Hamburg, 3rd edn, 1966), vol. 1, p. 257; *The Quest of the Historical Jesus* (London, 3rd edn, 1954), p. 242. (Note that the English translation is based upon the first German edition; the third German edition contains material not found in the English translation).

2 The phrase is derived from the English translation of the subtitle of the first edition of Schweitzer's *Von Reimarus zu Wrede: Eine Geschichte der Leben-Jesu-Forschung* (Tübingen, 1906). The second and third editions are known by the shorter title *Geschichte der Leben-Jesu-Forschung*. A more prosaic translation would be 'A History of Research into the Life of Jesus'. Other German designations of the movement were, of course, in circulation at the time – for example, Martin Kähler's phrase *Leben-Jesu-Bewegung*: see his famous *Der sogenannte historische Jesus und der geschichtliche, biblische Christus* (Leipzig, 1892), p. 5.

3 George Tyrrell, *Christianity at the Cross-Roads* (London, 1963), p. 47. Cf. the perhaps more famous quotation (p. 49): 'The Christ that Harnack sees, looking back through nineteen centuries of catholic darkness, is only the reflection of a liberal Protestant face, seen at the bottom of a deep well.' This comment is certainly correct in the case of Renan or Holtzmann, but is questionable in the case of Harnack himself.

4 For a useful discussion, see J. M. Robinson, *A New Quest of the Historical Jesus* (London, 1959), pp. 26–31.

5 See Ernst Troeltsch, 'Die kleine Göttinger Fakultät von 1890', *Christliche Welt* 18 (1920), pp. 281–3 (actually an obituary for one of its chief members, Wilhelm Bousset). For an excellent introduction to the 'History of Religions School', see G. W. Ittel, 'Die Hauptgedanken der religionsgeschichtliche Schule', *Zeitschrift für Religions- und Geistesgeschichte* 10 (1958), pp. 61–78.

6 See H. Schmidt, 'In memoriam Hermann Gunkel', *Theologische Blätter* 11 (1932), pp. 97–103 for useful insights. Of particular interest was the changing understanding of the nature (and, indeed, the *possibility*) of New Testament theology within the school: see the excellent introduction of Robert Morgan, *The Nature of New Testament Theology: The Contribution of William Wrede and Adolf Schlatter* (London, 1973), pp. 1–67.

7 The second edition of 1900 was expanded to 210 pages.

8 For an excellent study of the challenge posed to the Ritschlian understanding of *das Reich Gottes* by Weiss, see R. Schäfer, 'Das Reich Gottes bei Albrecht Ritschl und Johannes Weiss', *Zeitschrift für Theologie und Kirche* 61 (1964), pp. 68–88. The more general study of Christian Walther, *Typen des Reich-Gottes-Verständnisses* (Munich, 1961) is useful here also.

9 Johannes Weiss, *Die Idee des Reiches Gottes in der Theologie* (Giessen, 1901), pp. 1–4. Weiss draws upon Richard Wegener, *Albrecht Ritschls Idee des Reiches Gottes im Lichte der Geschichte kritisch untersucht* (Leipzig, 1897) to support the suggestion already made in the first edition of *Die Predigt Jesu* to the same effect.
10 See Schweitzer, *Geschichte der Leben-Jesu-Forschung*, vol. 1, pp. 245–54; *Quest of the Historical Jesus*, pp. 222–37.
11 Ernst Issel, *Die Lehre vom Reich Gottes im Neuen Testaments* (Leiden, 1891); Otto Schmoller, *Die Lehre vom Reich Gottes in den Schriften des Neues Testaments* (Leiden, 1891). Schmoller's views are much closer than Issel's to those of Weiss himself.
12 See the preface to the first edition: *Jesus' Proclamation of the Kingdom of God* (London, 1971), p. 56. It is possible that Weiss delayed publication of the work out of respect for his late master, who died in 1889.
13 *Die Predigt Jesu vom Reich Gottes* (Göttingen, 2nd edn, 1900), p. v.
14 See D. L. Holland, 'History, Theology and the Kingdom of God: A Contribution of Johannes Weiss to Twentieth Century Theology', *Biblical Research* 13 (1968), pp. 54–66.
15 *Jesus' Proclamation of the Kingdom of God*, p. 133. Cf. pp. 84–96; 129–31.
16 *Jesus' Proclamation of the Kingdom of God*, pp. 105–7. For the development of this theme, see his later *Die Nachfolge Christi und die Predigt der Gegenwart* (Göttingen, 1895).
17 *Jesus' Proclamation of the Kingdom of God*, p. 114.
18 This is particularly clear from the second edition of *Die Predigt Jesu*, as well as his later suggestion that it was possible to separate the historical and theological aspects of the question: see particularly *Die Idee des Reich Gottes*, p. 113, in which he asserts that Jesus' ideas are invariably transposed and reinterpreted *(umgestimmt und umgedeutet)*.
19 See Schweitzer, *Geschichte der Leben-Jesu-Forschung*, vol. 1, pp. 254–6; *Quest of the Historical Jesus*, pp. 237–40.
20 *Die Predigt Jesu vom Reich Gottes* (Gütersloh, 2nd edn, 1900), pp. 134–8.
21 See Schweitzer, *Geschichte der Leben-Jesu-Forschung*, vol. 2, pp. 382–450; *Quest of the Historical Jesus*, pp. 328–95. (Note that the English translation merges three chapters of the original into one.)
22 See the title of chapter 19 of the English translation: Schweitzer, *Quest of the Historical Jesus*, p. 328.
23 Schweitzer, *Geschichte der Leben-Jesu-Forschung*, vol. 2, p. 630 'Als ein Unbekannter und Namenloser kommt er zu uns, wie er am Gestade des Sees an jene Männer, die nicht wußten, wer er war, herantrat'; *Quest of the Historical Jesus*, p. 401.
24 According to Rudolf Bultmann, *Jesus Christus und die Mythologie* (Hamburg, 1964), p. 9. As Bultmann notes, however, Kaftan later became convinced that Weiss was, in fact, correct.

25 See Robert Morgan, 'Non Angli sed Angeli: Some Anglican Reactions to German Gospel Criticism', in *New Studies in Theology I*, ed. Stephen Sykes and Derek Holmes (London, 1980), pp. 1–30; id., 'Historical Criticism and Christology: England and Germany', in *England and Germany: Studies in Theological Diplomacy*, ed. S. W. Sykes (Frankfurt, 1982), pp. 80–112, especially pp. 90–2.

26 Its hypothesis was then taken up and developed by Rudolf Bultmann, 'Die Frage nach dem messianischen Bewußtsein Jesu und des Petrus-Bekenntnis', *Zeitschrift für die neutestamentliche Wissenschaft* 19 (1919–20), pp. 165–74; reprinted in *Exegetica* (Tübingen, 1967), pp. 1-9. For the development of the theme of the 'Messianic Secret' to the onset of the Second World War, see H. J. Ebeling, *Das Messiasgeheimnis und die Botschaft des Marcus-Evangelisten* (Berlin, 1939). More recently, see Heikki Räisänen, *Das Messiasgeheimnis im Markusevangelium* (Helsinki, 1976).

27 C. G. Wilke, *Der Urevangelist* (Leipzig, 1838); H. J. Holtzmann, *Die synoptischen Evangelien* (Leipzig, 1863).

28 For an excellent introduction, see W. C. Robinson Jr., 'The Quest for Wrede's Secret Messiah', *Interpretation* 27 (1973), pp. 10–30; reprinted in *The Messianic Secret*, ed. Christopher Tuckett (Philadelphia/London, 1983), pp. 97–115. Cf. the comment of Eduard Schweizer, 'Zur Frage des Messiasgeheimnisses bei Markus', *Zeitschrift für die neutestamentliche Wissenschaft* 56 (1965), pp. 1–8; p. 8 'Schon 1901 hat W. Wrede erweisen, daß das Messiasgeheimnis redaktionelle Konstruktion des Markus ist und in die Dogmengeschichte, nicht ins Leben Jesu gehört. Dahinter kann man nicht mehr zurückgehen.'

29 See Morgan, 'Historical Criticism and Christology', p. 90.

30 For what follows, see William Wrede, *Das Messiasgeheimnis in den Evangelien* (Göttingen, 1901), pp. 2–4; *The Messianic Secret* (Cambridge/London, 1971), pp. 5–7.

31 See Schweitzer, *Geschichte der Leben-Jesu-Forschung*, vol. 2, pp. 382–450; *Quest of the Historical Jesus*, pp. 328–95. See note 21.

32 Thus John Macquarrie, *An Existentialist Theology: A Comparison of Heidegger and Bultmann* (London, 1973), pp. 159–62.

33 Thus Carl E. Braaten, in his translation of Martin Kahler, *The so-called Historical Jesus and the Historic, Biblical Christ* (Philadelphia, 1964), p. 21.

34 See Martin Kähler, *Geschichte der protestantischen Dogmatik im 19. Jahrhundert*, ed. Ernst Kähler (Munich, 1962); Rolf Schäfer, 'Die Rechtfertigungslehre bei Ritschl und Kähler', *Zeitschrift für Theologie und Kirche* 62 (1965), pp. 66–85, especially pp. 77–80.

35 Kähler, *Der sogenannte historische Jesus*, p. 4; *The so-called Historical Jesus*, p. 43. For an excellent introduction in English, see C. E. Braaten, 'Martin Kähler on the Historic, Biblical Christ', in *The Historical Jesus and the*

Kerygmatic Christ, ed. C. E. Braaten and R. A. Harrisville (Nashville, 1964), pp. 79–105.

36 The term is introduced without comment in the first edition: *Der sogennante historische Jesus*, p. 6.

37 *Der sogennante historische Jesus*, pp. 10-11; *The so-called Historical Jesus*, pp. 52–4.

38 This criticism of the principle of historical analogy may be detected in his earlier works: see Hans-Georg Link, *Geschichte Jesu und Bild Christi: Die Entwicklung der Christologie Martin Kählers in Auseinandersetzung mit der Leben-Jesu-Theologie und der Ritschl-Schule* (Neukirchen, 1975).

39 *Der sogennante historische Jesus*, p. 7; *The so-called Historical Jesus*, p. 48.

40 *Der sogennante historische Jesus*, p. 43; *The so-called Historical Jesus*, p. 92.

41 *Der sogennante historische Jesus*, p. 45; *The so-called Historical Jesus*, p. 95. For the term 'soterology', see Kähler, *Die Wissenschaft der christlichen Lehre* (Leipzig, 1883). The term appears to have been introduced in a letter to his father, dated 15 November 1865: see C. Seiler, *Die theologische Entwicklung Martin Kählers bis 1869* (Göttingen, 1966), pp. 124–30.

42 *Der sogennante historische Jesus*, pp. 22; 35–6; *The so-called Historical Jesus*, pp. 66; 82–4. The context of the first citation is here reproduced in full: 'Das ist der erste Zug seiner Wirksamkeit, daß er seinen Jüngern den Glauben abgewann. Und der zweite ist und bleibt, daß dieser Glaube bekannt wird. Daran hängt seine Verheißung; daran hängt für uns die Entscheidung; daran hängt die Geschichte der Christenheit. Der wirkliche, d.h. der wirksame Christus, der durch die Geschichte der Völker schreitet, mit dem die Millionen Verkehr gehalten haben in kindlichen Glauben, mit dem die großen Glaubenszeugen ringend, nehmend, siegend und weitergebend Verkehr gehalten haben – der wirkliche Christus ist der gepredigte Christus. Der gepredigte Christus, das ist aber eben der geglaubte; der Jesus, den wir mit Glaubensaugen ansehen in jedem Schritt, den er thut, in jeder Silbe, die er redet; der Jesus, dessen Bild wir uns einprägen, weil wir darauf hin mit ihm umgehen wollen und umgehen, als mit dem erhöhten Lebendigen.' The equation of *wirklich* with *wirksam* is of decisive significance here. For a sympathetic exposition of Kähler's maxim, see Alister E. McGrath, 'Justification and Christology: The Axiomatic Correlation between the Historical Jesus and the Proclaimed Christ', *Modern Theology* 1 (1984–5), pp. 45–54.

43 *Der sogennante historische Jesus*, p. 36; *The so-called Historical Jesus*, p. 83.

44 Wilhelm Herrmann, 'Der geschichtliche Christus: Der Grund unseres Glaubens', *Zeitschrift für Theologie und Kirche* 2 (1892), pp. 232–73, especially p. 253.

45 Otto Ritschl, 'Der historische Christus, der christliche Glaube und die theologische Wissenschaft', *Zeitschrift für Theologie und Kirche* 3 (1893),

pp. 371–426; A similar criticism was made in the same year by Willibald Beyschlag, in the revised preface to the third edition of *Das Leben Jesu* (Halle, 1893). For two of the most important essays on this theme, written in response to Drews' *Christusmythe* (1909), see Wilhelm Bossuet, 'Die Bedeutung der Person Jesu für den Glauben: Historische und rationale Grundlagen des Glaubens', in *Fünfter Weltkongress für freies Christentum*, ed. Max Fischer and Michael Schiele (Berlin, 1911), pp. 291–305; Georg Wobbermin, *Geschichte und Historie in der Religionswissenschaft* (Supplement to *Zeitschrift für Theologie und Kirche* 21: Tübingen, 1911).

46 See the excellent introduction by James M. Robinson, in Schweitzer, *Geschichte der Leben-Jesu-Forschung*, vol. 1, pp. 7–24.

47 *Geschichte der Leben-Jesu-Forschung*, vol. 1, p. 254; *Quest of the Historical Jesus*, p. 237. As Robinson points out (p. 14), a fourth may be added to this list: 'Entweder muß man, wie Bruno Bauer, ganz skeptisch sein und bei Markus alle berichteten Tatsachen und Zusammenhänage in gleicher Weise beantstanden, oder, wenn man darauf ein historisches Leben-Jesu erbauen will, das Evangelium als Ganzes, wegen der durchgehenden Zusammanhänge, als historisch anerkennen und dann erklären, warum nun einzelne Berichte, wie die Speisung und die Verklärung, von übernatürlichem Lichte umflossen sind, und was ihnen historisch zugrunde liegen kann' (*Geschichte der Leben-Jesu-Forschung*, vol. 2, pp. 354–5; *Quest of the Historical Jesus*, p. 306). In fact, as we noted earlier, Schweitzer rejected such a consistent scepticism, as may be seen from *Das Messianitäts- und Leidensgeheimnis*, although he is clearly aware of its full force and significance. For more recent reflections on the Wrede-Schweitzer debate on Mark, see Eduard Schweizer, 'Die theologische Leistung des Markus', *Evangelische Theologie* 24 (1964), pp. 337–55.

48 Ernst Käsemann, 'Zum Thema der urchristlichen Apokalyptik', *Zeitschrift für Theologie und Kirche* 59 (1962), pp. 257–84; pp. 257–8 n. 2. For the background to this important essay, see Gerhard Ebeling, 'Der Grund christlicher Theologie', *Zeitschrift für Theologie und Kirche* 58 (1961), pp. 227–44; Ernst Fuchs, 'Über die Aufgabe einer christlichen Theologie', *Zeitschrift für Theologie und Kirche* 58 (1961), pp. 245–67. Both these essays took up Käsemann's references to apocalyptic in his important essay 'Die Anfänge christlicher Theologie', *Zeitschrift für Theologie und Kirche* 57 (1960), pp. 162–85, especially p. 180 'Apocalyptic . . . was the mother of all Christian theology'. We shall return to Käsemann's attitudes to apocalyptic in the seventh chapter of the present study.

49 Karl Barth, *Der Römerbrief* (Zürich, 8th edn, 1947), p. 298. It is difficult to bring out the full force of the German original.

50 For useful introductions, see Wilhelm Pauck, *Harnack and Troeltsch* (New

York, 1968), pp. 43–94; Trutz Rendtorff and Friedrich Wilhelm Graf, 'Ernst Troeltsch', in *Nineteenth Century Religious Thought in the West*, ed. Ninian Smart, John Clayton, Patrick Sherry and Steven T. Katz (3 vols: Cambridge, 1985), vol. 3, pp. 305–32. See also the excellent essays by Robert Morgan in *Ernst Troeltsch: Writings on Theology and Religion*, trans. and ed. Robert Morgan and Michael Pye (London, 1977), pp. 1–51; 208–33. The *religionsgeschichtliche Schule* (particularly Bousset) also made important contributions to the study of apocalypticism, of particular relevance to Schweitzer's thesis: see Hans Dieter Betz, 'Zum Problem des religionsgeschichtlichen Verständnisses der Apokalyptik', *Zeitschrift für Theologie und Kirche* 63 (1966), pp. 391–409.

51 For example, see Hermann Diem, *Dogmatik, ihr Weg zwischen Historismus und Existentialismus* (Munich, 3rd edn, 1960), pp. 9–13; Gotthold Müller, 'Die Selbstauflösung der Dogmatik bei Ernst Troeltsch', *Theologische Zeitschrift* 22 (1966), pp. 334–46.

52 Ernst Troeltsch, *Gesammelte Schriften* (4 vols: Tübingen, 1912-25), vol. 1, pp. vii–viii.

53 Ernst Troeltsch, *Vernunft und Offenbarung bei Johann Gerhard und Melanchthon* (Göttingen, 1891), pp. 212–3. The importance of this work is emphasised by Walter Bodenstein, *Neige des Historismus: Ernst Troeltschs Entwicklungsgang* (Gütersloh, 1959). For a criticism of Bodenstein, see Karl-Ernst Apfelbacher, *Frömmigkeit und Wissenschaft: Ernst Troeltsch und sein theologisches Programm* (Munich/Paderborn/Vienna, 1978).

54 Gustav Ecke, *Die theologische Schule Albrecht Ritschls* (Berlin, 1897), especially pp. 119–27.

55 For Harnack's review, see *Christliche Welt* 11 (1897), 627. For the most significant statements of Kattenbusch's review, see *Christliche Welt* 12 (1898), 76–81. For Troeltsch's rejoinder, see *Christliche Welt* 12 (1898), 627–31. The changing allegiance of this important journal over the period 1890–1910 is of considerable significance to the development of later liberal Protestantism: see Johannes Rathje, *Die Welt des freien Protestantismus: Ein Beitrag zur deutsch-evangelischen Geistesgeschichte* (Stuttgart, 1952).

56 'Geschichte und Metaphysik', *Zeitschrift für Theologie und Kirche* 8 (1898), pp. 1–69. For an analysis, see Eckardt Lessing, *Die Geschichtsphilosophie Ernst Troeltschs* (Hamburg, 1965). In this study, Troeltsch amplifies and defends statements in his earlier article 'Die Selbständigkeit der Religion', *Zeitschrift für Theologie und Kirche* 5 (1895), pp. 361-436; 6 (1896), pp. 71–110; 167–218, in response to the critical comments of the Ritschlian Julius Kaftan, 'Die Selbständigkeit des Christentums', *Zeitschrift für Theologie und Kirche* 6 (1896), pp. 373–94. For the latter's subsequent rejoinder, see Julius Kaftan, 'Erwiederung: (1) Die Methode; (2) Der Supernaturalismus', *Zeitschrift für Theologie und Kirche* 8 (1898), pp. 70–96.

57 For this phrase, see 'Geschichte und Metaphysik', p. 69. A related phrase is *religionsgeschichtliche Theologie*, found in the 1900 essay 'Über historische und dogmatische Methode in der Theologie', in *Gesammelte Schriften*, vol. 2, pp. 729–53; p. 738. (The essay is mistakenly assigned to the year 1898 in this edition.) The work is reprinted in *Theologie als Wissenschaft*, ed. Gerhard Sauter (Munich, 1971), pp. 105–27. It must be emphasized that Troeltsch does not use the term *historische Theologie* in the significantly different sense established by Schleiermacher in his *Kurze Darstellung des theologische Studiums*, §§26–8.

58 For an excellent study, see B. A. Gerrish, 'The Possibility of a Historical Theology: An Appraisal of Troeltsch', in *The Old Protestantism and the New: Essays on the Reformation Heritage* (Edinburgh, 1982), pp. 208–29.

59 'Über historische und dogmatische Methode in der Theologie', pp. 734–5. Cf. 'Geschichte und Metaphysik', p. 5. Two important contributions to this debate from the Ritschlian school should be noted: Max Reischle, 'Historische und dogmatische Methode der Theologie', *Theologische Rundschau* 4 (1901), pp. 261–75; 305–24; Friedrich Traub, 'Die religionsgeschichtliche Methode und die systematische Theologie', *Zeitschrift für Theologie und Kirche* 11 (1901), pp. 301–40.

60 'Geschichte und Metaphysik', pp. 8–9. See the highly critical appraisal of this approach by H. R. Mackintosh, 'Does the Historical Study of Religions yield a Dogmatic Theology?', *American Journal of Theology* 13 (1909), pp. 505–19; id., *Types of Modern Theology* (London, 1937), pp. 181–217.

61 'Über historische und dogmatische Methode in der Theologie', p. 738. See further Hans-Georg Drescher, *Glaube und Vernunft bei Ernst Troeltsch: Eine kritische Deutung seiner religionsphilosophische Grundlegung* (n.p., 1957).

62 On the question of whether it is possible to eliminate *all* presuppositions from questions of method, see his important essay 'Voraussetzungslose Wissenschaft', in *Gesammelte Schriften* vol. 2, pp. 183–92.

63 The question of the nature and identity of 'das Wesen des Christentums', and the means by which this may be established, is of significance here: see Hans Wagenhammer, *Das Wesen des Christentums: Eine Begriffsgeschichtliche Untersuchung* (Mainz, 1973); S. W. Sykes, 'Ernst Troeltsch and Christianity's Essence', in *Ernst Troeltsch and the Future of Theology*, ed. J. P. Clayton (Cambridge, 1976), pp. 139–71.

64 See the highly critical comments of Johannes Weiss, *Jesus von Nazareth: Mythus oder Geschichte?* (Tübingen, 1910). For a useful assessment of the debate in English, see Shirley Jackson Case, *The Historicity of Jesus* (Chicago, 1912), and his earlier article, 'The Historicity of Jesus: An Estimate of the Negative Argument', *American Journal of Theology* 15 (1911), pp. 20–42.

65 For a useful account of this work, see B. A. Gerrish, 'Jesus, Myth and

History: Troeltsch's Stand in the Christ-Myth Debate', in *The Old Protestantism and the New*, pp. 230–47.

66 See Ernst Troeltsch, *Die Bedeutung der Geschichtlichkeit Jesu für den Glauben* (Tübingen, 1911), especially p. 23.

67 *Die Bedeutung der Geschichtlichkeit Jesu*, pp. 27–30.

68 *Die Bedeutung der Geschichtlichkeit Jesu*, pp. 10–17; 19–23.

69 See W. E. Wyman, *The Concept of Glaubenslehre: Ernst Troeltsch and the Theological Heritage of Schleiermacher* (Chico, Cal., 1983), for a useful introduction in English.

70 *Die Bedeutung der Geschichtlichkeit Jesu*, p. 31.

71 See the excellent study of Robert Morgan, 'Ernst Troeltsch and the Dialectical Theology', in *Ernst Troeltsch and the Future of Theology*, pp. 33–77.

5

Dialectical and Dialogical Christology: Barth and Brunner

On the evening of 4 August 1914, as the First World War began to embed itself in the consciousness of the German nation, perhaps her greatest contemporary theologian drafted an appeal on behalf of the Kaiser to his people in support of the war effort. The same theologian shortly afterwards added his signature to those of 92 other intellectuals, addressing a similar public appeal to the 'world of culture'. That theologian was Adolf von Harnack, and he was joined in that appeal by Adolf Deissmann, Wilhelm Herrmann, Adolf von Schlatter, Friedrich Naumann and Reinhold Seeberg.[1] It seemed that the German theological establishment, liberal and conservative alike, was committed to the war effort, with all that this entailed. For many, the 'manifesto of the intellectuals' (*Manifest der Intellektuellen*) represented the simultaneous collapse and discrediting of the bourgeois idealism of the nineteenth century, and the theological programme it had engendered. One such individual was Karl Barth:

> For me personally, one day in the beginning of August of that year stands out as *dies ater*, on which ninety-three German intellectuals, among whom I was horrified to discover almost all of my hitherto revered theological teachers, published a profession of support for the war policy of Kaiser Wilhelm II and his counsellors. Amazed by their attitude, I realised that I could no longer follow their ethics and dogmatics, or their understandings of the bible and history, and that the theology of the nineteenth century no longer had any future for me.[2]

As a student, Barth had come to 'absorb Herrmann through every pore',[3] and his publications over the period 1908-16 demonstrate the influence of the great Marburg liberal, particularly in relation to the theological significance of the critical historical method. A theological student beginning his studies in Germany in the first decade of the twentieth century could scarcely have failed to encounter the tension between the historical theology of Troeltsch and the ahistorical theology of Herrmann.[4] It is important to appreciate that, despite all the differences between Barth or Gogarten and Herrmann, they remain united in their hostility to historicism in general, and the historicism of Troeltsch in particular.[5] Writing to Thurneysen on 1 January 1916, Barth admitted

> ...how frightfully indifferent historical questions have become to me. Of course, this is nothing new for me, as even under the influence of Herrmann, I always regarded [historical] criticism merely as a means of achieving freedom in relation to the tradition, rather than a constitutive factor in a new liberal tradition, as Wernle and company apparently want it to be.[6]

The strongly ahistorical character of 'dialectical theology' has often been noted, and it is therefore important to observe that, at least in this respect, there is a significant continuity between Herrmann and the 'dialectical theology' of Barth and Gogarten.[7]

The origins of the great turning point in modern Christology are to be sought in Barth's *Römerbrief* of 1918, a work of prophecy rather than theology. Now that dialectical theology is an aspect of the history of Christian thought, rather than a contemporary theological force, it is difficult for the modern scholar to appreciate the full force of this violent work when it broke upon an unprepared theological world. It was perhaps through this work that the full power of Søren Kierkegaard's critique of Hegelian historical pantheism was first channelled into the German theological consciousness.[8] The *Römerbrief* returns time and time again to stress the Kierkegaardian 'infinite qualitative distinction' (*unendliche qualitative Unterschied*) between God and man. Like an Old Testament prophet, Barth emphasizes the utter holiness and remoteness of God from man and from human culture and religion. God 'stands over and against man and everything human in an infinite qualitative distinction (*in unendlichem qualitativem Unterschied dem Menschen und allem Menschlichen gegenüberstehend*), and is never (*nie und nimmer*) identical with anything which we name, experience, conceive or worship as God.'[9] Time and time again Barth emphasises the vastness of the gulf fixed between God and man, and the impossibility of the abrogation of this gulf. Barth substitutes for Lessing's *garstige, breite Graben* ('ugly great ditch') of history the *Gletscherspalte* ('crevasse') of time and eternity. God is *totaliter aliter*, wholly and absolutely different from man. How, then, may mediation between God and man take place? Barth's answer is significant:

If I have any system, it is restricted to bearing in mind, as much as possible, what Kierkegaard called the 'infinite qualitative distinction' between time and eternity, in its negative and positive aspects. 'God is in heaven, and you are on earth'. For me, the relation of *this* God and *this* man, the relation of *this* man and *this* God, is, in a nutshell, the theme of the Bible and the totality of philosophy. The philosophers term this crisis of human knowledge the prime cause; the bible sees Jesus Christ at this cross-roads (*Kreuzweg*).[10]

It is perhaps worth noting that Barth replaces Kierkegaard's *existential* dialectic between the temporal and the eternal with a corresponding *eschatological* dialectic, in which time is annihilated by eternity. *Christentum, das nicht ganz und gar und restlos Eschatologie ist, hat mit Christus ganz und gar und restlos nichts zu tun!* Any possibility of interpreting Jesus' relationship to God in the terms of liberal Protestantism is ruthlessly destroyed. His religious consciousness is only the consciousness of his abandonment by God: God remains unknown and unknowable, and all that may be seen of the reality of this unknown God in the history of the world or of Jesus of Nazareth are his effects, rather than that reality itself (Barth, with the battlefields of the First World War in mind, refers to these effects as *Einschlagstrichter und Hohlraüme* – 'shell-holes and craters'). God cannot be thought of as 'entering into' history, in that his revelation is a 'non-historical event' (*unhistorisches Ereignis*), which impinges upon human history only as a tangent touches a circle[11] – at a 'mathematical point'. God's revelation can no more be pinned down in human history than a bird in flight, concealing more than it reveals (in that it reveals the 'otherness' of God in the chasm fixed between God and man), having no 'stationary point' (*Standpunkt*). Revelation comes 'perpendicularly from above' (*senkrecht von oben*). In Jesus, God becomes a secret, making himself known as the unknown, speaking in eternal silence.[12] The concept of 'incarnation' is thus utterly inconceivable, in that God cannot be seen as entering into history.[13]

For many of Barth's critics, the 'theology of crisis' was merely an uncritical emotional reaction to the aftermath of the First World

War.[14] In response to this, it is necessary to point out that, since the war of 1870, the possible religious consequences of a national 'war' had begun to embed themselves within the German theological consciousness.[15] The enormous influence of the First World War upon German preaching[16] may thus be regarded as developing this theme. Barth's reaction to the war fits easily into a well-established pattern in the theology of German-speaking Protestantism.[17] Where Barth differed from others lay not so much in his ideas, as the force and consistency with which he proclaimed them. The new pessimism of the period, nourished by political and economic crises and the collapse of bourgeois idealism, was unquestionably extraordinarily receptive to the 'theology of crisis' (*Theologie der Krisis*). It seems, however, that this *Zeitgeist* merely provided a 'point of contact' for the new theology, establishing a context within which the full force of 'dialectical theology' could be felt.

The impact of the First World War upon European culture cannot be overstated. The years 1918-22 saw remarkable alterations in western European self-consciousness. Although the publication of Oswald Spengler's *Decline of the West* in 1918 (which drew heavily upon the degenerative theories of Max Nordau and Cesare Lombroso) is probably the most famous manifestation of this shift in culture, others soon followed. On 29 May 1919, observation of a solar eclipse confirmed two crucial predictions of Einstein's special theory of relativity, the third being confirmed in 1923. The concept of a 'relativistic universe' appeared to be as revolutionary to the twentieth century as the Newtonian mechanical universe was to the eighteenth, calling man's understanding of his world into question. On 23 June 1919, Marcel Proust initiated his remarkable experiment in subliminal sexual emotions and disjointed time with the publication of *A l'ombre des jeunes filles*. J. B. Bury's *Idea of Progress* (1920) poured scorn upon the idea of continuous development of human culture, civilization and ideas. The ideas of Sigmund Freud suddenly broke free of their captivity within specialized medical and psychiatric circles in 1920, with the founding of the first psychiatric polyclinic at Berlin, and the launching of the *International Journal of Psycho-Analysis*. James Joyce's *Ulysses* appeared in 1922, shocking the literary world, and causing T. S. Eliot to remark that it 'destroyed the whole of the nineteenth century'. It is no exaggeration to state that the immediate post-war years saw the final collapse of the cultural heritage of the nineteenth century, with shock-waves which were felt in every sphere of intellectual and creative activity. The *theological* consequences of this shift in cultural attitude may be seen in the reaction (and especially Karl Barth's lecture 'Unerledigte Fragen an die heutige Theologie') to Franz Overbeck's *Christenthum und Kultur*, published posthumously in 1919. The 'theology of crisis' thus developed *within*, rather than *as a result of*, the cultural situation of the post-war period. It may also be pointed out that a number of theological factors conspired to bring about a rediscovery of the deity of God, the Luther renaissance and the publication of Rudolf Otto's *Das Heilige* (1917) being the most significant,[18] in addition to the widespread dissatisfaction with the pseudo-historical theology of the liberal school noted in the previous chapter. In every sphere of thought, the situation was ripe for radical new development – and Barth's *Römerbrief* happened to be the occasion of that development in the sphere of Christian theology.

The impact of the Barthian emphasis upon the absolute and unqualified (*schlechthinnig*) distinction between God and the world may be judged from the exchange of views between Barth and the ageing Harnack in the January and February issues of the journal *Christliche Welt* for 1923.[19] In many ways, the Barth-Harnack correspondence may be seen as symbolic, representing an encounter not merely between two different schools of thought, but two different theological eras, with irreconcilably opposed ways of speaking and thinking about God. In this exchange, Harnack put fifteen questions to the 'despisers of intellectually defensible theology', of which the fourteenth identified the central Christological issue thrown up by the rise of dialectical theology:

> If the person of Jesus Christ stands at the centre of the gospel, how can the foundation for a reliable and generally accepted knowledge of that person (*die Grundlage für eine zuverlässige und gemeinschaftliche Erkenntnis dieser Person*) be gained other than through critical-historical investigation, in order that an imagined Christ (*erträumte Christus*) is not substituted for the real one? What else, other than scientific theology, is able to undertake such a study?

In many respects, Harnack's question to Barth is similar to Herrmann's question to Kähler, discussed in the previous chapter, and relates to precisely the same issue – the relationship between the Jesus of history and the Christ of faith. For Barth, as for Kähler, it is the risen Christ, rather than the historical Jesus, who is central to theology.[20] As Barth stated this in his reply to Harnack:

The 'reliable and generally accepted' knowledge of the person of Christ as the centre of the gospel can only be that of faith awakened by God. Critical-historical study represents the deserved and necessary end (*das verdiente und notwendige Ende*) of those 'foundations' of this knowledge (that is, the knowledge of *faith*). Such foundations do not exist except where they are laid by God himself. Whoever does not know that we do *not* know Christ according to the flesh any more – and this applies to all of us! – should let the critical study of the Bible tell him so. The more radically he is terrified, the better it is for him and for the subject in question. This could well be the service which 'historical science' can render to the real task of theology.[21]

In effect, Barth may be regarded as emphasizing the *dogmatic* consequences of the critical historical studies of the gospel tradition (such as those of Weiss, Wrede and Schweitzer), in a manner similar to, although more consistent and radical than, Martin Kähler. It is thus significant that Barth suggested, in an essay of 1925, that even Herrmann himself implicitly adopted the risen Christ of faith as the point of departure for his Christological speculation: Herrmann's fault was merely a lack of consistency.[22]

In 1920–1, Barth was publicly joined in his reaction against both historicism and *Kulturprotestantismus* by Friedrich Gogarten and Emil Brunner. The former delivered his celebrated lecture on 'the crisis of our culture' to the *Freunden der Christliche Welt* at the Wartburg in 1920, causing a mild sensation by doing so. His great emphasis upon the 'annihilating and creative act of God' (*Gottes vernichtender, schaffender Tat*) in the present crisis of European civilization, by which the distinction between God and the world was brought home as it had never been brought home before, reminded many of his audience of some of the more forceful pronouncements of Luther, and horrified Troeltsch, who saw in the lecture a programmatic critique of the relation between religion and culture.[23] Gogarten's essay *Zwischen den Zeiten*, published in 1920, was widely recognized as a theological manifesto, setting out the programme which dialectical theology would undertake in the years ahead.[24] In the following year, the movement gained a new supporter in the person of Emil Brunner, who identified the enemies of the new theology as *Historismus* and *Psychologismus*.[25] By the year 1925, dialectical theology had established itself as a leading force in German theology – despite its Swiss pastoral origins. By the year 1935, however, it was clear that there were serious tensions within the movement, particularly between Barth and Brunner. Despite their common theological presuppositions, the leading figures of the dialectical theology movement developed Christologies which were different to the extent of near-incompatibility. In the remainder of the present chapter, we propose to analyse the main features of the Christologies of Emil Brunner and Karl Barth, in terms of their main Christological works. The first major Christological work to emerge from the school of dialectical theology was Brunner's *Der Mittler*, and we therefore begin our analysis of the Christology of the movement with reference to Brunner.

In his works prior to 1921, Brunner developed a pre-critical, pre-dialectical Christology.[26] The transition to a dialectical Christology may be detected in the 1921 work *Erlebnis, Erkenntnis und Glaube*, with its emphasis upon the objectivity of faith, and a clear move away from the liberal interest in the inner life of Jesus or the psychological phenomenon of his religious personality.[27] However, in this work a tendency can already be detected to construct Christology in terms of a dialogical analogy between God and man, with the move towards an anthropology which would ultimately lead to the rupture between Brunner and Barth in 1934.[28]

In *Der Mittler* (1927), Brunner argued that Christianity was essentially an incarnational-mediatorial phenomenon, deriving from and constituted by the person and work of Christ.[29] Arguing that this point had been ignored or distorted during the period of the nineteenth century, Brunner suggested that the Christological tradition from Schleiermacher to Harnack was essentially based upon a general conception of religion, of which Christianity was the highest and most developed manifestation. Thus he interpreted Ritschl as having understood Christianity primarily as the introduction of an eternal divine idea into history in a definite historical event – the life of Jesus. As such, Ritschl's system does not make reference to a 'unique fact of history' (*einmaliges Faktum der Geschichte*).[30] The fact that Ritschl chooses to express his Christology in personal and historical forms must not be permitted to obscure the fact that it is essentially composed of rational and ethical ideas, with only the loosest of connections with history. Of the possible Christological titles available to him from the tradition, Ritschl chose that of 'royal prophet' rather than 'priestly mediator', thus indicating that he understood Christ's relationship to Christianity to be essentially factual and causal (*tatsächlich-kausal*) rather than essential and necessary (*sachlich-notwendig*).[31] Jesus is effectively treated by Ritschl as nothing more than the historical point of departure for a self-sufficient idea. In other words, Ritschl affirms that Christ was the first to introduce the 'Christian idea' into history as a *matter of historical fact*, thus giving the impulse for the subsequent historical development of that idea in Christianity; for Brunner, this amounted to a matter of *historical contingency*, where what was required was a matter of *historical necessity* (in that it was Christ, and only Christ, who could do this). A *theological* rather than an *historical* justification for the central significance of Jesus of Nazareth is required, according to Brunner. This point is encapsulated in his choice of the term *Mittler* as the title for the work, thus pointing to the need to ground the history of Jesus of Nazareth in the concept of special revelation[32] and the absolute necessity of redemption,[33] rather than the accidental truths of history. By doing so, he totally rejects such Jesuologies as the 'religious hero', the 'religious genius' or the 'moral personality': for Brunner, a Christ who is merely *primus inter pares* is not a Christ who can be preached.[34] Brunner argues that modern theology, in its attempt to ground and interpret Christian faith in terms of human experience, has virtually removed from it any sense of sin or guilt, and thus rendered the idea of a 'Mediator' unnecessary. It is for this reason that Brunner must be regarded as constructing his Christology 'from above', rather 'from below' (to use the later terms) at this stage. However, Brunner insists that God must be conceived *biblically* rather than *philosophically* – in other words, as a *person* rather than as the originator or embodiment of a self-sufficient *idea*. Brunner is implacably opposed to the 'false [theological] objectivism' which he considers to have arisen through the intrusion of Greek philosophical thought into the theology of the early church (and his approximation to Harnack here is significant), and attempted to overcome it through a reinterpretation of the idea of the 'Word' of God. Although his initially resulting Christology, as found in *Der Mittler*, is unquestionably docetic,[35] Brunner's developing theological personalism, evident in his rejection of idealism, contains the germs of his later solution to this deficiency.[36]

To understand this later development, it is necessary to appreciate the significance of the development of the concept of *dialogical personalism* in the early 1920s. In 1921, Ferdinand Ebner's *Das Wort und die geistigen Realitäten* appeared, to be followed by Martin Buber's *Ich und Du* in 1923.[37] Both works developed a powerful critique of contemporary idealism, and particularly the concept of the isolation of the self, in terms of the analysis of all human existential life in *dialogical* terms.[38] Buber analyses human experience as follows:

The world is twofold for man according to his twofold attitude (*Haltung*).
The attitude of man is twofold according to the two basic words he can utter.
The basic words are not single words, but pairs of words.
One basic word is the word pair I-You (*Ich-Du*).
The other basic word is the word pair I-It (*Ich-Es*).[39]

For Buber, the I-It relationship defines the world of experience (*Erfahrung*), which may be regarded as the interaction of a subject and object.[40] The I-You relationship, however, establishes the world of encounter (*Begegnung*), which must be regarded as the mutual interaction of two subjects. Whereas in the world of experience the subject is active and the object passive, the world of encounter opens up the possibility of both activity and passivity on the part of the subject as he engages in a dynamic relationship with another subject. It is this concept of the mutual interaction of two subjects which Buber attempts to encapsulate in the untranslatable formula *Ich-wirkend-Du und Du-wirkend-Ich*.[41] Buber thus emphasizes the importance of the relationship (*das Zwischen*) between the 'I' and the 'You', which prevents the improper reification or hypostasization of either. 'Actuality' (*Wirklichkeit*) cannot be objectified. While Buber locates the world of encounter primarily in human relationships, he is clearly aware of its potential application of the relationship between God and man.[42] The development of Buber's dialogical critique of the subject-object dichotomy was a major theme of the theology of the second quarter of the twentieth century, and its most significant Christological application may be found in Brunner's 1938 work on truth as 'encounter', *Die Wahrheit als Begegnung*.

In this work, Brunner argued that faith was primarily a personal encounter with the God who meets us personally in Jesus Christ. The anti-intellectualism of this concept of divine revelation will be evident, and reflects Brunner's conviction that the early church misunderstood revelation as the divine impartation of doctrinal truth *about God*, rather than the *self-revelation of God*.[42] For Brunner, 'truth' is itself a personal concept, and the subject-object dichotomy a destructive element within Christian theology. The biblical revelation lies 'beyond objectivism and subjectivism', in that revelation is understood to be an event in history. This should not be interpreted to mean that history reveals God, but that God reveals himself within the historical process, and supremely in the work and person of Jesus Christ. By the phrase 'personal correspondence' (*personale Korrespondenz*, or, less frequently, *personhafte Korrespondenz*), employed extensively in this work, Brunner intends to convey the fact that revelation cannot be conceived propositionally or intellectually, but must be understood *as an act of God*, and supremely the act of Jesus Christ. God reveals himself personally and historically, by communicating himself in Jesus Christ. The concept of 'truth as encounter' thus conveys the two elements of a correct understanding of revelation: it is *historical* and it is *personal*. By the former, Brunner wishes us to understand that truth is not something permanent within the eternal world of ideas which is disclosed or communicated to man, but something which *happens* in space and time. Truth comes into being, as the act of God in time and space. By the latter, Brunner intends to emphasize that the content of this act of God is none other than God himself, rather than a complex of ideas or doctrines concerning God. The revelation of God is the 'imparting of himself' to man.[43] For Brunner, divine revelation is necessarily Christocentric: he counters the false objectivism of Orthodoxy's doctrine of propositional revelation with Luther's *dictum* to the effect that the scriptures are 'the manger in which Christ is laid'. The concept of man's encounter with God necessarily implies that the person of God is historically and personally actualized in Jesus Christ. It is through the recognition that Jesus Christ establishes the 'point of contact' (*Anknüpfungspunkt*) between God and man that this encounter takes place.[44] It will therefore be clear that Brunner's understanding of the term 'Mediator' (*Mittler*) altered significantly from the 1927 work of that name, in that the original anti-intellectualist sense of the term was supplemented with the concept of Christ as the *Anknüpfungspunkt* between God and man.

The transition from Brunner's early dialectical Christology to his later 'historical-dialogical' (*geschichtlich-dialogisch*) Christology involved a shift in his understanding of the manner in which God encounters man. For the later Brunner, that encounter does not take place in a vacuum (as he appeared to suggest in *Der Mittler*), but in history itself, the sphere in which man is active.[45] That encounter presupposes that man possesses a capability to respond to the personal, historical revelation of God in Christ, a capacity which Brunner terms *Angesprochsein und Sichansprechenlassen*.[46] This significant development inevitably meant that anthropological considerations came to exert an increasing influence over Brunner's Christology. From 1930 onwards, Brunner envisages a direct correlation between the man who hears the word of God and the appearance of the word of God in Christ, effectively treating man as God's 'conversation partner' (*Gesprächspartner*) in the continuum of history.[47]. It is this aspect of Brunner's 'historical-dialogical' Christology which distinguishes it so radically from the purely dialectical Christology of Karl Barth.[48] The definitive statement of Brunner's 'historical-dialogical' Christology, found in the second volume of his *Dogmatik* (1950), indicates how closely his anthropology and Christology have become interrelated, without substantially developing any of the points noted above.[49]

The development of the later Christology of Karl Barth is of considerable interest, in that his earlier theology – especially as enunciated in the *Römerbrief* – appeared to leave no room for a 'Christology' in any meaningful sense of the term. Barth's move away from this earlier dialectical position is therefore of the greatest significance. In his earlier theology, Barth's thought is dominated by the 'diastasis' of God over and against man; in his later theology, 'diastasis' is replaced by 'dialogue'. How are we to account for this development?

Perhaps Hans Urs von Balthasar comes nearest to the truth when he identifies two critical turning points in Barth's theological development: 'The first was the turning away from liberalism to Christian radicalism, which took place during the First World War, and received its expression in the *Römerbrief*; the second was the final liberation from the dross of philosophy, in order that an unadulterated and independent theology might result.'[50] Barth later appears to have realised that the decisive influence of Kierkegaard on his earlier dialectical theology represented the outcome of the hidden intrusion of philosophy and anthropology into theology so that his dialectical theology, far from representing the *destruction* of anthropocentric theology, actually represented its *consolidation*. In this second phase, Barth may therefore be thought of as attempting to base his theology upon a *theological* rather than an *anthropological* foundation – and as identifying Jesus Christ, the Word of God, as that foundation. This development may be seen in his study of Anselm of Canterbury's theological method (1931). In this study, Barth argued that theology should be autonomous in relation to philosophy. At the heart of this work is the recognition of the importance of Anselm's insight that there is a '*ratio* peculiar to the Word of God', a '*ratio* of God', a 'Word spoken from God' which stands over and against human concepts of *ratio*.[51] Truth is thus the consequence of God's own action, which Barth comes to identify with the event of God's own self-revelation in his Word in Jesus Christ, rather than a product of the human rational faculty.

Whereas Barth once emphasized the enormity of the gulf fixed between God and man, he later came to emphasize the 'togetherness' (*Zusammensein*) or the 'dialogue' (*Zwiesprach*) between God and man in history itself. The introduction of this idea of a 'dialogue' between God and man clearly raises the question of the relation between Barth and Brunner on this point.

The liberal theology of the nineteenth century tended to treat God as an *object*, in the sense of his being at the disposal of human enquiry. Early dialectical theology insisted that God must be regarded as a *subject*, thus reversing his hitherto prevailing cognitive status. Indeed, Barth plays upon the two German terms usually employed to signify 'object': God is not subject to man's passive scrutiny as *Objekt*, but stands over and against him as *Gegen-stand*. Brunner adopted a similar attitude. The difference between Barth and Brunner lies in their understanding of man's relation with respect to God as subject. The situation may be summarized as follows:

Liberal Theology: God as *object*, man as *subject*.
Brunner: God as *subject*, man as *subject*.
Barth: God as *subject*, man as *object*.

For the theologians of the nineteenth century in general, particularly those associated with the Ritschl–Herrmann–Harnack tradition, man was the active partner in discovering the nature, identity and character of God. As we saw above, Brunner insists upon the *mutual activity* of God and man within the sphere of history, in order that the insights of dialogical personalism may be exploited theologically. Man is thus the reciprocating *Gesprächspartner* of God. It is therefore inevitable, as we noted above, that Brunner's theology in general, and particularly his Christology, is heavily dependent upon his anthropological presuppositions. Barth, however, totally inverts the cognitive structure of the God-man relation, as expressed by the liberal school, insisting that man must be regarded as an *object* to whom the divine subject addresses his Word.[52] By emphasizing man's passivity and God's activity in the process of revelation, Barth believes it is possible to exclude *anthropological* considerations altogether from theology. Just as he believed the theologians of the nineteenth century to have been forced to reduce theology to anthropology by their insistence that man was subject and God object, so Barth believes that theology may maintain an intellectual autonomy if it is God who is treated as subject, and man as object, in the process of revelation. The crucial anthropological question arising from the liberal theology concerned the *possibility* of revelation: for Barth, the proper question concerned the *reality* of revelation. Revelation is a divinely initiated and actuated unitary event, in which it is God (rather than man) who responds to God in faith. Barth thus effectively reduces the 'dialogue' between God and man to a 'monologue'.[53]

Barth's later works may be regarded as an attempt to unfold the objective knowledge given to man in a real historical event, whereas he earlier disregarded the unique revelation of God in Christ in favour of what can only be termed a general theological agnosticism. It is this later approach which is to be found in the more explicitly Christological sections of the *Kirchliche Dogmatik*. We are obliged to qualify 'Christological' in this manner, in that Barth frequently emphasises that the entire contents of the *Dogmatik* may be regarded as Christological:

> When Holy Scripture speaks of God, it concentrates our attention and thoughts upon one single point...And if we look closer, and ask: who and what is at this point upon which our attention and thoughts are concentrated, which we are to recognise as God?...then from its beginning to its end the Bible directs us to the name of Jesus Christ...Our eyes see God and our thoughts are centered upon God...when they are directed towards Jesus Christ.[54]

All theology necessarily possesses an implicit Christological perspective and foundation, which it is the task of theology to make explicit, in the manner of *fides quaerens intellectum* 'Christological thinking *per definitionem* constitutes the unconditional basis for all theological thinking.[55] Reacting against the Christology represented by A. E. Biedermann, Barth explicitly rejects any deductive Christology based upon a 'Christ-principle' in favour of one based upon 'Jesus Christ himself as witnessed to in Holy Scripture'.[56] Every theological proposition in the *Kirchliche Dogmatik* may be regarded as Christological, in the sense that it has its point of departure in Jesus Christ. It is this feature of Barth's later thought which has led to it being described as 'Christological concentration' or 'Christomonism'. It must be made clear at this point that Barth is *not* suggesting that the *doctrine* of either the person or work of Christ (or both, if they are deemed inseparable) should stand at the centre of a Christian dogmatics, nor that a Christological *idea* or *principle* should constitute the systematic speculative midpoint of a deductive system. Rather, Barth is arguing that the *act of God* which is Jesus Christ underlies theology in its totality.[57] A 'Church Dogmatics' must be 'christologically determined', in that the very possibility and reality of theology is determined by the actuality of the act of divine revelation, by the speaking of the Word of God, by the event of Jesus Christ. To think theologically is essentially to take seriously the fact that the being of God is prior to the enterprise of human theological speculation and questioning; that God's being in its character as 'being in motion' (*gehende*) both establishes the foundation and directs the subsequent course of theology. Christology must be *presupposed from the outset*, rather than arrived at subsequently. Christological doctrine can at best approximate to the greater truth of the *event* of Jesus Christ, which Barth is reluctant to objectify propositionally. Barth's fundamental contention is that Christology is essentially the obedient orientation of the theologian towards the being and act of God: his apparent failure to remain consistent to this principle (evidenced by his obvious committment to a specific Christology) should not be permitted to obscure this point. Jesus Christ constitutes the perspective from which all of theology may and must be surveyed. But what, it may be asked, does Barth understand by the phrase 'Jesus Christ'?

In his earlier dialectical phase, Barth understood Christology to encapsulate the paradoxical nature of theology, providing a brilliant illustration and defence of the paradoxical sitation of the theologian, as he had identified it in the 1922 essay *Das Wort Gottes als Aufgabe der Theologie*: 'As theologians, we should speak about God. We are, however, men, and as such are unable to speak about God.'[58] This 'theology of paradox' served only to infuriate his critics, such as Erik Peterson. In 1925, Peterson published a penetrating critique of dialectical theology, based upon Barth's 1922 essay, in which he illustrated the total futility of the 'dialectical' approach to theology with particular reference to the incarnation:

> To speak of the incarnation . . . as a 'dialectical possibility' actually means not to speak of it at all. And that is precisely what Barth does. For when he says that the impossible has itself become the possible, that death has become life, that eternity has become time, or that God has become man, all that he has said in these different variations is exactly the same – basically, nothing whatsoever. Thesis and antithesis are brought together in a formal and empty synthesis, in which everything and yet nothing is said.[59]

There are clear indications, however, that Barth was moving away from this purely dialectical and paradoxical approach to Christology even before his seminal work on Anselm's theological method.[60] The idea of *paradox* is now replaced by the idea of *analogy*. Barth, however, insists that this analogy be understood as *analogia revelationis* or *analogia fidei*, rather than *analogia entis* – in other words, that an analogy between God and the world is not presupposed (which would be to constitute theology anthropologically), but is itself caused by God's being and action in creation, which creates a correspondence in the creaturely realm to God.[61] The analogy always leads from the creator to the creature, and never from the creature to the creator. Nevertheless, despite this important qualification, it is clear that Barth has moved away from the idea of the paradox of grace to the idea of an all-embracing – although God-given – analogy between God and man, nature and grace, and creation and redemption. By the year 1932, in which the first half-volume of the *Kirchliche Dogmatik* appeared, Barth had moved away from his earlier Kierkegaardian 'Christology of paradox' (which seems to us to be more a 'Christology of protest') towards his mature 'Christology of the Word', based upon the concept of the Christological concentration of the divine revelation to man.

It is important to appreciate that Barth's later Christology is totally integrated within a trinitarian context. In asserting that Barth's thought is totally Christological, it is necessary to add that this has as its corollary that it is totally trinitarian. The entire panorama of the history of salvation is surveyed from the standpoint of the Trinity.[62] Barth thus does not begin his theological reflection (and it is worth remembering how much Barth enjoys pointing out the a posteriori character of *Nach-Denken*) from the history of Jesus of Nazareth, or even from the theologoumenon of the incarnation: the proper starting point for such speculation is eternity, with the pre-existent Christ, with the second person of the Trinity. Viewed from this standpoint, the history of Jesus Christ is recognized not merely as a 30-year episode in time and space, but as an event encompassing and embracing the entire history of God and man, beginning from eternity and stretching into eternity.[63] History is thus *theatrum gloriae Dei*, the arena within which the glory of God may be discerned and recognized. This discernment and recognition, however, is to be treated as an act of God himself, in that man is an epistemic object, rather than a subject. For Barth, *Erkenntnis* ('knowledge') is thus *Anerkenntnis* ('recognition'), and *Denken* ('thinking') is *Nach-Denken* ('contemplation' – but by thus splitting the word, Barth suggests it should be interpreted as 'thinking afterwards'): our knowledge of God is moulded by God himself, a process in which God is active and man is passive. The *locus* of this recognition, however, is defined by Barth in exclusively *Christological* terms. Hans Urs von Balthasar illustrates this 'christological concentration' by comparing it to an hour-glass, in which the sand pours from the upper to the lower section through a constriction. Similarly, the divine revelation proceeds from God to the world, from above to below, only through the central event of the revelation of Christ, apart from which there is no link between God and man.[64] One could perhaps say that Barth regards theology as a spiral round about the self-expression of God in time, in that Barth's Christology is essentially concerned with the contemporaneity of 'above' and 'below' in the history of the humiliation of Christ on the cross.[65] Incarnation and reconciliation (and the reader is reminded that the the German term *Versöhnung* might also be translated as 'atonement') are different sides or aspects of the one movement or action of God in Jesus Christ. The diverse aspects and elements of the question of the person and work of Christ are inextricably interwoven, in that God is merely declaring to man what he had consummated in eternity, by a decree which anticipates everything temporal.[66] In three different ways, Barth develops the manner in which the reconciliation of God and man in Christ is made known[67] – but it must be stressed that Barth's emphasis is unquestionably upon the making known, or revealing, to man of something which has already happened from all eternity. This point is of sufficient importance to warrant further discussion.

We have already noted the trinitarian dimension of Barth's Christology. That trinitarian dimension is particularly linked with the man-ward divine movement of revelation. Distinguishing between the revealer, the revelation, and the 'revealedness' (*Offenbarsein*),[68] Barth argues that the revelation of God the Father is totally determined and constituted by the person of the revealer, Jesus of Nazareth, in that the *content* of this revelation cannot be separated from its *form*.[69] In this way, Barth is able to avoid a total detachment of Christology from the historical figure of Jesus of Nazareth. Equally, however, Barth avoids the suggestion that God is ontologically bound up with and conditioned by the facticity of human existence by his insistence that God is 'antecedently in himself' what he reveals to man. God does not require creation in order to realise or interpret himself. It is for this reason that Barth refers to revelation as the *repetitio aeternitatis in aeternitate*, an eternal recapitulation of what God already is. In Christ, God reveals himself *as himself*, as he already is, without introducing the necessity of a created arena within which such potentiality may be actualised (which would, of course, introduce an anthropologically conditioned necessity into God where it is clearly out of place).[70] The subjectivity of God precludes any such anthropological intrusions into what is, properly speaking, theological territory. The history of Jesus Christ can therefore only recapitulate in time what has already happened antecedently in eternity.[71]

We have made this point at some length because of its inherent Christological importance. Barth's reluctance to engage with historical questions, evident in the *Römerbrief*, can be shown to have culminated in the *Kirchliche Dogmatik*, with the result that a Christology is constructed with only the most superficial contacts with human history. As we have emphasised, Barth's concept of the divine freedom in revelation necessitates that the ensuing revelation merely recapitulates its eternal antecedents. The incarnation, death and resurrection of Christ merely declare what has already happened eternally. These events, so central to Christian theology as a whole (and two of which are unquestionably central to the New Testament *kerygma*), are thus minimized in their significance, in that the emphasis is seen to have shifted from God's revelation in time to the eternal antecedent of that revelation. Barth effectively proceeds from the pre-existence of Christ, thus seeing Christ as equally present at every stage in the historical process. Barth thus *denies the historical nature of revelation*. The consequences of this are considerable.

Perhaps the most surprising conclusion which must be drawn from this analysis is that, despite all differences in substance and emphasis, Barth's Christology is constructed within precisely the same framework as those of the *Aufklärung*, and the nineteenth century in general.[72] Although Barth inverts the nineteenth century subject-object relation in respect to God and man, his central interest remains the anthropologically conditioned question concerning man's knowledge of his situation. Christ is the *locus* in which the true knowledge of the human situation is disclosed, the *speculum* or mirror in which man sees himself reflected. For Barth, Christ's incarnation, passion, death and resurrection cannot in any way be said to change the relationship between God and man – they merely disclose the Christologically determined situation to man. Barth's apocatastasian tendencies have frequently been noted, in that it appears impossible for man to avoid being saved, whether he knows it or not, whether he wishes to be saved or not.[73] Those who find this conclusion questionable are invited to consider what, according to Barth, it is necessary (or, with Barth's doctrine of the *servum arbitrium* in mind, *possible*) for man to do in order *not* to be saved! Given that man *is* saved, it is therefore understandable that Barth's emphasis should fall upon the present knowledge of the real situation, and his tendency to use terms such as *Kenntnis* ('knowledge') and cognates where one would expect *Heil* or *Versöhnung* may easily be explained upon this basis. Thus in his discussion of both the positive and negative aspects of the judgement and sentence of God executed and revealed in the death and resurrection of Jesus Christ, Barth's emphasis falls upon the *knowledge* thus made available to man:

In the mirror of Jesus Christ who was offered up for us and who was obedient in this offering, it becomes known (*wird offenbar*) who we ourselves are . . . we are exposed and known (*erkannt*), and have to know (*erkennen*) ourselves, as the proud creatures who ourselves want to be God and Lord . . . The knowledge (*Erkenntnis*) of the grace of God, and the comfort which flows from it in this sentence, the knowledge (*Erkenntnis*), therefore, of its positive sense, is bound up with the fact that we do not cease to know (*erkennen*) ourselves as those who are condemned.[74]

It is on the basis of the present temporal knowledge of the eternally actualised situation (that is, of the reconciliation of the world to God through Jesus Christ) that the community of faith stands or falls:

If there is no knowledge (*Erkenntnis*) of the overruling righteousness of God, or knowledge only in the form of a mistaken apprehension (*Verkennen*), distorted by partial or total misunderstandings, how can the community escape error and decay, how can faith be kept from doubt and dissolution into all types of unbelief and superstition?[75]

If man does not know what has already happened in eternity, he cannot act upon its basis. The crucial emphasis is therefore not so much upon what *has* happened, as upon what *must yet happen* – man's knowledge or recognition of the real Christologically-determined situation. Despite all Barth's protests to the contrary, there are excellent reasons for supposing that he regards man's knowledge and insight, rather than God's activity, as constituting the centre of theological reflection, precisely because that 'activity' belongs to eternity, rather than time.

The temporal recapitulation of that 'activity' can only be regarded as the 're-presentation' of what has already taken place in eternity, in order that man may learn of what has already happened. The 'eternalization' (*Äternisierung*) of revelation, necessary for Barth on the basis of his presupposition of the divine freedom and the exclusion of anthropological considerations from theology, inevitably means that the emphasis is actually shifted from that revelation itself to man's recognition and appropriation of that revelation – and hence from God's activity to man's insights and knowledge (or, more accurately, to man's epistemic capacities and incapacities). As God 'is in revelation what he is antecedently in himself', it is impossible to speak of revelation 'happening' in time unless one refers to the event of the human appropriation of that revelation *qua* revelation. It is significant that Barth's doctrine of the person and work of Christ makes no reference to any engagement with sin or evil (unless these are understood in the epistemically reduced sense of human 'ignorance' or 'confusion' concerning man's true situation).[76] Barth has simply inverted the liberal Christology, without in any way altering its fundamental point of reference or its preoccupations.

A further difficulty arising from Barth's 'eternalization' of revelation relates to the critical historical questions raised since the time of Lessing concerning the 'ugly great ditch' of history. How can Barth avoid the difficulties which eventually proved fatal to Harnack? Like his great teacher, Wilhelm Herrmann, Barth appears to dismiss them as being of little significance:

> The problem does indeed have this temporal or spatial aspect. It has the form of the problem of the historical (*geschichtlich*) distance between the being and activity of Christ in its own place and ours, in a different place. That there is this difference cannot be denied. . . This distance-problem, however, which has become of such interest to modern Protestantism is, all things considered, more of a technical or conceptual difficulty rather than a spiritual, or a genuine theological, problem.[77]

This deliberate refusal to engage in dialogue with the critical questions raised by the historicization of reality inevitably means that Barth's Christology marks the end of a road in our study, rather than a significant contribution to the development of the Christological tradition of German-speaking Protestantism. Although Barth's insistence that revelation is not a predicate of history, linked with his conceptual distinction between the contemporaneous and coextensive 'secular form' and the 'divine content' of revelation, might seem to render him immune from such critical historical questions, the reality is actually rather different. Precisely because of the epistemic significance of man's recognition of revelation for what it is, the question of how the 'secular form' – let alone the 'divine content' – of that revelation may be discerned within the historical continuum becomes acutely pressing. If revelation demands historical predicates, as Barth insists it does,[78] the question of how those predicates may be recognized within the historical nexus cannot be evaded. It does not matter if revelation is merely 're-presentation' or 'recapitulation' of the Christologically determined situation: once the necessity of historical predicates is conceded, the full challenge of the critical historical method must be faced. Although Jüngel has argued with some force that the relationship between the 'form' and 'content' of revelation is not arbitrary,[79] the fact remains the the circumstantial historical act 'with and under' which revelation occurs *must* be open to critical historical enquiry *if it is an historical event*. Barth simply has not succeeded in freeing his Christology from the critical questions raised by the modern period.

It is therefore significant that Barth is often presented as the exponent of a 'classical Christology', reverting to the great themes of patristic Christology and their medieval and Reformation developments.[80] Barth tends to enter into debate with the theology of medieval and Reformed scholasticism on matters of Christology, rather than with the Christologies of the modern period. Of particular importance in this respect is Barth's discussion of the distinction between anhypostatic and enhypostatic manhood. Barth appears to have encountered this distinction for the first time during his Göttingen period, and to have seen in the latter a means of safeguarding the essential unity of Jesus Christ with God.[81] Similarly, Barth's frequent insistence that God is the subject of Jesus Christ's actions is articulated in terms of the patristic concept of the 'carrier' or 'bearer' (*Träger*): 'The Word became flesh: not man in general, but the carrier of our human essence.'[82] Barth's unhesitant affirmation that Christ assumed *fallen* human nature (in other words, that the Word became 'flesh' as well as 'man') has caused disquiet among some of his critics, in view of its unorthodox historical associations.[83] God thus performs the actions of Jesus through the human nature which he 'carries', this human nature not being an agent in itself. Barth emphasizes that God acts *directly*, rather than *indirectly*, in Christ. It is not a question of

God acting vicariously through Christ, or delegating Christ to act on his behalf with his authority: Christ *is* God, and as such God may be said to act when Christ acts:

> We deal with God himself when we deal with this man. God himself speaks when this man speaks in the words of men. God himself acts and suffers when this man acts and suffers as a man. God himself triumphs when this one triumphs as a man. The human speaking and acting and suffering and triumphing of this one man directly concerns us, in that his human history is ours, the salvation-history which, because God himself is its human subject in his Son, changes the entire human situation.[84]

Whereas the 'carrier' of the human nature in mankind is the individual man, Barth refuses to acknowledge the existence of any human carrier in the hypostatic union: the human nature is carried by the Word of God. In his polemic against the Christology of Lutheran Orthodoxy (as well as certain older representatives of Reformed Orthodoxy), Barth argues that the human nature of Christ may be thought of as a temple within which God dwells:

> Can one describe this in any way other than Calvin (*Inst.* II.14.1): *e virginis utero templum sibi delegit in quo habitaret?* Is 'temple' or 'dwelling' – a dwelling filled with Godhood, and exclusively and totally claimed and sanctified by God, but still a dwelling! – not really enough to describe what has to be said about human essence in relation to Jesus Christ and to the history which took place in him?[85]

This point is important, in that it illustrates Barth's tendency to treat Christ's humanity as a vehicle for his divinity, in a manner similar to Calvin and the Alexandrian tradition (which Calvin follows at this point). It is passages such as the above which may be interpreted as indicating that Barth constructs his Christology 'from above', and expose Barth to the criticism that he *presupposes* the divinity of Christ: whereas this presupposition might be permissible for Athanasius, Calvin or Bucanus, since the time of the *Aufklärung* it is no longer permissible to avoid the *historical* question of how this divinity is to be recognized from the history of Jesus of Nazareth and the tradition concerning him.[86] In effect, Barth merely reinterprets the earlier 'classical' Christological tradition in the light of his 'theology of the Word', rather than establishing its presuppositions in the first place.

In this respect, as in so many others, Barth must be regarded as deliberately disengaging himself from what is widely regarded as the most crucial question facing contemporary Christology: the relation between faith and history. If the 'modern' period is characterized by its critical-historical attitudes (as Troeltsch suggested in his famous study of the Reformer Philip Melanchthon and the Lutheran scholastic Johann Gerhard), then Barth's Christology belongs to the pre-modern period. It is perhaps significant that Barth seems to be most at home in his dialogue with the Christology of the sixteenth and seventeenth centuries, rather than with that of the modern period.

As we emphasized earlier, the development of the Christology of German-speaking Protestantism from 1750 to the present day is an essentially continuous process, an evolving dialogue during which possibilities are explored, in order that they may be accepted, rejected or modified. Barth's Christology represents a deliberate disengagement from that process of dialogue, apparently on the assumption that the 'theology of the Word' is immune from the critical questions raised by the modern period, particularly those arising from the historicization of reality. This attitude may be contrasted with that of Brunner, whose concept of a Christologically concentrated 'historical dialogue' between God and man leads him to attempt a systematic engagement with the questions of faith and history. Barth's contribution to the development of modern German Christology must therefore be regarded as an effective initial Kierkegaardian protest against 'Culture-Christologies', followed by the development of an idiosyncratic ahistorical Christology which, as the subsequent course of the Christological debate indicates, represents a 'blind alley' in the making of modern German Christology. The nature of Barth's early protest against the liberal *Christusbild*, particularly in its radical and sweeping appeal to eschatology, was such as to inhibit *any* systematic Christological reflections, other than awe in the presence of the *totaliter aliter*: his own later reflections must be regarded as effectively contradicting his earlier insights. Perhaps Barth's permanent significance, from the point of view of the present study, lies in his prophetic critique of any *Christusbild*, which he exposes as ultimately nothing more than an idol. We need our Barths to remind us of that fundamental point: having acknowledged it, however, the task of attempting to construct a *Christusbild* – however provisional we must recognize it to be – must continue. Christian theology cannot be reduced to silence concerning the object of its proclamation! The most fruitful Christological development to emerge from the early dialectical school was, in fact, the 'kerygmatic' Christology of Rudolf Bultmann, to which we now turn.

NOTES

1 For the text of the appeal, and names of the signatories, see G. F. Nicolai, *Die Biologie des Krieges* (2 vols: Zurich, 1919), vol. 1, pp. 7–10. Six other prominent theologians also signed the document. For useful background, see Wolfgang Huber, 'Evangelische Theologie und Kirche beim Ausbruch des Ersten Weltkrieges', *Studien zur Friedensforschung* 4 (1970), pp. 148–215.

2 Karl Barth, *Evangelische Theologie im 19. Jahrhundert* (Theologische Studien 49: Zurich, 1957), p. 6. (This monograph should not be confused with *Die protestantische Theologie im 19. Jahrhundert*, published at Zurich in 1947: in English, the titles are identical, both *evangelisch* and *protestantisch* being translated as 'Protestant', on account of the overtones of the English word 'evangelical'.) Elsewhere, he notes the absence of Martin Rade from the signatories: *Schleiermacher-Auswahl* (Munich, 1968), p. 293. See the useful study of Wilfried Härle, 'Der Aufruf der 93 Intellektuellen und Karl Barths Bruch mit der liberalen Theologie', *Zeitschrift für Theologie und Kirche* 72 (1975), pp. 207–24.

3 For an excellent introduction to Barth's days as a student, and the remarkable influence of Herrmann upon him at Marburg, see Eberhard Busch, *Karl Barth: His Life from Letters and Autobiographical Texts* (London, 1976), pp. 33–52. The significance of the influence of Harnack, Gunkel and Kaftan at Berlin should not be overlooked: Barth knew the later Ritschlian theology at first hand, as may be seen from the early essay, 'Moderne Theologie und Reichgottesarbeit', *Zeitschrift für Theologie und Kirche* 19 (1909), pp. 317–21. His later comments on this article may be noted, as found in the autobiographical sketch in the *Fakultätsalbum der evangelisch-theologischen Fakultät Münster* (Münster, 1927). It is interesting, in view of their subsequent disagreements, to note that Barth was a devoted regular (and probably the youngest) member of Harnack's Berlin seminars: see Agnes von Zahn-Harnack, *Adolf von Harnack* (Berlin, 2nd edn, 1951), pp. 414–5.

4 For example, see H. Diehl, 'Thesen und Antithesen: Herrmann und Troeltsch', *Zeitschrift für Theologie und Kirche* 18 (1908), pp. 473–8, especially p. 473; Karl Bornhausen, 'Ernst Troeltsch und das Problem der wissenschaftlichen Theologie', *Zeitschrift für Theologie und Kirche* 4 (1923), pp. 196–223, especially p. 196.

5 This point, all too easily overlooked, has been emphasized by Robert

Morgan, 'Troeltsch and the Dialectical Theology', in *Ernst Troeltsch and the Future of Theology*, ed. J. P. Clayton (Cambridge, 1976), pp. 33–77, and Wilfried Groll, *Ernst Troeltsch und Karl Barth: Kontinuität im Widerspruch* (Munich, 1978). See also Paul Althaus, 'Theologie und Geschichte: Zur Auseinandersetzung mit der dialektischen Theologie', *Zeitschrift für systematische Theologie* 1 (1923), pp. 763–76; Van A. Harvey, *The Historian and the Believer* (London, 1967), pp. 153–9, who illustrates the historical deficiencies of dialectical theology with reference to Barth on the 'historicity' of the resurrection.

6 *Briefwechsel Karl Barth-Eduard Thurneysen 1913–1921* (2 vols: Zurich, 1973–4), vol. 1, p. 121. For the relationship of Gogarten to Troeltsch, see H. Fischer, *Christlicher Glaube und Geschichte: Voraussetzungen und Folgen der Theologie Friedrich Gogartens* (Gütersloh, 1967), pp. 13–64. The anti-historical attitude of the early Brunner is well illustrated in his essay 'Geschichte oder Offenbarung? Ein Wort der Entgegnung an Horst Stephan', *Zeitschrift für Theologie und Kirche* 6 (1925), pp. 266–78. For an excellent study of the somewhat ambivalent relationship of Barth and Gogarten over the period 1922–33, see Peter Lange, *Konkrete Theologie? Karl Barth und Friedrich Gogarten 'Zwischen den Zeiten' (1922–1933)* (Zurich, 1972).

7 It should be noted that Bultmann, although now recognized as having close affinities with 'dialectical theology', was not regarded as being affiliated with the movement at the time. In the 1920s, 'dialectical theology' meant Barth and Gogarten, and to a lesser extent, Brunner and Thurneysen. The term 'dialectical theology' appears to have arisen from Barth's reference to 'die innere Dialektik der Sache' in the preface to the second edition of the *Römerbrief*. The statement: 'Offenbarung ist und setzt ein Oberhalb der Dialektik unserer Existenz' (*Die christliche Dogmatik im Entwurf* (Munich, 1927), p. 188) is also suggestive. Barth, of course, preferred the designation 'Theology of the Word of God'.

8 See Barth's estimate of the influence of the Danish philosopher upon his early thought: 'Dank und Reverenz', *Evangelische Theologie* 23 (1963), pp. 337–49. The best study of the relationship between Barth and the Danish philosopher is E. Brinkschmidt, *Sören Kierkegaard und Karl Barth* (Neukirchen, 1971). Ernst Troeltsch acknowledged this remarkable influence over Gogarten's *Theologie der Krisis* (which is primarily a 'crisis of culture') in his 1921 essay 'Ein Apfel vom Baume Kierkegaards': see *Anfänge der dialektischen Theologie II*, ed. J. Moltmann (Munich, 1963), pp. 140–53. Gogarten's 1920 lecture 'Die Krisis unserer Kultur' was the immediate occasion of this essay: see *Anfänge der dialektischen Theologie*, pp. 101–22. A full account of Kierkegaard's Christology is impossible here: the reader is referred to the excellent study of Hayo Gerdes, *Das Christusbild Sören Kierkegaards vergleichen mit der Christologie Hegels und*

Schleiermachers (Düsseldorf, 1960). For a useful study of the Christological legacy of Kierkegaard in English, see Paul Sponheim, *Kierkegaard on Christ and Christian Coherence* (London, 1968), pp. 267–320. See also notes 12, 13, and 59.

9 *Der Römerbrief* (Zurich, 8th edn, 1947), p. 315.

10 *Römerbrief*, p. xiii. The German term is ambiguous, and can be translated either as 'cross-roads' or 'way of the Cross'.

11 *Römerbrief*, p. 5 'Die Austrahlungen oder viehlmehr die erstaunlichen Einschlagstrichter und Hohlraüme, durch die er sich innerhalb der historischen Anschaulichkeit bemerkbar macht, sind, auch wenn die 'Leben Jesu' heißen, nicht die andre Welt die sich in Jesus mit unsrer Welt berührt'. Cf. p. 6 'Aber [die göttliche Offenbarung] berüht [die Welt] wie die Tangente einen Kreis, ohne sie zu berühren, und gerade indem sie sie nicht berührt, berührt sie sie als ihre Begrenzung, als neue Welt.'

12 *Römerbrief*, pp. 72–4. Note the reference to Kierkegaard. On Kierkegaard's view of time (which, as we noted earlier, is significantly altered by Barth), see J. Heywood Thomas, 'Kierkegaard's View of Time', *Journal of the British Society for Phenomenology* 4 (1973), pp. 33–40, and references therein. The contrast with Heidegger is illuminating: F. Seven, *Die Ewigkeit Gottes und die Zeitlichkeit des Menschen: Eine Untersuchung der hermeneutischen Funktion der Zeit in Karl Barths Theologie der Krisis und im Seinsdenken Martin Heideggers* (Göttingen, 1979).

13 For an excellent analysis of Barth's developing equivocal attitude to Hegel's doctrine of the 'reconciliation' (*Versöhnung*) of God and man in history, raised by this assertion, see Christophe Freyd, *Gott als die universale Wahrheit von Mensch und Welt: Die Versöhnungslehre Karl Barths im Lichte der Religionsphilosophie Hegels* (Stuttgart, 1982). The influence of Kierkegaard is once more important: see Stephen D. Crites, *In the Twilight of Christendom: Hegel vs. Kierkegaard on Faith and History* (Chambersburg, Pa., 1972), and references therein.

14 For example, K. Budde, 'Die Theologie der Krisis und der Weltkrieg', *Christliche Welt* 41 (1927), 1104–5; Gustaf Wingren, *Die Methodenfrage der Theologie* (Göttingen, 1957), pp. 114–5.

15 K. Hammer, *Deutsche Kriegstheologie (1870–1918)* (Munich, 1971).

16 See Wilhelm Pressel, *Die Kriegspredigt 1914–1918 in der evangelischen Kirche Deutschlands* (Göttingen, 1967).

17 For the impact of the outbreak of the war upon Barth's preaching, see the valuable study of Jochen Fähler, *Der Ausbruch des Ersten Weltkrieges in Karl Barths Predigten 1913–1915* (Bern, 1979), pp. 66–73.

18 *Das Heilige* went through twenty-five editions between 1917 and 1936, making it one of the most widely read theological works of the twentieth century. The Luther renaissance may be regarded as stemming from

Karl Holl's Berlin address of 31 October 1917, on the occasion of the 400th anniversary of the Reformation: see Karl Holl, 'Was verstand Luther unter Religion', reprinted in *Gesammelte Aufsätze zur Kirchengeschichte* (3 vols: Tübingen, 7th edn, 1948), vol. 1, pp. 1–110. In this address, Holl emphasized the holiness, glory and majesty of God, in contrast to the somewhat emasculated deity of liberal Protestantism.

19 See E. Rolffs, 'Adolf Harnack und die Theologie der Krisis', *Christliche Welt* 52 (1938), 61–5; D. Braun, 'Der Ort der Theologie: Entwurf für einen Zugang zum Verständnis des Briefwechsels zwischen Adolf von Harnack und Karl Barth aus dem Jahre 1923', in *Parrhesia: Festschrift für Karl Barth* (Zurich, 1966), pp. 11–49; E. Fascher, 'Adolf von Harnacks und Karl Barths Thesenaustausch von 1923', in *Frage und Antwort: Studien zur Theologie und Religionsgeschichte* (Berlin, 1968), pp. 201–31. For the full text of the exchanges in English, which dragged on until the May issue of that year, see H. M. Rumscheidt, *Revelation and Theology: An Analysis of the Barth-Harnack Correspondence of 1923* (Cambridge, 1972), pp. 29-53. Rumscheidt's translation of Barth's fourteenth thesis is incorrect. See also Rumscheidt's earlier study, 'The Barth–Harnack Correspondence: Conflict as Methodology', *Continuum* 7 (1969), pp. 143–52; 195–212.

20 Cf. *Römerbrief*, p. 5 'Jesus Christus unser Herr: das ist die Heilsbotschaft, das ist der Sinn der Geschichte'.

21 For the original of the Harnack citation, see *Christliche Welt* 37 (1923), p. 8; for the original of the Barth, see p. 91 of the same volume. For an excellent discussion of Barth's mature attitude to the critical-historical method, foreshadowed here and in the *Römerbrief*, see Friedrich Wilhelm Marquardt, 'Exegese und Dogmatik in Karl Barths Theologie. Was meint: Kritischer müßten mir die historisch-kritischen sein!', in *Registerband zu Karl Barths Kirchliche Dogmatik*, ed. H. Krause (Zurich, 1970), pp. 651–76.

22 Barth, 'Die dogmatische Prinzipienlehre bei Wilhelm Herrmann', *Zwischen den Zeiten* 3 (1925), pp. 246–75.

23 For Troeltsch's response, see note 8. Gogarten developed his implicit critique of Troeltsch in the 1922 essay *Wider die romantische Theologie*; reprinted in *Anfänge der dialektischen Theologie II*, pp. 140–53. See further Hans–Georg Drescher, 'Entwicklungsdenken und Glaubensentscheidung: Troeltschs Kierkegaardverständnis und die Kontroverse Troeltsch–Gogarten', *Zeitschrift für Theologie und Kirche* 79 (1982), pp. 80–106.

24 The new journal founded by Barth, Gogarten and Thurneysen in 1922 took its name from this lecture.

25 Emil Brunner, *Erlebnis, Erkenntnis, und Glaube* (Tübingen, 1921), p. 1. Note the caustic references to Troeltsch (and also the remarkably

superficial treatment of him!), characteristic of early dialectical theology – for example, p. 2. It is, incidentally, clear that Brunner was not initially regarded as a member of the dialectical circle: in an exchange of letters between Thurneysen and Barth of 12–16 February 1923, certain misgivings concerning him are expressed (*Briefwechsel*, vol. 2, pp. 141–5). For a later, somewhat garbled, attack on Troeltsch, see his *The Theology of Crisis* (New York, 1930), pp. 7–10.

26 See Brunner, *Das Symbolische in der religiöse Erkenntnis: Beiträge zu einer Theorie des religiösen Erkennens* (Tübingen, 1914). On this pre-critical phase, see Stephan Scheld, *Die Christologie Emil Brunners: Beitrag zur Überwindung liberaler Jesuologie und dialektisch-doketischer Christologie in Zuge geschichtlich-dialogischen Denkens* (Wiesbaden, 1981), pp. 48–92. On the 'pre-critical' and 'pre-dialectical' phase in general, see Roman Roessler, *Person und Glaube: Der Personalismus der Gottesbeziehung bei Emil Brunner* (Munich, 1965), pp. 19–20; Heinrich Leipold, *Missionarische Theologie: Emil Brunners Weg zur theologischen Anthropologie* (Göttingen, 1974), p. 20.

27 *Erlebnis, Erkenntnis und Glaube*, pp. 10; 55–6. Cf. Scheld, *Christologie*, pp. 93–102 for an excellent analysis. Brunner's 1919 review of Barth's *Römerbrief* is significant, suggesting that he was aware of the significance of the work: *Kirchenblatt für die reformierte Schweiz* 34 (1919), pp. 29–32.

28 This point is emphasized by Christoph Gestrich, *Neuzeitliches Denken und die Spaltung der dialektischen Theologie* (Tübingen, 1977), p. 33.

29 For an excellent analysis, see Scheld, *Christologie*, pp. 103–99.

30 *Der Mittler: Zur Besinnung über den Christusglauben* (Tübingen, 1927), p. 35; *The Mediator: A Study of the Central Doctrine of the Christian Faith* (London, 1934), p. 56 (This English translation is inaccurate at points of importance, and should be used in parallel with the German original.) The concept of *Einmaligkeit*, introduced without further discussion here, is further developed in the important essay 'Das Einmalige und der Existenzcharakter', *Blätter für deutsche Philosophie* 3 (1929), pp. 265–82. In this essay, Brunner points out that philosophers of history, such as Dilthey and Rickert, emphasize the uniqueness and individuality of every historical event (in the sense of *das Einzigartige*, however, rather than *das Einzige*), whereas Christianity recognizes the 'once-for-all-ness' of the Christ-event.

31 *Der Mittler*, p. 73; *The Mediator*, p. 97.

32 See the important introduction: *Der Mittler*, pp. 3–21; *The Mediator*, pp. 21–41. Cf. Scheld, *Christologie*, pp. 104–28.

33 See Scheld, *Christologie*, pp. 162–75 for an excellent study of Brunner's Anselmian satisfaction theory.

34 *Der Mittler*, p. 42; *The Mediator*, p. 64 'Weder ist ein Christus als primus inter pares der Christus, der man predigen könnte, noch ist die Behauptung wissenschaftlich haltbar, Jesus sei der erstmalige Gestalter

des ethisch-rationalen Zweckprinzips Reich Gottes oder Liebe Gottes.'

35 This point was emphasized by Brunner's contemporary Paul Althaus, 'Brunners Mittler: Zur Aufgabe der Christologie', in *Theologische Aufsätze* (2 vols: Gütersloh, 1935), vol. 2, pp. 174–7. Cf. Scheld, *Christologie*, p. 196 for comments on 'das dialektisch-doketische Verständnis der Fleischwerdung und Gott-Menschheit Jesu Christi'.

36 In his exposition of John 1.14 ('The Word became flesh'), Brunner develops the concept of *logos* – which he argues to be a central concept of Greek religious philosophy, and somewhat inaccurately terms *der platonisch-stoisch-philonischen Logosbegriff* – in a strongly historical and personal direction, thus foreshadowing his later work *Wahrheit als Begegnung* (1938): see Scheld, *Christologie*, pp. 128–32, for further references.

37 Ferdinand Ebner, *Das Wort und die geistigen Realitäten: Pneumatologische Fragmenten* (Innsbruck, 1921); reprinted in *Schriften* (2 vols: Munich, 1963), vol. 1, pp. 75–342; Martin Buber, *Ich und Du* (Leipzig, 1923); reprinted in *Werke* (3 vols: Munich/Heidelberg, 1962–4), vol. 1, pp. 77–170.

38 On the history of the concept, see Buber, 'Zur Geschichte der dialogischen Prinzips', *Werke*, vol. 1, pp. 291–305; B. Casper, *Das dialogische Denken: Eine Untersuchung der religionsphilosophischen Bedeutung Franz Rosenweigs, Ferdinand Ebners und Martin Bubers* (Freiburg, 1967). For an excellent study of Buber's personalism, see Michael Weinrich, *Der Wirklichkeit begegnen . . . Studien zu Buber, Grisebach, Gogarten, Bonhoeffer und Hirsch* (Neukirchen, 1980), pp. 51–129. For a useful study in English, see Steven T. Katz, 'Dialogue and Revelation in the Thought of Martin Buber', *Religious Studies* (1978), pp. 57–68.

39 Buber, *Werke*, vol. 1, p. 79.

40 The best study of the *Ich-Es* relationship remains that of Z. Balogh, *Martin Buber und die Welt des Es* (Meisenheim, 1969).

41 *Werke*, vol. 1, p. 92.

42 *Die Wahrheit als Begegung: Sechs Vorlesungen über das christliche Wahrheitsverständnis* (Zurich, 2nd edn, 1963), pp. 164–7. For an excellent study of Brunner's views on 'personal revelation' up to this point, see Y. Salakka, *Person und Offenbarung in der Theologie Emil Brunners während der Jahre 1914–1937* (Helsinki, 1960).

43 *Wahrheit als Begegnung*, p. 114 'Gott hält mir in seinem Wort kein Dogmatikkolleg, er legt mir nicht den Inhalt eines Glaubensbekenntnisses aus oder vor, sondern er erschließt mir *sich selbst* . . . Er teilt mir nicht *etwas* sondern *sich* mit' (my italics).

44 *Wahrheit als Begegnung*, pp. 107–8. See also the important essay of 1932, 'Die Frage nach dem Anknüpfungspunkt als Problem der Theologie', in *Ein offenes Wort: Vorträge und Aufsätze 1917–1962* (2 vols: Zurich, 1981),

vol. 1, pp. 239–67. It was, of course, on account of their disagreement over the anthropological dimensions of this *Anknüpfungspunkt* that Barth and Brunner went their separate ways: see Brunner's 1934 essay 'Natur und Gnade: Zum Gespräch mit Karl Barth', in *Ein offenes Wort*, vol. 1, pp. 333–66. Barth's hostility to the *spekulative Ich-Du-Philosophie* (as taken up by Gogarten) was expressed in a circular letter to Thurneysen and others, dated 7 October 1922: *Briefwechsel*, vol. 2, pp. 102–7; especially pp. 105–6. The essence of Barth's concern was that this philosophy attributed to man an excessive natural capacity to know and relate to God. On the use made of 'personalism' in the theology of Gogarten, see Lange, *Konkrete Theologie*, pp. 112–7; Weinrich, *Der wirklichkeit begegnen*, pp. 131–212.

45 'Das Einmalige und der Existenzcharakter', p. 279.

46 'Das Einmalige und der Existenzcharakter', p. 271.

47 For example, see *Gott und Mensch: Vier Untersuchungen über das personhafte Sein* (Tübingen, 1930), p. 21; 'Die Christusbotschaft im Kampf mit den Religionen', *Basler Missionstudien* 8 (1931), pp. 1–20; especially pp. 8–9.

48 See Scheld, *Christologie*, pp. 212–20. Cf. the much less perceptive study of Hermann Volk, 'Die Christologie bei Karl Barth und Emil Brunner', in *Das Konzil von Chalcedon: Geschichte und Gegenwart*, ed. Aloys Grillmeier (3 vols: Würzburg, 1951–4), vol. 3, pp. 644–73. For a useful comparison of Barth and Brunner on the doctrine of the *imago Dei*, see David Cairns, *The Image of God in Man* (London, 1973), pp. 152–86. Brunner's anthropological concerns are best studied from *Der Mensch im Widerspruch: Die christliche Lehre vom wahren und vom wirklichen Menschen* (Zurich, 1937), the first theological anthropology to emerge from the by then not-so-dialectical school. For an excellent study of his anthroplogical development and its theological ramifications, see Leopold, *Missionarische Theologie*, *passim*.

49 *Die christliche Lehre von Schöpfung und Erlösung* (Zurich, 1950), especially pp. 281–308. For an excellent analysis, see Scheld, *Christologie*, pp. 221–316. Volk suggests that the Christology of the *Dogmatik* is *less* Chalcedonian than that of *Der Mittler*: Volk, 'Christologie bei Karl Barth und Emil Brunner', p. 663.

50 See Hans Urs von Balthasar, *Karl Barth: Darstellung und Deutung seiner Theologie* (Cologne, 1962), p. 101.

51 *Fides quaerens intellectum: Anselms Beweis der Existenz Gottes im Zusammenhang seines theologischen Programms* (Zurich, 1981), pp. 44–7.

52 On this, see James Brown, *Subject and Object in Modern Theology* (London, 1955), pp. 34–82 (on the Kierkegaardian concept of the 'subjectivity of God') and pp. 140–67 (on Barth). The important essay of Wolfhart Pannenberg should also be noted: 'Die Subjectivität Gottes und die Trinitätslehre: Ein Beitrag zur Beziehung zwischen Karl Barth und der

Philosophie Hegels', *Kerygma und Dogma* 23 (1977), pp. 25–40.

53 See the caustic comments of von Balthasar, *Karl Barth*, pp. 225–6; 380 (with particular reference to the 'monologue of the cross').

54 *Kirchliche Dogmatik*, II/2, pp. 56–7; *Church Dogmatics*, II/2, p. 52–4. There are a number of useful introductions and general surveys of Barth's Christology in English to which the reader may be directed: John Thompson, *Christ in Perspective: Christological Perspectives in the Theology of Karl Barth* (Edinburgh, 1978), is particularly recommended as an overview of the Christology of the *Kirchliche Dogmatik*; Charles Waldrop, *Karl Barth's Christology: Its Basic Alexandrian Character* (Berlin, 1984), is also valuable, although it seems to the present writer that the attempt to interpret Barth as a representative of the 'Alexandrian' or 'Antiochene' Christology involves the use of anachronistic frames of reference ill suited to the analysis of Barth's highly idiosyncratic theology. For the claim that Barth was a Nestorian, see Henri Bouillard, *Karl Barth* (2 vols: Paris, 1957), vol. 1, p. 122; R. Prenter, 'Karl Barths Umbildung der traditionellen Zweinaturlehre in lutherischer Beleuchtung', *Studia Theologica* 11 (1957), pp. 1–88. Both these studies appear unclear as to what 'Nestorianism' actually is, and in what sense it differs from the general 'Antiochene' position. For a careful justification of the claim that Barth was Alexandrian, see Waldorp, *Karl Barth's Christology*, pp. 87–164. Pannenberg suggests that Barth is the foremost representative of 'Alexandrian' Christology within modern Protestantism, but bases this conclusion upon the presupposition that Barth's Christology begins 'from above': Wolfhart Pannenberg, *Grundzüge der Christologie* (Gütersloh, 6th edn, 1982), p. 27. As may be seen from Klappert's taxonomy of Christologies, this presupposition is open to question: see note 65.

55 *Kirchliche Dogmatik*, IV/3, p. 200; *Church Dogmatics*, IV/3, p. 175.

56 *Kirchliche Dogmatik*, IV/3, p. 199; *Church Dogmatics*, IV/3, p. 174.

57 Barth thus praises Bultmann for recognizing that the Christ event is *der Tat Gottes*: *Rudolf Bultmann: Ein Versuch ihn zu verstehen* (Zurich, 1964), pp. 37–48. Some scholars have suggested, on the basis of his statements concerning the role of Jesus Christ in dogmatics, that Barth, in fact, reverts to a theology of the *Christusprinzip*: see Colin Brown, *Karl Barth and the Christian Message* (London, 1967), pp. 138–9; E. H. Friedmann, *Christologie und Anthropologie: Methode und Bedeutung des Lehre vom Menschen in der Theologie Karl Barths* (Münsterschwarzach, 1972), pp. 121–2. For a useful analysis of this general problem, see S. W. Sykes, 'Barth on the Centre of Theology', in *Karl Barth – Studies of His Theological Methods*, ed. S. W. Sykes (Oxford, 1979), pp. 17–54.

58 Karl Barth, 'Das Wort Gottes als Aufgabe der Theologie', in *Das Wort Gottes und die Theologie* (Munich, 1925), pp. 156–78; p. 158 'Wir sollen als Theologen von Gott reden. Wir sind aber Menschen und könne als

solche nicht von Gott reden. Wir sollen Beides, unser Sollen und unser Nicht-Können, wissen und eben damit Gott die Ehre geben. Das ist unsre Bedrängnis. Alles Andre ist daneben Kinderspiel.'

59 Eric Peterson, 'Was ist Theologie'; reprinted in *Theologie als Wissenschaft: Aufsätze und Thesen*, ed. Gerhard Sauter (Munich, 1971), pp. 132–51; p. 137. For an excellent analysis, see Eberhard Jüngel, 'Von der Dialektik zu Analogie: Die Schule Kierkegaards und der Einspruch Petersons', in *Barth Studien* (Zurich/Cologne/Gütersloh, 1982), pp. 127–79. For the origins of this 'Christology of paradox', see Hermann Fischer, *Die Christologie des Paradoxes: Zur Herkunft und Bedeutung des Christusverständnisses Sören Kierkegaards* (Göttingen, 1970).

60 See his essay 'Kirche und Theologie', in *Die Theologie und die Kirche: Gesammelte Vorträge II* (Munich, 1928), p. 302–28; p. 319 'Die Offenbarung . . . ist nicht dialektisch, ist kein Paradox.' The interesting reference to God speaking 'das undialektische Wort' (*Christliche Dogmatik*, p. 460) should be noted.

61 On the distinction between *analogia entis* and *analogia fidei*, and its significance within Barth's theology of revelation, see Gottlieb Söhngen, 'Analogia entis in analogia fidei', in *Antwort: Karl Barth zum siebzigsten Geburtstag* (Zurich, 1956), pp. 266–72; Walter Kreck, 'Analogia fidei oder analogia entis?', in *Antwort*, pp. 272–86. The most valuable general study remains H. G. Pöhlmann, *Analogia Entis oder Analogia Fidei? Die Frage nach Analogie bei Karl Barth* (Göttingen, 1965). For the contextualization of Barth's polemic against the *analogia entis*, see E. Mechels, *Analogie bei Erich Przywara und Karl Barth: Das Verhältnis von Offenbarungstheologie und Metaphysik* (Neukirchen, 1974).

62 For an excellent study of Barth's doctrine of the Trinity, of considerable importance in this respect, see R. D. Williams, 'Barth on the Triune God', in *Karl Barth – Studies of His Theological Methods*, pp. 147–93.

63 Inevitably, this has implications for Barth's understanding of the nature of time and the relative priority of creation and redemption: for useful introductions, see A. Brandenburg, 'Der Zeit- und Geschichtsbegriff bei Karl Barth', *Theologie und Glaube* 45 (1955), pp. 357–78; R. H. Roberts, 'Barth's Doctrine of Time: Its Nature and Implications', in *Karl Barth – Studies of His Theological Methods*, pp. 88–146; Konrad Stock, *Anthropologie der Verheißung: Karl Barths Lehre vom Menschen als dogmatisches Problem* (Munich, 1980), pp. 191–233.

64 Von Balthasar, *Karl Barth*, p. 210.

65 See Berthold Klappert, *Die Auferweckung des Gekreuzigten: Der Ansatz der Christologie Karl Barths im Zusammenhang der Christologie der Gegenwart* (Neukirchen, 1971), pp. 3–5, for a taxonomy of Christologies. Klappert distinguishes five different starting points and methods employed in modern theology:

(1) Christology *from above to below*, exemplified by classical incarnational theology.
(2) Christology *from below*, exemplified by Friedrich Gogarten's concept of pure personality.
(3) Christology *from below to above*, exemplified by Wolfhart Pannenberg.
(4) Christology *from both above and below* in the encounter with the kerygma, exemplified in different manners by Rudolf Bultmann and Otto Weber.
(5) Christology *from both above and below* in the history of the humiliation of Jesus Christ, as seen in Barth.

The celebrated distinction between Christology 'from above' and 'from below' is unworkable in practice, as has often been pointed out – e.g., see Nicholas Lash, 'Up and Down in Christology', in *New Studies in Theology I*, ed. Stephen Sykes and Derek Holmes (London, 1980), pp. 31-46. However, it seems to us that Klappert's characterization of Barth begs too many questions to be acceptable. The best study of this aspect of Barth's thought remains von Balthasar, *Karl Barth*. Barth's Christology may be regarded as 'from above' as a working hypothesis, although it must be subjected to refinement along the lines suggested by von Balthasar.

66 *Kirchliche Dogmatik* II/2, p. 57; *Church Dogmatics* II/2, pp. 53–4.
67 See Klappert, *Auferweckung des Gekreuzigten*, pp. 85–99. See also the useful analysis of IV/1–3 in Eberhard Jüngel, 'Einführung in Leben und Werk Karl Barths', in *Barth Studien*, pp. 22–60; pp. 54–8.
68 See Eberhard Jüngel, *Gottes Sein ist im Werden: Verantwortliche Rede vom Sein Gottes bei Karl Barth. Eine Paraphrase* (Tübingen, 1965) – but see also note 79.
69 *Kirchliche Dogmatik* I/1, p. 411; *Church Dogmatics* I/1, p. 448.
70 *Kirchliche Dogmatik* I/1, pp. 411–3; *Church Dogmatics* I/1, pp. 448–50. Note also the statement that 'we come to the doctrine of the Trinity by no other way than through an analysis of revelation': *Kirchliche Dogmatik* I/1, p. 329; *Church Dogmatics* I/1, p. 358.
71 This point is made with particular force in the important essay of Jacques de Senarclens, 'La concentration christologique', in *Antwort: Karl Barth zum siebsigsten Geburtstag*, pp. 190–207, especially p. 202 'Jésus-Christ récapitule en lui-même toute la réalité.' See also Helmut Thielicke, *Theologische Ethik* (3 vols: Tübingen, 2nd edn, 1958–9), vol. 1, p. 596.
72 See Alister E. McGrath, 'Karl Barth als Aufklärer? Der Zusammenhang seiner Lehre vom Werke Christi mit der Erwählungslehre', *Kerygma und Dogma* 30 (1984), pp. 273–83 for a full analysis. Cf. von Balthasar, *Karl Barth*, p. 210, who argues that Schleiermacher determines Barth's concerns as 'der Prägstock, der ein nicht mehr auszulöschendes Zeichen

aufdrückt, die Form, aus der man bei aller materiellen Entgegensetzung sich nicht mehr befreit'.

73 See Emil Brunner, *Die christliche Lehre von Gott* (Zurich, 1946), pp. 375–9; E. Buess, *Zur Prädestinationslehre Karl Barths* (Zurich, 1955); G. Gloege, 'Zur Prädestinationslehre Karl Barths', in *Heilsgeschehen und Welt: Theologische Traktate I* (Göttingen, 1965), pp. 77–132; Gestrich, *Neuzeitliches Denken*, pp. 211–20; McGrath, 'Karl Barth als Aufklärer?', pp. 275–9. For a perceptive analysis of the anthropological dimensions of Barth's idiosyncratic doctrine of election, see Stock, *Anthropologie der Verheißung*, pp. 44–61.

74 *Kirchliche Dogmatik* IV/1, pp. 574–5; *Church Dogmatics* IV/1, pp. 515–16.

75 *Kirchliche Dogmatik* IV/1, p. 578; *Church Dogmatics* IV/1, p. 518.

76 See Alister E. McGrath, 'Karl Barth and the Articulus Iustificationis: The Significance of His Critique of Ernst Wolf within the Context of His Theological Method', *Theologische Zeitschrift* 39 (1983), pp. 349–61. In this study, we develop criticisms made of Barth's epistemically reduced concept of salvation by Gustav Wingren, *Die Methodenfrage der Theologie* (Göttingen, 1957).

77 *Kirchliche Dogmatik* IV/1, pp. 316–7; *Church Dogmatics* IV/1, p. 288.

78 See Jüngel, *Gottes Sein ist im Werden*, pp. 76–7; 106–8.

79 See Jüngel, *Gottes Sein ist im Werden*, pp. 87–90. Jüngel argues that the revelatory event, in so far as it expresses (or, perhaps we might say, *recapitulates*) the *Urgeschichte* of the being and act of God, is necessarily related to that original divine act.

It must be emphasized that this work is not merely an account of Barth's doctrine of God, but also an important early statement of Jüngel's own views on responsible discussion of God, in response to the debate in the early 1960s between Herbert Braun and Helmut Gollwitzer. Jüngel effectively employs his exposition or 'paraphrase' of Barth to criticize Braun's proposals for 'non-objectifying' accounts of God.

80 See Hans Stickelberger, *Ipsa assumptione creatur: Karl Barths Rückgriff auf die klassische Christologie und die Frage nach der Selbständigkeit des Menschen* (Berne, 1979).

81 Stickelberger, *Ipsa assumptione creatur*, pp. 79-211.

82 *Kirchliche Dogmatik* IV/2, p. 101; *Church Dogmatics* IV/2, p. 92.

83 For example, see D. M. Baillie, *God was in Christ: An Essay on Incarnation and Atonement* (London, 1973), pp. 16–17. For Barth's comments on this work, see *Kirchliche Dogmatik* IV/2, pp. 61–2; *Church Dogmatics* IV/2, pp. 55–6.

84 *Kirchliche Dogmatik* IV/2, p. 54; *Church Dogmatics* IV/2, p. 51.

85 *Kirchliche Dogmatik* IV/2, p. 97; *Church Dogmatics* IV/2, pp. 88–9.

86 See Pannenberg, *Grundzüge der Christologie*, pp. 27–8.

6

The Kerygmatic Christ: Bultmann, Tillich and Ebeling

Dialectical theology was unquestionably the dominant theological force within the Germany of the Weimar Republic. The disagreements within the movement would not become serious until the late 1930s, by which time the practical and ethical problems posed for the German churches initially by the Third Reich, and subseqently by the Second World War, served to inhibit the development of any serious alternative to the 'theology of the Word of God'. Although it is possible to argue that, considered as a *theological* force, dialectical theology was on the wane by the year 1935, its moral intensity in the face of National Socialism earned it a legitimate and continuing place in the religious consciousness of Germany both in the Nazi and the immediate post-war periods. Nevertheless, a new theological force had developed within Germany in the pre-war period, although it only came to public attention during the war itself. On 4 June 1941, Rudolf Bultmann delivered a lecture at the Alpirsbach conference of the *Gesellschaft für Evangelische Theologie* entitled 'Neues Testament und Mythologie'. The same work was published later the same year as a pamphlet, less than 50 pages in length. The lecture introduced a phrase into the German theological vocabulary which summarizes the Christological programme with which we are concerned in the present chapter – *die Entmythologisierung des Neuen Testaments* ('the demythologization of the New Testament') – as well as occasioning a crisis within popular German Protestantism.[1] In view of the considerable degree of misunderstanding still surrounding Bultmann's theology in English-speaking circles, we propose to introduce it at greater length than usual. Bultmann's Christology is of importance in that it arises from a major new development in contemporary understandings of the nature of the New Testament documents, based upon the *kerygma* as the unifying principle between the Jesus of history and the Christ of faith. In the present chapter, we shall consider Bultmann's approach to Christology, as well as the developments and criticisms of this approach associated with Paul Tillich and Gerhard Ebeling.

The fundamental contention of Bultmann's controversial lecture of 1941[2] was that the New Testament proclamation or *kerygma* concerning Christ was conceived in mythological terms (deriving from Jewish apocalyptic and the Gnostic redemption myths) which, although perfectly legitimate and intelligible in the first century, cannot be accepted today:

> It is impossible to use electric light and radio equipment and, when ill, to claim the assistance of modern medical and clinical discoveries, and at the same time believe in the New Testament world of spirits and miracles (*die Geister- und Wunderwelt des Neuen Testaments*). Anyone who thinks he can manage this must be clear that, by explaining the content of the Christian faith in this manner, he is making the Christian proclamation unintelligible and impossible in the present day.[3]

Man's understanding of the world and of his own existence has changed radically since the first century, with the result that modern man finds the mythological world-view of the New Testament unintelligible and unacceptable. A man's *Weltanschauung* is given to him with his age, and he is in no position to alter it. The modern scientific and existential *Weltanschauung* means that the New Testament *Weltanschauung* is now discarded (*erledigt*) and unintelligible (*unverständlich*. Furthermore, it is impossible to be selective in relation to the New Testament *kerygma*: the liberal theologians thought that they could eliminate 'mythological' elements (such as apocalypticism) after the manner of Harnack, by distinguishing the mythological 'husk' from the religious or ethical 'kernel', and the *religionsgeschichtliche Schule* – particularly Troeltsch – interpreted him as an eternal symbol for the cultus of the Christian church. Bultmann declares this process of reduction to be illegitimate, in that it compromises the *kerygma* by failing to bring out clearly that the New Testament speaks of an event (*Ereignis*) through which God has brought about the salvation of the world (even if it articulates this event in mythological terms). For Bultmann, there are two, and only two, possibilities for the contemporary theologian: *either* the mythical world-view is accepted in its totality, *or* it is rejected in its totality. The resolution of the contradiction between the *Weltanschauungen* of the first and twentieth centuries can only be overcome, according to Bultmann, by *demythologizing* the New Testament. It must be emphasized that Bultmann has no time for those who suggest that the gospel is concerned with timeless moral truths or the historical manifestation of a self-sufficient idea: the gospel is, and remains, gospel – the decisive intervention of God in history through Christ in the 'Christ-event' (*Christusereignis* - note the deliberate contrast with *Christusprinzip*). In Christ something has *happened* of relevance not merely to the New Testament writers of the first century, but to everyone to whom the Christian gospel is proclaimed. The difficulty lies in articulating precisely *what* it is that has happened.

The liberals had attempted to *eliminate* the mythological elements in the New Testament, and thus found themselves totally incapable of dealing with the consequences of Schweitzer's 'consistent eschatology', which demonstrated that the entire synoptic *Christusbild* was conditioned by eschatological considerations. Bultmann, recognizing the futility of half-measures, sought to *interpret* the mythological framework of the New Testament, and thus confronted the problem which the liberals had unsuccessfully attempted to evade. It cannot be overemphasized that Bultmann does not understand the purpose of his programme of *Entmythologisierung* to be the elimination of myth: Bultmann placed far too high a value on 'myth' to adopt so simplistic a course of action. For Bultmann, 'myth' is a primitive means of objectifying the forces which impinge upon and determine human existence, and thus conveys insights concerning man's own existence. For Bultmann, it is necessary to reinterpret the mythology of the New Testament anthropologically, or *existentially*. Bultmann thus takes as his point of departure the understanding of existence found in the New Testament, and his theological programme may thus be defined as the existential demythologization of the New Testament. One could perhaps say that Bultmann was substituting a twentieth century myth in the place of its first century equivalent.

In order to understand Bultmann's Christology fully, it will be necessary to consider his understanding of the nature of the New Testament *kerygma*, and his use of the existentialist philosophy of Martin Heidegger. Before this is appropriate, however, it is necessary to consider Bultmann's relation to the liberal and *religionsgeschichtlich* schools. The rise of dialectical theology in the early 1920s provided one alternative to these traditions: how, then, does Bultmann relate to them, and, indeed, to dialectical theology itself? It may seem outrageous to suggest that Barth and Bultmann have anything in common: is not one the pillar of neo-orthodox dogmatic theology, and the other a radical New Testament critic? In fact, however, the two have much in common, arising from the cultural aftermath of the First World War.

In his important essay of 1924, *Die liberale Theologie und die jüngste theologische Bewegung* ('The Liberal Theology and the Latest Theological Movement'),[4] Bultmann deals with the relationship between Barth and Gogarten (whom he treats as the leading figures of dialectical theology) and 'liberal theology' (which, significantly, he identifies with the positions of Herrmann and Troeltsch, apparently glossing over their manifest differences). Bultmann stresses the significance of two facts: first, that dialectical theology did not originate from within Orthodoxy, but from within liberal theology itself (Barth was a student at Marburg, Gogarten at Heidelberg, and Thurneysen at both); second, that dialectical theology was not a protest against any *individual* theologian, but against a *specific theological trend (eine bestimmte theologische Richtung)*.[5] Bultmann himself shared that liberal heritage, and emphasized its intellectual integrity, and its opposition towards compromise, whether intellectual or spiritual. The distinctive character of the liberal school, according to Bultmann, was its use of the critical-historical method, which it believed would free men from the burden of dogmatic theology, and permit the real historical figure of Jesus to become the foundation of faith. For Bultmann, this very method, so characteristic of what he somewhat loosely terms 'liberal' theology, in fact contained the seeds of its own destruction: 'Historical research can never lead to any conclusion which can serve as the basis of faith, because all *its results have only relative validity (Geltung)*.'[6] Bultmann cites two works originating from the 'liberal school' which identified this crucial point, and yet apparently failed to recognize its full implications. The first was Troeltsch's *Die Bedeutung der Geschichtlichkeit Jesu* (1911), which, for Bultmann, made Christian faith dependent upon the research of 'scholars and professors'; the second was the fourteenth question which Harnack addressed to Barth in their exchanges of 1923. For Bultmann, Barth's response (see p. 99) to this was totally correct:

> Historical criticism cannot be set aside; we must, however, understand its true significance: it educates us in freedom and truth – not only by freeing us from a specific traditional understanding of history (*ein gewisses Geschichtsbild der Tradition*), but because it frees us from every understanding

of history (*Geschichtsbild*) possible for scientific knowledge, and brings us to the realisation that the world which faith wishes to lay hold of is totally unattainable with the assistance of scientific knowledge.[7]

Developing this point further, Bultmann emphasised that the results of the application of the critical historical method possess a purely relative validity, in that the original historical phenomena, to which the method may be applied, are themselves relative entities existing within an immense nexus of interrelated entities, none of which may claim absolute validity. 'Even the historical Jesus himself is one phenomenon among others, not an absolute entity.'[8] Furthermore, the liberal approach to history assumes that man may be treated as standing outside that history, apart from it, as an indifferent observer, similar to the observer of the world of nature. But – and here we may see Bultmann's distinctively existential understanding of history being employed as a *theological* weapon, effective even against the *Theologie des Historismus* of Troeltsch – man is, in fact, a part of that history. Existentialism demonstrates to man that history is the *historicity* of his own existence. Man is not a subject who stands at a distance from the historical process and comprehends it as the object of his thought: he himself is apprehended by history, and drawn into it as part of it. In other words, man's understanding of history arises through an *encounter* with history, in which he experiences history as the expression of the possibilities of human existence. Man himself is part of history, and in enquiring about history, he is enquiring about a nexus of circumstances in which he and his own being are involved. The only appropriate manner in which history may be approached is that of a *dialogue*, in which man is not a neutral and disinterested observer, but a part of the process in question. Therefore, Bultmann argues, it is legitimate to assert that 'liberal theology' is based upon a 'pantheism of history' – an assertion which he justifies by considering the Ritschlian Christology.[9] For Bultmann, the liberal account of the religious significance of Jesus may be equally applied to, or inferred from, any other individual in history. There is simply no coherent or legitimate criterion by which Jesus may be singled out in this manner as *the* historical entity to possess such permanent significance. For Bultmann, as for Barth and Gogarten, *God is not a 'given' entity*[10] – in history, in experience, or anywhere else. Bultmann therefore agreed with Barth when the latter emphasized the purgative nature of New Testament criticism: as he remarked in an important essay of 1927:

I have never yet felt ill at ease (*unbehaglich*) in my critical radicalism, but quite at ease. However, I often have the impression that my conservative New Testament colleagues feel rather ill at ease; for I see them always engaged in salvage work (*Rettungsarbeit*). I just let the fire burn, for I see that all that is burned are the imaginary portraits (*Phantasiebilder*) of the 'Life of Jesus' theology, and that it is 'Christ according to the flesh'.[11].

Thus far, it will be clear that Barth and Bultmann have much in common with each other. Both were educated within the liberal school, and both realized and rejected its radically unsatisfactory foundations (although in different manners: Bultmann's critique of Troeltsch, based on an existential understanding of history, is far more penetrating than anything Barth or Brunner produced, and remains of permanent value). Barth and Bultmann alike constantly emphasize, particularly during the period 1921-27, that Christian theology is about God, rather than man, and that Christology necessarily cannot content itself with dealing with 'Christ according to the flesh'. The critical study of the New Testament is therefore to be welcomed, as it simply destroys the foundations of the liberal 'Jesuologies', without calling into question the fact that God *acted* in Christ to redeem the world. But how is that 'act' of God to be described? It is at this point that we must return to an analysis of Bultmann's programme of demythologization.

For Bultmann, the New Testament makes statements about God – and therefore about human existence. Bultmann follows the great Marburg liberal, Wilhelm Herrmann, in emphasizing that theological statements cannot, in principle, be made about God as he is in himself, but rather as he relates to us – and therefore, according to Bultmann, must consist in statements concerning man's existential situation.[12] As such, Bultmann argues that it is both possible and necessary to interpret the New Testament myths in existentialist terms.[13] A provisional definition of 'myth' could be 'a religious story which is in principle incapable of verification': it must be emphasized, and indeed, cannot be emphasized too strongly, that the term 'myth' does not in any way imply that the 'religious story' is in any sense *untrue*.[14] The New Testament relates 'stories' concerning remote and inaccessible times and places (such as 'in the beginning'; 'in heaven'), and involving supernatural agents or events. Perhaps the most important of these is the eschatological myth of the imminent end of the world through direct divine intervention, leading to judgement and subsequent reward or retribution. For Bultmann, such 'myths' may be reinterpreted existentially. Thus, in the case of the eschatological myth, the recognition that history has not, in fact, come to an end does not necessarily invalidate the myth: interpreted existentially, the 'myth' refers to the *hinc et nunc* of human existence – the fact that man does indeed face the *eschaton* of his own death, and that in the decisions which he is obliged to make concerning his existence, he is effectively working out his own judgement. Man is forced to make existential decisions, which determine his existential situation. Bultmann's theology may be regarded as an ellipse constructed around two foci: first, the programme of demythologization, or existential interpretation, of the New Testament; second, the idea of the *kerygma*, the proclamation of a divine word addressed to man, occasioning a crisis and demanding an existential decision on his part. Beneath the strange language of the New Testament lies the proclamation of a way of life which is a present possibility for man and which he may appropriate as his own. The 'husk' of the myth contains the 'kernel' of the *kerygma*: by translating the mythical 'husk' into contemporary existential terms, the heart of the Christian proclamation may be recovered and made intelligible to modern man.

Bultmann argues that precisely this sort of demythologizing may be found in the Fourth Gospel,[15] written towards the end of the first century, when the early eschatological expectations of the Christian community were fading. The *eschaton* is interpreted by Bultmann to refer to the moment of existential crisis, as man is confronted with the divine *kerygma* addressed to him. In a manner similar to Brunner, Bultmann develops the concept of *Angesprochensein* – the idea that man is addressed directly by the *kerygma* here and now. The 'realized eschatology' of the Fourth Gospel arises through the fact that the redactor of the gospel has realized that the *parousia* is not some future event, but one which has already taken place, in the confrontation of the believer with the existential *kerygma*:

To the 'Now' of the coming of the Revealer (*Offenbarer*) there corresponds exactly the 'Now' of the proclamation of the word as an historical (*geschichtlich*) fact, the 'Now' of the present, *of the moment*. That is, Jesus is not the Revealer, since the 'Word became flesh', through his effects upon the history of the world (*weltgeschichtlichen Wirkungen*), which obviously affects everyone, and is universally available for evaluation and decision, but through the preaching of the word as a concrete event at a specified time (*in der Predigt des Wortes als einem jeweils konkreten Geschehen*).

This 'Now' of being addressed at a specific moment (*jeweiliges Jetzt des*

Angesprochenseins), this moment, is *the eschatological 'Now'*, because in it the decision is made between life and death. It is the hour which is coming, and, in being addressed, now is... Therefore it is not true that the *parousia*, expected by others as an event occuring in time, is now denied or transformed by John into a process within the soul, an experience. Rather, John opens the reader's eyes: the *parousia* has already occurred![16]

Bultmann thus regards the Fourth Gospel as partially reinterpreting the eschatological myth in terms of its significance for human existence. Christ is not a past phenomenon, but the ever-present word of God, expressing not a general truth, but a concrete proclamation addressed to man demanding an existential decision. For Bultmann, the eschatological process became an *event* in the history of the world, and becomes an event once more in contemporary Christian proclamation. Thus Bultmann is able to argue that Christian theology, while speaking of faith in 'objective' terms, must realize that it must go beyond 'objective' formulations in order to maintain its existential character. But what understanding of human existence is appropriate for this programme of demythologization (which, once more, we wish to emphasize does not concern the total or – still worse! – partial *elimination* of myth, but its *interpretation* and the restatement of its content)?

'Existentialism' denotes a class of philosophy concerned with human existence, which attempts to understand this existence in terms of the concrete experience of existing individuals. As such, it is primarily a philosophical method rather than a specific body of doctrines,[17] a type of philosophy of such flexibility that it can embrace the nihilism of Jean-Paul Sartre or the Catholicism of Gabriel Marcel.[18] Although it is particularly associated with the modern era, it appears to make spasmodic appearances throughout history, whenever man has wished to distinguish between two fundamentally different modes of existence: the individual being of man, and the being of objects in nature. This distinction is expressed by existentialist thinkers in different manners: for Martin Buber, the former is expressed in terms of the world of *Du* and the latter in terms of the world of *Es*; for Martin Heidegger, the former is expressed in terms of *Existenz* and the latter in terms of *Vorhandenheit*. For Bultmann, the 'right' existentialist philosophy is that of Heidegger (whose lectures Bultmann attended as a professor at Marburg – certainly the most senior, and probably the most appreciative, member of his audience), in that it appears to interpret human existence in the most appropriate practical and conceptual terms, revealing the *structure* of human existence, in order that Christian theology may address itself directly to those structures. We must therefore consider Heidegger's analysis of the structure of existence in order to understand Bultmann's theology.

Heidegger's distinction between *Existenz* and *Vorhandenheit* is of crucial importance. An inanimate object, such as a stone, clearly 'exists' in some sense of the word ('being extant') which is quite distinct from the existence of a conscious thinking and reflecting individual (which Heidegger broadly intends to convey by the use of the term *Dasein*). It is through the reflection of this existing individual *upon his own existence* that the distinctive characteristics of existence may be established. 'We ourselves are the entities to be analysed. The being of any such entity is mine (*Das Seiende, dessen Analyse zur Aufgabe steht, sind wir je selbst. Das Sein dieses Seienden ist je meines*).'[19] The four main characteristics of human existence, as established by Heidegger, are the following.[20] First, man (that is, to use Heidegger's terms, *Dasein*) has a relation to himself, in that he may legitimately be said to be 'at one with himself' or 'at odds with himself'. In other words, man is not simply an object (whereas a stone unquestionably is), but is actually both subject and object to himself, transcending the subject-object dichotomy in his relation to himself. Second, man is a possibility, rather than a predetermined actuality. Man is never complete or fixed in his being, but is open to various possibilities of existence, which he himself may choose. Third, every man's existence is individual, unique to him, and defying classification (Heidegger refers to this characteristic of *Existenz* as *Jemeinigkeit*). Fourth, man exists in the world (a characteristic which is rather awkwardly designated as *In-der-Welt-sein*), and as such is caught up with it, conditioned by it, limited by it, and concerned with it. This is not merely a statement about the physical location of man's existence: it is an existential statement concerning the way in which man's *Existenz* is inextricably linked with the world itself. Man is in the world, and yet not of it; his ways of being are distinctive – this, after all, is the essential distinction between *Existenz* and *Vorhandenheit*. Yet there is the possibility that man's *Existenz* will be compromised by the world, and that it will, in effect, be reduced to the level of *Vorhandenheit*. There is every possibility that man will come to regard himself as an object *extant*, but not *existing*, in the world. There is thus an important ambiguity in the existential significance of the 'world': it may be conceived neutrally, as the arena of man's activity, his *Spielraum*; it may also be considered negatively, as a threat to authentic existence, in that man may lose himself in it, losing sight of his own *Existenz* as he 'falls' into the world. It is this possibility which underlies the important distinction between authentic (*eigentlich*) and inauthentic (*uneigentlich*) existence – a distinction which underlies Bultmann's soteriology, and hence his Christology.

For Heidegger, 'inauthentic existence' arises from man's absorption in his concern with the world, in a way of being which is directed towards the world, dehumanized, and ultimately based upon misunderstanding and delusion.[21] Man deludes himself that he is master of his own destiny and of his world. Such a life is both meaningless and worthless. The final demonstration of the illusion of inauthentic existence is provided by death itself, which finally exposes the transience of this self-deception. Heidegger regards the concept of *Angst* ('anxiety') as a catalyst in the transition from inauthentic to authentic existence, revealing to man that fact that he has been 'thrown' into a world in which he is not at home (this characteristic of existence is referred to by Heidegger as *Geworfenheit*). Man may be said to have 'fallen' from existence (and here Heidegger's seminary background seems to bring his thought and terms close to those of Christianity). Man's 'fallenness' (*Verfallenheit*) has several characteristics, of which the following are the most important. First, he is fallen *into the world*, which may absorb him into the impersonal mass of collective existence. Second, he is fallen *away from (abgefallen) his own true self*. Man may thus exist in a state of 'alienation' (*Entfremdung*) from his own true self and his true existence. It is therefore necessary for 'fallen' man to recover his true way of being, recognizing his illusions of security as ontological anxiety discloses to him that he is 'not at home' (*nicht zu Hause*) in the world (and, once more, Heidegger's seminary background equipped him to note the importance of ontological anxiety for Christian theologians such as Augustine and Luther). For Heidegger, in fact, 'authentic' existence is an existence of recognized despair, free from illusion, as man lives in the anticipation of his own death:[22] however, it is important to appreciate that Bultmann will only follow Heidegger in his *descriptions* of the structures of existence (and particularly the important distinction between 'authentic' and 'inauthentic' existence), and does not commit himself to following Heidegger's *prescriptions* concerning them. Furthermore – and it is vitally important that this point be appreciated – Heidegger treats 'fallenness' *as an existential possibility open to man*, whereas Bultmann treats it *as a present existential actuality*. With Heidegger's analysis of existence in mind, we may turn to consider its theological application in the work of Bultmann.

According to Bultmann,[23] the New Testament recognizes two modes of human existence: unbelieving and unredeemed existence (that is, inauthentic existence); and believing and redeemed existence (that is, authentic existence). The former is characterized by the delusion of self-sufficiency, and by the adhesion to (and hence the dependence upon) the visible and transitory world. Although the goal of man's endeavours (to attain his essential and authentic existence) is appropriate, the means which he adopts towards this end are inappropriate and, ultimately, self-defeating: man attempts to find himself through his own unaided efforts, and, by doing so, merely becomes more and more deeply embedded in the transitory world of death and despair. Believing and redeemed existence, however, arises through man's abandoning every hope that he may attain his essence through his own efforts or on the basis of the visible and transitory world in which he exists: he recognizes that his life is given to him as a gift, and in an act of 'desecularization' (*Entweltlichung*), chooses to base his life upon what is invisible and intangible. Although he continues to exist in the world, his attitude to it is now one of freedom from it. Although he is in the world, he is no longer of the world (John 17. 15–16). This existentialist approach to the New Testament may be illustrated from Bultmann's 1928 essay on the eschatology of the Fourth Gospel.

In this essay, Bultmann identifies existentialist categories as underlying the 'Johannine dualism', in which concepts such as light and darkness, truth and falsehood, life and death, are set in permanent antithesis. These antitheses serve to express the double possibility in man's existence, and derive their meaning from the threat which is perceived to be posed to man's existence by the world, and the means by which this threat may be overcome. Thus we find Bultmann interpreting the key Johannine term *kosmos* ('world') in the twofold manner indicated by Heidegger – the world as the *sphere of existence*, and the world as the *threat to existence*:

Through the *event of revelation*, therefore, *two possibilities* are actualized for the world: 1. 'To be world' (*Weltsein*) in the new sense of 'remaining world' (*Weltbleiben*) – to set the seal on one's fallenness (*Verfallenheit*), to hold fast to it, to hold fast to one's self. 2. 'Not to be world' (*Nicht-Welt-sein*), not to be 'of (*aus*) the world', and thus to be 'of (*aus*) the world' in the new sense of being 'out of' (*aus*) the world, namely, 'outside' (*heraus aus*) it, no longer belonging to it.[24]

Bultmann is also able to apply an existential analysis to the Pauline soteriology (and particularly to the Pauline anthropological terms: his analysis of the Pauline term 'body' is particularly significant in this respect).[25]

It is significant that Bultmann regards Paul and the Fourth Gospel as being of greater value for Christology than the synoptic gospels, on account of their kerygmatic foundations. Thus for Bultmann, the fact that the Fourth Gospel is a source for the *kerygma* of the early church, rather than the historical Jesus, merely serves to *increase*, rather than (as with the liberal school) to *diminish*, its Christological importance. For Bultmann, the New Testament in general asserts that man's true nature is no longer to be attained by his own efforts, which merely serve to further enmesh and embed him in his existential alienation. Man cannot liberate himself from this existential alienation by his own efforts: such liberation must come from without. The most fundamental difference between Heidegger and Bultmann is that the latter regards authentic existence as a possibility which man may achieve for himself, whereas the latter regards it as a possibility which only comes about *by a gratuitous act of God*: at the very point at which man can do nothing, God steps in and acts – indeed, has acted already – on behalf of man. 'So here is the crucial distinction between the New Testament and existentialism, between the Christian faith and the natural understanding of being. The New Testament speaks, and faith knows, of an act of God (*Tat Gottes*), which first makes possible abandonment (*Hingabe*), faith, love, and the authentic (*eigentlich*) life of man.'[26] It is at this point that Bultmann's soteriology finds its Christological concentration, in that this act of God is identified with the 'Christ-event' (*Christusereignis*) – the cross and resurrection of Jesus Christ.[27]

At this point, it is necessary to formally introduce the term *kerygma*, which has already been employed without adequate discussion. For Bultmann, the *kerygma* is the word of proclamation through which the Christ-event confronts the individual here and now. The Word of God becomes a *personal* word of God, addressed to the individual, striking his conscience and demanding a decision. It confronts man here and now, in a specific historical situation, with the necessity for a decision on his part, if his state of inauthentic existence and fallenness is to be replaced with that of authenticity. The *kerygma* concentrates and compresses the history of salvation into an eschatological demand. Good Friday and Easter Day become the 'Today' of proclamation, in that it is the proclamation of the saving event which occasions the transition from the state of inauthentic to that of authentic existence. The existential significance of the history of salvation, as it is concentrated and focused in the death and resurrection of Jesus Christ, is distilled into the *kerygma*. Through his programme of demythologization, Bultmann is able to extract the existential significance of the history of Jesus of Nazareth by removing the mythical 'husk' from the cosmic apocalyptic drama narrated by the New Testament, culminating in the resurrection, thus revealing the 'kernel' of the proclamation of the permanent significance of Jesus Christ for human existence throughout the ages. Although the New Testament writers such as Paul (or, to a significantly lesser extent, John) used the mythological thought-forms of their day, their fundamental intention was, according to Bultmann, to present their readers with a new possibility of existence. This approach to the relation between the historical Jesus and the *kerygma* is particularly well expressed in an essay of 1929 dealing with the relation between Jesus and Paul.[28]

For Bultmann, the significance of the historical person of Jesus for the theology of Paul may be expressed in a single sentence: it is the historical person of Jesus which makes Paul's proclamation the gospel.[29] Paul does not proclaim any new ideas about God, but an act of God in human history in Jesus the Messiah. Similarly, the primitive Christian community itself proclaimed no new apocalyptic or messianic ideas, save that Jesus was the Messiah – and hence that the historical person of Jesus was the decisive saving act of God (*die entscheidende Heilstat Gottes*). The death of Christ on the cross was implicitly recognized by the primitive community, and explicitly so by Paul, as the judgement of God upon man's previous self-understanding. For Paul, the actual historical event of the cross – which was most emphatically *not* a symbol or image of an eternal divine idea – lays down a challenge to man to relinquish his former self and way of being in favour of the new way of being offered to him. Questions such as whether Jesus understood himself to be the Messiah are thus of little significance – if he did understand himself as *Messias designatus*, all that would be implied for Bultmann was that Jesus employed a contemporary Jewish conception in order to bring home to his hearers the need for a decision on their part. Bultmann thus excludes the three great and influential portraits of Christ drawn by the theologians of the *Aufklärung* and the liberal school (Christ as teacher; Christ as example; Christ as hero), in that they merely correspond to 'Christ according to the flesh', a secular phenomenon (*Weltphänomen*) to be treated in a manner similar to other such phenomena. For Bultmann, the cross and the resurrection are indeed secular phenomena (in that they took place within human history) – but they must be discerned by faith as divine acts. The cross and the resurrection are linked in the *kerygma* as the divine act of judgement and the divine act of salvation. It is this divine act, pregnant with existential significance, which is of continuing significance, and not the historical phenomenon which acted as its bearer. The *kerygma* is thus not concerned with matters of historical fact, but with conveying the necessity of a decision on the part of its hearers, and thus transferring the eschatological moment from the past to the here and now of the proclamation itself:

> This means that *Jesus Christ encounters (begegnet) men in the kerygma and nowhere else*, just as he confronted Paul himself and forced him to a decision. The *kerygma* does not proclaim universal truths or a timeless idea – whether it is an idea of God or of the redeemer – but an historical fact (*ein geschichtliches Faktum*)... Therefore the *kerygma* is neither a vehicle for timeless ideas nor the mediator of historical information: what is of decisive importance is that the *kerygma* is Christ's 'that' (*Dass*), his 'here and now', a 'here and now' which becomes present in the address itself.
>
> One cannot therefore go behind the *kerygma*, using it as a 'source' (*Quelle*), in order to reconstruct an 'historical Jesus' with his 'messianic consciousness', his 'inner life', or his 'heroism'. That would merely be 'Christ according to the flesh', who no longer exists. It is not the historical (*historisch*) Jesus, but Jesus Christ, the one who is preached, who is the Lord.[30]

Bultmann may thus be regarded as developing the insights of Martin Kähler in relation to the correlation between the historical Jesus and the Christ of faith – or, as we might describe him in this context, the Christ of the *kerygma*. The *existentially significant* Christ is not 'Christ according to the flesh', but the 'preached Christ', the Christ who is present in the *kerygma*. Although Bultmann does not reduce the theological significance of the resurrection to a single point, it is certainly true to assert that the *theological* significance of the resurrection relates primarily to the presence of Christ in the faith and preaching of his disciples – that is, in the *kerygma*. Thus Bultmann has no hesitation in asserting that the Easter faith consists of faith that 'Jesus Christ is present in the *kerygma*'.[31]

In many respects, Bultmann may be regarded as developing the biblical theology of Martin Kähler, although with a sophistication which eluded the latter. The contemporary experience of the truth of Christ may be regarded as identical with the confrontation by the *kerygma*, and the existential decision it occasions. Faith comes into being through an encounter with an historical event – the event of Christ, as this event is occasioned by the *kerygma* itself. Although that *kerygma* is based upon the history of Jesus of Nazareth, it now transcends it. Bultmann thus has no time for critical questions concerning the nature of the historical Jesus, and his relation to the Christ of faith, insisting that it is, in principle, both impossible and illegitimate to go behind the Christ of the *kerygma* to its historical foundations. All that it is necessary to state about Jesus is that the fact he has come, and that he is present in the *kerygma*; the mere fact of Jesus' existence ('das Dass'), apart from any concrete historical characteristics or predicates, is all that need be presupposed in order to account for the transition from unbelief to faith, from inauthentic to authentic existence: in other words, that the *kerygma* contains in itself an adequate account of Jesus.[32] The *kerygma* is not historically verifiable:

> In the Christian proclamation, man is not presented with an historical report or a piece of the past, which he can inspect and critically verify or falsify; but he is told that God has acted in what happened then, whatever it might have been (*es möge gewesen sein wie es wolle*), and that through this act of God, the word of divine judgement and forgiveness which now confronts him is authenticated (*legitimiert*); that the meaning of that act of God is nothing other than the actual establishment of this word, the proclamation of this word itself. No historical science can affect or confirm or reject this affirmation. The fact that this word and this proclamation are the acts of God stands on the other side of historical observation.[33]

It may therefore be stated that the German repudiation of the 'Quest of the Historical Jesus' reached its zenith in the theology of Rudolf Bultmann. On the basis of his form-critical (*formgeschichtlich*) research (a full discussion of which lies beyond the present study)[34], he concluded that such a quest was *impossible* (thus confirming the general conclusions of Wrede and Schweitzer), and on the basis of his existential theology, he concluded that such a quest was *illegitimate*. The recognition that the *kerygma* was the centre, not only of the gospels, but also of primitive Christianity, must be regarded as Bultmann's most significant contribution to the making of modern German Christology, in that this insight resulted in a decisive shift of emphasis away from the nineteenth century preoccupation with the *historical* foundations of Christology towards an apparently legitimate *existential* concern with the underlying meaning of history (and thus found a formal analogy with contemporary understandings of historiography as concerned with underlying 'meaning', rather than a mere record of the brute facts of the past *wie es eigentlich gewesen*). For Bultmann, history only survived as *kerygma*, in both senses of the term (that is, as the content of the message, and the act of preaching itself): the tradition concerning Jesus survived only to the extent that it served some specific kerygmatic function in the life and worship of the primitive church as its *Sitz im Leben*.[35] The gospels are kerygmatic documents, proclaiming a faith in which the historical (*historisch*) Jesus and the facts concerning him have been transformed irreversibly into the mythological proclamation of a divine pre-existent being who became incarnate, died for the sins of men, was raised from the dead, and whose return in triumph was shortly expected. It is impossible to get behind these mythological and theological images to the bare historical facts, although it is possible to assert (1) the continuity of the *kerygma* with the historical Jesus, and (2) the possibility of reinterpreting the mythical elements of the *kerygma* existentially to relate to the modern *Weltanschauung*. The *kerygma* thus serves the dual function of witnessing to past events and interpreting the experience of present events.[36]

Bultmann may therefore be regarded as having completed the destruction of the *Leben-Jesu-Forschung* begun in the closing decade of the nineteenth century by establishing the kerygmatic foundations of the New Testament, primitive Christianity and contemporary proclamation, thus giving a remarkably unified structure to his Christology. The twentieth century recognized that the gospels are primary sources for the history of the early church (and only secondarily for the history of Jesus), whereas the nineteenth century tended to regard the gospels as primary sources for the history of Jesus. This scholarly development is of incalculable Christological significance, and underlies Bultmann's kerygmatic Christology. It would be inept to characterize his Christology as a 'Christology from below', despite its heavy anthropological conditioning, for the obvious reason that Bultmann does not begin from the historical figure of Jesus of Nazareth, but from 'above' and 'below' *as they are simultaneously given in the kerygma*.[37] This observation not merely demonstrates the futility of the 'above-below' Christological dichotomy, but indicates how it is possible for a theology to be based upon anthropological considerations (in this case, the structures of human existence) without being reduced to anthropology.

The main line of criticism directed against Bultmann's kerygmatic Christology concerns the relation between *kerygma* and history, and will be discussed at greater length in the chapter which follows. A further point of criticism relates to Bultmann's programme of demythologization. It was pointed out that Bultmann's method was heavily dependent upon *Religionsgeschichte*. His programme of demythologization was based on the earlier *religionsgeschichtliche Schule*, which identified the influence of Gnostic redeemer myths on the New Testament.[38] However, it is now generally considered that gnosticism was a post-Christian phenomenon,[39] so that Bultmann's thesis requires substantial revision. In answer to this, however, it may be pointed out that the New Testament *Weltanschauung* is still to be treated as mythical, the scholarly question concerning the origins and background of the specific mythology being secondary to the theological task of reinterpreting it. Bultmann's programme does not require the identification of the components of the kerygmatic formulations as features of incipient gnosticism. The 'de-apocalypticizing' which he detects in the Fourth Gospel is a feature of demythologizing, and most, if not all, of his programme may be accomplished on the assumption of a Jewish apocalyptic background to the New Testament, without resorting to the presupposition of pre-Christian gnostic influences. Other criticisms concerned Bultmann's somewhat simplistic approach to *Formgeschichte*, and his insistence that the only 'pre-understanding' (*Vorverständnis*) appropriate in the modern period was based upon the 'modern scientific world-view' and the 'self-understanding' of existentialism.[40]

It will be clear that Bultmann's Christology marks a decisive turning point in the making of modern German Christology. The new emphasis upon the centrality of the *kerygma* established the school of Bultmann as the dominant theological force in Germany in the immediate post-war period. The theme of the 'kerygmatic Christ' was incorporated into a philosophical theology by an *émigré* from National Socialist Germany, who also exploited existentialism theologically. Paul Tillich left Germany in 1933 as the first non-semitic university teacher to be dismissed by Hitler, to settle in the United States and develop his existential theology unimpeded by political considerations. The result is clearly continuous with the general trend evident in German

Christology over the period 1933–65, and must be considered as an aspect of that development, although Tillich's influence upon the German Christological tradition itself has not been significant. We shall therefore briefly examine Tillich's Christology before turning to the more important exposition of the 'kerygmatic Christ' associated with Gerhard Ebeling.

For a short period in 1924–5, Tillich and Heidegger were colleagues at Marburg, and it is evident, both from Tillich's own personal reflections, as well as the substance of his ontology, that he was greatly influenced by the Marburg existentialist.[41] The theological importance which Tillich attaches to existentialism may be judged from the following passage in his *Systematic Theology*:

> Theology, when dealing with our ultimate concern, presupposes in every sentence the structure of being, its categories, laws and concepts. Theology, therefore, cannot escape the question of being any more easily than can philosophy. The attempt of biblicism to avoid non-biblical, ontological terms is doomed to failure as surely as are the corresponding philosophical attempts.[42]

Tillich therefore follows a programme similar, in respects, to Bultmann's programme of demythologization, attempting to extract the existential significance of the New Testament soteriological and Christological statements (which Tillich understands to be expressed 'symbolically').[43] Thus Tillich refers to 'the Fall' as a symbol, where Bultmann designates it as a myth.[44] The story of 'the Fall' should not be interpreted literally, as an account of an event which happened 'once upon a time', but as a symbol for the human situation universally. For Tillich, 'existence' is estrangement, characterized by *Angst*, unbelief, concupiscence and *hubris* (pride). Nothing that exists is 'as it ought to be'.[45] Tillich's somewhat confused distinction between 'essence' and 'existence' is perhaps best understood if 'essence' is understood to correspond to Heidegger's concept of *authentic existence*, and 'existence' to *inauthentic existence*. Man knows of no other existence other than 'estranged' or 'inauthentic' existence.[46] This raises the interesting question as to how man's 'essence' became corrupted to 'existence', a question which Tillich answers in a manner which will satisfy only his most uncritical admirers.[47] It is, however, evident that Tillich is chiefly concerned with the question as to how the gap between existence and essence may be overcome (rather than the more tantalizing question as to how it got there in the first place). It is in this context that we encounter the Christologically related concept of 'New Being', the 'restorative principle' of Tillich's theological system.[48]

For Tillich, the event upon which Christianity is based has two aspects: the fact which is called 'Jesus of Nazareth', and the reception of this fact by those who received him as the Christ.[49] The factual, or objective-historical Jesus is not the foundation of faith apart from his reception as the Christ. In fact, it is obvious that Tillich has no interest in the historical figure of Jesus of Nazareth: all that he is prepared to affirm about him (in so far as it relates to the foundation of faith) is that it was a 'personal life', analogous to the biblical picture, who might well have had another name other than 'Jesus'. 'Whatever his name, the New Being was and is active in this man.'[50] The symbol 'Christ' or 'Messiah' means 'he who brings the new state of things, the New Being', and the significance of Jesus of Nazareth lies in his being the historical manifestation of the New Being, who subjects himself to the conditions of existence, and by doing so conquers existential estrangement.[51] 'It is the Christ who brings the New Being, who saves men from the old being, that is from existential estrangement and its destructive consequences.'[52] In one personal life, that of Jesus of Nazareth, 'essential manhood' has appeared under the conditions of existence without being conquered by them. In other words, the significance of Jesus of Nazareth resides in his being the historical manifestation of a self-sufficient existential principle, which may be discussed without any reference to that original manifestation, save that it actually took place. Thus Tillich is able to follow Bultmann in stating that 'Christology is a function of soteriology', in that it is the soteriological problem which creates the Christological question.[53] It is, however, very difficult to avoid the conclusion that the intense theological *seriousness* which characterizes Bultmann's discussion of the relation between faith and history is absent from Tillich. The total divorce of faith and history in Tillich's thought, suggesting his Christology is actually idealist, thus appears inevitable.[54] We are, in effect, presented with a philosophy of existence which attaches itself to the existence of Jesus of Nazareth in the most tenuous of manners, and which is not significantly disadvantaged if the specific historical individual Jesus of Nazareth did not exist. Thus Tillich does not follow Bultmann in asserting that the revelation which makes the transition from inauthenticity to authenticity is to be sought only in Jesus of Nazareth, although he does make it clear that he considers this revelation to be perfect (and hence 'final'). The revelation in Jesus may be said to illuminate the mystery of being, although other sources of illumination are available. Unfortunately, Tillich here appears to return to the discredited Jesuologies of the liberal school, which regarded Jesus of Nazareth as the supreme exemplar of a particular moral or religious principle, without – as Bultmann appreciated – being able to justify this assertion in the first place.

In turning to deal with Gerhard Ebeling, we encounter one of the most significant theologians of recent years. Although it is probably an exaggeration to suggest that his *Das Wesen des christlichen Glaubens* (1959) was comparable in its significance to Harnack's *Das Wesen des Christentums*,[55] there is no doubt that he represents the most important and influential thinker in the tradition of Bultmann. The starting point of Ebeling's theological development was determined by his engagement in questions of historical theology (many English-speaking theologians still think of Ebeling only as a brilliant Luther scholar!) and particularly Luther's hermeneutics,[56] in which he may be regarded as attempting to correlate the theology of the young Luther with the existential hermeneutics of Bultmann.[57] This programme may be regarded as culminating in his *Wesen des christlichen Glaubens*, in which his differences with Bultmann over the significance of the historical Jesus became clear. These differences were more substantially developed in the important work *Theologie und Verkündigung* (1962).[58] The culmination of Ebeling's theological insights may be seen in his three-volume *Dogmatik des christlichen Glaubens*,[59] which is, regrettably, unlikely ever to be translated into English.

The most appropriate point at which to begin an analysis of Ebeling's Christology is his understanding of faith. For Ebeling, faith is to be interpreted existentially: 'faith concerns what gives existence stability (*was der Existenz Bestand gibt*), and thus concerns Being and Non-Being (*Sein oder Nichtsein*).[60] Faith is an existential attitude, and most emphatically does not have an object: Ebeling engages in a programme of *Entobjektivierung* which is parallel, in respects, to Bultmann's programme of *Entmythologisierung*, in order to exclude any possibility that Christian faith will be interpreted as *fides historica*. The concept of non-intellectual experiential knowledge has, according to Ebeling, been legitimized by Luther and neo-Kantian epistemology. Ebeling argues that the Reformers excluded all substantial and objectifying understandings of the relationship between man and God, so that man is to be regarded as a person constituted and determined by the relations which he has with external reality. As such, Ebeling is able to insist that the 'ontology of relation' (*die Ontologie der Relation*)[61] is a general method for analysing human experience which is significant theologically. The threat posed to man's existence by death is for Ebeling, as for existentialism in general, a means by which the inauthenticity of his present existence (which Ebeling terms *Nichtsein*) is brought home to man.[62] This inauthenticity may be overcome as man receives the foundation and meaning of his existence from outside in a relation of faith.[63] The parallels between Bultmann and Ebeling will thus be evident. Similarly, Ebeling employs the results of Bultmann's programme of *Entmythologisierung* to overcome the contradiction between 'biblical realism' and 'modern experiential knowledge' by arguing that the New Testament *Weltanschauung* arises from a 'deficient historical consciousness' (*mangelndes Geschichtsbewusstsein*) on the part of the New Testament writers, which the modern period has a duty to remedy.[64] For Ebeling, the only historical fact (*historisches Faktum*) on which Christology is based is the cross:[65] the remainder of the New Testament account of the 'history' of Jesus (such as the virgin birth, the descent into Hell and the resurrection) cannot be regarded as objective history (*Historie*).[66] The application of the critical historical method thus serves to eliminate all mythological elements from the essence of the Christian faith: like Bultmann, Ebeling sees the method as purely negative, having a valuable purgative function in that it destroys false Christologies, although unable to erect anything in their place.[67]

The differences between Bultmann and Ebeling only fully emerge in their assessment of the theological significance of the historical figure of Jesus of Nazareth. For Bultmann, all that could be, and could be required to be, known about the historical Jesus was the fact that ('das Dass') he existed. For Ebeling, the person of the historical (*historisch*) Jesus is the fundamental basis (*das Grunddatum*) of Christology,[68] and if it could be shown that Christology was a misinterpretation of the significance of the historical Jesus, Christology would be brought to an end (*erledigt*).[69] In this, Ebeling may be seen as reflecting, or even exemplifying, the concerns of the 'new quest of the historical Jesus', to be discussed in the following chapter. Even Bultmann's minimal 'das Dass' actually requires justification in terms of 'das Was' or 'das Wie' – that is, in terms of the implicit content of the *kerygma*.[70] Ebeling argues that it is necessary to demonstrate the manner in which the historical Jesus and modern man are related – a manner which is necessarily independent of time and place. Ebeling locates this point of contact in the faith of Christ – the total dependence of Christ upon God, evident throughout his mission, and culminating in the historical event of the cross.[71] Indeed, Ebeling is able to assert that the cross is the fulfilment of the proclamation of Jesus for this very reason.[72] The resurrection serves two functions in this context. First, it denotes the end of the possibility of factual historical statements concerning Jesus;[73] second, it demonstrates that the faith of Jesus in God was not in vain, thus justifying his own faith, and the faith of those who followed him.[74] Ebeling also emphasises that the resurrection does not amount to the communication of new or additional revelation to that given in Jesus, but the continued witness to the faith of Jesus. The post-Easter Christ is not disinct from the pre-Easter Jesus, but rather represents the 'right understanding' of Jesus himself; through the resurrection, Jesus is present in the *kerygma* as the basis of faith. The cross is thus a manifestation of the manner in which existential doubt may be replaced with certainty – a transition which underlies Ebeling's 'deobjectified' concept of 'pure faith'. 'Das Was' of Christology, according to Ebeling, is thus Christ as an example (*Vorbild*) and evoker of faith. The crucial transition from *Historie* (objective history) to *Geschichte* (experiential history) is thus effected through understanding the historical (*historisch*) Jesus as the example of the existential attitude which corresponds to and occasions an identical (or at least an analogous) attitude in the personal experiential history of the individual who receives the *kerygma*.[75] The faith of Jesus is hence the fundamental theological and historical (*historisch*) essence of the Christian faith, which may be transferred to the present day, and upon doing so, proves to be relevant to the existential sitation of contemporary man. Jesus is thus the 'pioneer and perfecter of faith' (Hebrews 12.2). Thus the *event* of the cross becomes the *word* of the cross, evoking belief even to this day.[76] This is, of course, perfectly consistent with Ebeling's deobjectified concept of faith: Jesus is not the *content* of faith, but merely its basis and its evoker, or cause; as the *witness* of faith, he is the *ground* of faith. Nevertheless, it will be clear that Ebeling has not resolved the vexed problem of the relation of faith and history, even though he evidently attaches considerably more significance to 'das Was' of the historical Jesus than Bultmann.[77] Ebeling's positive approach to the question of the historical Jesus – seen, for example, in his assertion that the situation qualified by Jesus 'legitimizes' the keryma[78] – should be understood to refer to the demonstration of the relation of the *kerygma* to Jesus, rather than a demonstration of the truth of the *kerygma* itself.[79] Of particular importance in this respect is Ebeling's observation that, whereas in other historical phenomena a complex relationship of diversity and discrepancy exists between an historical individual and his perceived significance, a remarkable exception must be conceded in the case of Jesus: in Jesus everything in his actions, attitudes and preaching is concentrated and focused upon the evoking of faith – a function which is continued in the *kerygma* of today. In this, Ebeling follows Ernst Fuchs' insistence that the *kerygma* is essentially the 'echo' of the existential decision which Jesus himself made.[80]

For Ebeling, the crucial aspect of Christology is that the *event* of the cross has become the *word* of the cross. The existential certainty which Jesus demonstrated upon the cross is transmitted through the *kerygma*, the Christologically determined word-event which mediates the essence of the Christian faith in the historical process. The concepts of 'faith' and 'the cross' are correlated in a 'theology of the cross' (*theologia crucis*) which is both concentrated and constituted Christologically.[81] As the disciples acquired the existential certainty of faith, they transmitted the experience of this existential certainty in the 'word-event',[82] which presents contemporary man with the possibility of that certainty. It is this aspect of his theology (and, indeed, similar aspects of the theology of Fuchs) which has been criticized, in that Ebeling appears to be too heavily dependent upon actual linguistic affinities between Jesus and the early church – for example, in the case of the concept of 'faith'. Thus Robinson points out the necessity of demonstrating a *continuity of intention*, rather than mere linguistic affinities, between the teaching of Jesus and the *kerygma*.[83] It is considerations such as these which underlie the so-called 'New Quest of the Historical Jesus', which we shall consider in the following chapter.

In the present chapter, we have been concerned with Christologies based upon an existential analysis of the human predicament, which see in the *kerygma* the means by which this predicament may be resolved. The significance of Christ is developed in terms of his relation to the *kerygma*, with three important consequences. First, a minimum of attention is paid to the historical figure of Jesus of Nazareth: for Bultmann, it is merely necessary that he existed ('das Dass'). In many respects, Jesus of Nazareth is treated as having been the historical occasion for the introduction of a self-sufficient existential principle, henceforth expressed and transmitted in the *kerygma*. The critical-historical method is thus seen as possessing an essentially negative function, in that it destroys the inadequate Jesuologies of the liberal and *religionsgeschichtliche Schule*. While it might be suggested that this approach to the theological significance of the historical Jesus is simply an attempt to make a virtue out of necessity (in that it appeared impossible to obtain reliable information concerning him in the first place), it must be emphasised that Bultmann and his circle were developing already existing theological insights, associated especially with Martin Kähler, which they regarded to have been *justified* by the new insights of the first four decades of the twentieth century concerning the nature of the New Testament documents. It thus follows that Christology follows soteriology, in that the *kerygma* is concerned with articulating the existential significance of Christ *pro nobis*, his perceived significance for believers, rather than his identity *per se*. The *kerygma* does not merely rehearse a factual account of history, or a sequence of historical events – rather, it directs an *interpretation* of these events (now independent of these events) to man in the form of an imperative. Faith recognizes in the history of Jesus of Nazareth the hand of God, and responds to the latter, rather than the former. Bultmann cites Philip Melanchthon's *dictum* 'to know Christ is to know his benefits' (*Christum cognoscere, eius beneficia cognoscere*) in justifying his assertion of the priority of soteriology over Christology. If Christology is based upon the *kerygma*, as Bultmann and his circle suggest, its foundations are necessarily soteriological, for the simple reason that the *kerygma* articulates the *perceived significance of Christ for believers*.

It is for this reason that Bultmann and his school maintain that the historical Jesus and his message have no significance – or at any rate, no *decisive* significance – for the Christian faith. At first sight, this assertion may appear utterly absurd.[84] Is not Christianity an historical religion, claiming to be based upon its historical founder and his message? However, the belief that the facts about Jesus of Nazareth and his message are not of decisive significance to the Christian faith is rendered plausible, as we have seen, by the recognition of the theological (more specifically, the *kerygmatic*) character of the New Testament documents, and the impossibility of obtaining reliable biographical information concerning the historical figure of Jesus of Nazareth. The *kerygma* does not preserve detailed historical memories concerning Jesus, but is an evaluation of his historical person. For Bultmann and his school, history cannot pass judgement upon the claims of the Christian faith concerning Jesus, for the simple reason that it lacks the competence to do so. Perhaps paradoxically, the *critical* application of the historico-critical method is self-defeating, in that it demonstrates the inability of the historian to engage in a serious critique of the *kerygma*.

Second, the realistic conceptual framework of the New Testament is demythologized or treated as symbolic, so that it comes to have a general reference to the universal existential situation of man. Thus the eschatological statements of the New Testament are treated by Bultmann,[85] Tillich,[86] Ebeling[87] and Fuchs[88] as referring to the present, in that every moment is the eschatological moment of existential decision. Similarly, the resurrection is treated as mythical or symbolical, something which most emphatically cannot be described as an objective historical fact (*historisches Faktum*), but which, when properly interpreted, refers to the universal human existential situation. The resurrection may thus be described as an 'historical (*geschichtlich*) event', in that it is an event which takes place in the personal experience of individuals – initially in the case of the primitive Christian community, and subsequently, through the *kerygma*, in the existential histories of all believers. The dual sense of the English word 'historical' obscures this vital point.

Third, a new concept of history was introduced into the German theological consciousness, with devastating results for the *Theologie des Historismus*. The rise of the existentialist understanding of history discredited historicism, and with it an understanding of the nature of reality. The increasing realization that history concerns the meaning of external events for those involved, and the growing emphasis upon the notion of historical encounter, called into question the presuppositions of the historicist understanding of reality. The full significance of the rise of historicism for Christian theology had been emphasized by Troeltsch (see chapter 4): it will therefore be clear that the discrediting of historicism had equally great, and perhaps even greater, significance. Indeed, it is possible to argue that it was on the basis of this new understanding of history, rather than any new understanding of the available sources, that a 'new quest of the historical Jesus' was undertaken. Bultmann's appreciation of the full significance of the existentialist understanding of history for Christian theology must be regarded as a major contribution to the development of modern German theology in general, and Christology in particular.

Although the approach to Christology considered in this chapter was enormously influential in the 1950s and 1960s, it was clear that there were certain fundamental deficiencies which required correction.

For example, it was pointed out that Bultmann appeared to be inconsistent in his programme of demythologization, in that his Christocentrism itself appeared to be a mythological construction which required elimination: any existential philosophy which recognized that authentic existence was a *gift* was expressing precisely the same as Bultmann's supposedly 'demythologized' *kerygma*.[89] A fully demythologized *kerygma* would, according to Bultmann's critics, merely proclaim the possibility of authenticity, without any claim to exclusivity, in that it would be seen as an 'intense awareness of existence as grace' conveyed through a symbol or myth.[90] For Buri, in fact, this amounts to the elimination of the *kerygma*, rather than its mere demythologization. In many ways, Tillich may be regarded as having taken this step, reducing the gospel to the timeless and self-sufficient truth that 'God' (Tillich is actually reluctant to use the word, preferring neuter terms such as 'Being') encounters man in history. For Bultmann, however, the *kerygma* did not proclaim *mythological* ideas, no matter how many mythological concepts it may have exploited in attempting to get its message across to its hearers: it was concerned with the existential significance of an historical person. If the *kerygma* were to be 'demythologized', it would be reduced to the 'meaning of Jesus of Nazareth'. For Bultmann, the concept of *kerygma* itself is not definitely not mythological, despite its use of evidently mythological concepts and language at points. The *kerygma* could not be regarded as a new myth, embodying and objectifying in a realistic manner some 'Christian religious principle'; it was rather the objectification of an historical encounter with God in Jesus of Nazareth, which could not itself be 'demythologized'.

The radicalization of Bultmann's theological programme in the direction suggested by Buri is probably best seen in the works of the Mainz New Testament scholar Herbert Braun. On the basis of his analysis of the three main Christological traditions in the New Testament (the synoptic gospels, John and Paul), Braun concluded that the Christological titles of the New Testament were merely Christological 'cyphers' (*Chiffren*) (similar, in fact, to Tillich's 'symbols') employed to refer to a deeper phenomenon – the self-understanding of faith.[91] In their encounter with Jesus of Nazareth, believers are brought to a new self-understanding: it is this same self-understanding which underlies the different Christologies of the three main traditions to be found in the New Testament.[92] Braun thus asserts: 'Anthropology is the constant; Christology is the variable.'[93] This assertion, however, went further than the mere legitimation of the use of an existential 'pre-understanding' (*Vorverständnis*) in Christology: it appeared to amount to a total secularization of the *kerygma*, including the demythologization of the idea of 'God', in that what was proclaimed was merely a new (or perhaps not-so-new) understanding of existence and the world, 'initiated' by Jesus of Nazareth and 'signified' or 'encoded' in the cypher of the kerygmatic Christ. For Braun's critics, such as Helmut Gollwitzer, Braun merely reduced the *kerygma* to anthropological insights.[94] All that remains of the *kerygma* is an idea of man, which is actualized whenever it is proclaimed and received, and which is essentially independent of Jesus of Nazareth.

Perhaps most fundamental of all was the perceived danger that 'das Was' would be eliminated in favour of 'das Dass', so that there would be no means available by which the *content* of the *kerygma* might be verified, or at least shown to be plausible. For Bultmann, it was necessary to have a 'minimum core of factuality'[95] upon which the *kerygma* could be held to be based – but Bultmann appears to conceive this 'minimum core' essentially in terms of the *continuity* of the history of Jesus and the *kerygma*. How, then, can the possibility that the association of the historical figure of Jesus of Nazareth with the Christ of the *kerygma* is simply an accident, or even a mistake, be excluded? For Ebeling, the answer lies in the assertion that there was an historical instance of the pattern of life which the *kerygma* proclaims. But is this enough? It was the serious threat which was perceived to be posed to the legitimacy of the Christian proclamation of Christ that led to the development of the 'New Quest of the Historical Jesus' within the later Bultmannian school – a development to which we now turn.

NOTES

1 See Eduard Lohse, 'Die evangelische Kirche vor der Theologie Rudolf Bultmanns', *Zeitschift für Theologie und Kirche* 82 (1985), pp. 173–91, for an excellent survey of this period.

2 For a useful analysis in English, see Ian Henderson, *Myth in the New Testament* (London, 1952), pp. 9–20.

3 'Neues Testament und Mythologie', in *Kerygma und Mythos I*, ed. H. W. Bartsch (Hamburg, 2nd edn, 1951), p. 18. For comment, see L. Malevez, *Le Message Chrétien et le Mythe: La Théologie de Rudolf Bultmann* (Brussels/Bruges/Paris, 1954), pp. 13–24.

4 *Theologische Blätter* 3 (1924), pp. 73–86; reprinted *Glaube und Verstehen I* (Tübingen, 5th edn, 1964), pp. 1–25. Reference is to this latter edition. An English translation may be found in *Faith and Understanding*, ed. Robert W. Funk (London, 1966), pp. 28–52.

5 'Die liberale Theologie', p. 1; 'Liberal Theology', pp. 28–9.

6 'Die liberale Theologie', p. 3; 'Liberal Theology', p. 30.

7 'Die liberale Theologie', p. 4; 'Liberal Theology', p. 31.

8 'Die liberale Theologie', p. 4; 'Liberal Theology', p. 31.

9 'Die liberale Theologie', pp. 5-13; 'Liberal Theology', pp. 32–0.

10 'Die liberale Theologie', pp. 6; 18; 'Liberal Theology', pp. 33; 45.

11 'Zur Frage der Christologie', *Zwischen den Zeiten* 5 (1927), pp. 41–69; reprinted *Glaube und Verstehen I*, pp. 85–113; p. 101. For an English translation, see *Faith and Understanding*, pp. 116–44; p. 132. Compare this with Barth's fourteenth thesis against Harnack, cited in the previous chapter of the present study. This essay is actually a review of Emanuel Hirsch, *Jesus Christus der Herr* (Göttingen, 1926), and the following comment may be noted: 'What Hirsch portrays is 'Christ according to the flesh', because he is not seen according to faith, but according to the manner of pietism and rationalism' (p. 95; English translation, p. 126). For Bultmann, 'to speak theologically of Jesus Christ means. . . to speak of him as he is seen by faith, and only as he is seen by faith' (p. 92; English translation, p. 123). Bultmann thus makes the important point that it cannot be assumed that faith is intellectually comprehensible, viewed from *outside* the context of faith.

12 See Malevez, *Le message chrétien*, pp. 46–62.

13 The reader is referred to two standard works by John Macquarrie, *An Existentialist Theology: A Comparison of Heidegger and Bultmann* (London, 1973); *The Scope of Demythologizing* (London, 1960). For more detailed studies of specific aspects of Bultmann's existentialism, see Gerhard Kuhlmann, 'Zum theologischen Problem der Existenz: Fragen an Rudolf Bultmann', *Zeitschrift für Theologie und Kirche* 10 (1929), pp. 28–58; Emil Brunner, 'Theologie und Ontologie, oder die Theologie am Scheideweg', *Zeitschrift für Theologie und Kirche* 12 (1931), pp. 111–22; W. Ernst, 'Theologische Begriffe in der modernen Existential-philosophie', *Zeitschrift für systematischen Theologie* 10 (1933), pp. 589–612; Felix Flückiger, *Existenz und Glaube: Kritische Betrachtungen zur existentialen Interpretation* (Wuppertal, 1966), pp. 17–47; Jean-Paul Resweber, *La théologie face au défi herméneutique* (Louvain, 1975), pp. 147–96 (ignore incorrect page headings); Jean Beaufret, 'Heidegger et la théologie', in *Heidegger et la question de Dieu*, ed. Richard Kearney and J. S. O'Leary (Paris, 1980), pp. 19–36.

14 A point which needs to be borne in mind when attempting to make sense of the confusion to be found within the pages of *The Myth of God Incarnate*, ed. John Hick (London, 1977). See further Dietrich Ritschl, '"Story" als

Rohmateriel der Theologie', *Theologische Existenz heute* 192 (Munich, 1976), pp. 7–41. (The term 'story' is more neutral and more fruitful theologically than 'myth'). For some more general perceptive comments on this question, see Ben Halpern, "Myth' and 'Ideology' in Modern Usage', *History and Theory* 1 (1960–61), pp. 129–49.

15 See the essay 'Die Eschatologie des Johannes-Evangeliums', *Zwischen den Zeiten* 6 (1928), pp. 4–22; reprinted *Glaube und Verstehen I*, pp. 134–52. For an English translation, see *Faith and Understanding*, pp. 165–83.

16 'Eschatologie des Johannes-Evangeliums', p. 144; 'Eschatology of the Gospel of John', p. 175.

17 For example, see Emmanuel Mounier, *Existentialist Philosophies: An Introduction* (London, 1948); David E. Roberts, *Existentialism and Religious Belief* (New York, 1957).

18 On Sartre, see Roberts, *Existentialism*, pp. 195–226; on Marcel, see ibid., pp. 275–332; Joseph C. Mihalich, *Existentialism and Thomism* (Totowa, NJ, 1969), pp. 23–35.

19 *Sein und Zeit* (Tübingen, 8th edn, 1957), p. 41; *Being and Time*, trs. John Macquarrie and Edward Robinson (London, 1962), p. 67. For an invaluable glossary of the terms used by Heidegger in this work, see Macquarrie and Robinson, op. cit., pp. 505–23. The practice of translating *Seiendes* as 'entities' is questionable – 'beings' is much to be preferred: see *The Later Heidegger and Theology*, ed. James M. Robinson and John B. Cobb (New Frontiers in Theology 1: New York, 1962), pp. ix–xii.

20 See, for example, Macquarrie, *An Existentialist Theology*, pp. 32–9.

21 For what follows, see Macquarrie, *An Existentialist Theology*, pp. 52–123.

22 On the existential significance of death, in Heidegger and elsewhere, see John Macquarrie's 1963 Birks Lectures, published in Macquarrie, *Studies in Christian Existentialism* (London, 1966), pp. 45–96, especially pp. 45–57.

23 See Maurice Boutin, *Relationalität als Verstehenprinzip bei Rudolf Bultmann* (Munich 1974), pp. 29–146; Resweber, *La théologie*, pp. 15–33. On the concept of *Entweltlichung* in Bultmann's theology, see the important study of Bernhard Dieckmann, *'Welt' und 'Entweltlichung' in der Theologie Rudolf Bultmanns* (Munich/Paderborn/Vienna, 1977). On Bultmann's use of the concept in his analysis of the Fourth Gospel, see Dieckman, *'Welt' und 'Entweltlichung'*, pp. 159–67.

24 'Eschatologie des Johannes-Evangeliums', p. 139; 'Eschatology of the Gospel of John', p. 170. The German term *aus* can bear the sense of 'of' or 'out of', and Bultmann is merely exploiting the theological potentialities of this ambiguity. This entire essay is, in fact, a brilliant reinterpretation of the Fourth Gospel in terms of Heidegger's analysis of the structures of existence.

25 Macquarrie, *Existentialist Theology*, pp. 39–45.

26 'Neues Testament und Mythologie', pp. 39–40.
27 See 'Neues Testament und Mythologie', pp. 41–6.
28 'Die Bedeutung des geschichtlichen Jesus für die Theologie des Paulus', *Theologische Blätter* 8 (1929), pp. 137–51; reprinted *Glaube und Verstehen I*, pp. 188–213; English translation in *Faith and Understanding*, pp. 220–46.
29 'Bedeutung des geschichtlichen Jesus', p. 202; 'Significance of the Historical Jesus', p. 235.
30 'Bedeutung des geschichtlichen Jesus', p. 208; 'Significance of the Historical Jesus', p. 241. Note the obvious appeal to Kähler (and the close correspondence with Barth) over and against the liberal school in the statement: 'Nicht der historische Jesus, sondern Jesus Christus, der Gepredigte, ist der Herr'.
31 *Das Verhältnis der urchristlichen Christusbotschaft zum historischen Jesus* (Heidelberg, 3rd edn, 1962), p. 27.
32 See *Kerygma und Mythos I*, pp. 133–4; 'Der Begriff des Wortes Gottes im Neuen Testaments', in *Glaube und Verstehen I*, pp. 268–93; p. 292; 'Die Bedeutung des geschichtlichen Jesus', p. 211; *Das Verhältnis der urchristlichen Botschaft*, p. 10.
33 'Die Krisis des Glaubens' (1931); in *Glaube und Verstehen II* (Tübingen, 4th edn, 1965), pp. 1–19; p. 16.
34 His early work *Die Geschichte der Synoptischen Tradition* (Göttingen, 1921) remains a classic, and should be consulted in the third edition (Göttingen, 1957), which contains an important *Ergänzungsheft*. This edition is available in English translation: *The History of the Synoptic Tradition* (Oxford, 1963). For discussion and further references, see W. G. Kümmel, *Das Neue Testament: Geschichte der Erforschung seiner Probleme* (Freiburg, 1958), pp. 415–520. The importance of the study of K. L. Schmidt, *Der Rahmen der Geschichte Jesu* (Berlin, 1919) should be noted in this connection: Schmidt demonstrated that the order of events varied from one gospel to another, thus indicating that the 'historical' framework of the gospels was nothing more than a skeleton upon which the evangelists could place their material concerning Jesus. This material was actually transmitted as discrete units, and it was only at a comparatively late stage in the transmission process that they were grouped together, roughly on a chronological, geographical or thematic basis.
35 On this, see Oscar Cullmann, '*Kyrios* as Designation for the Oral Tradition concerning Jesus', *Scottish Journal of Theology* 3 (1950), pp. 180–97. The concept of history as an objective reconstruction of past events 'as it actually was' is particularly associated with Leopold von Ranke. It is for this reason that he was dubbed 'the great ocularist' by Count von Yorck (see *Briefwechsel zwischen Wilhelm Dilthey und dem Grafen Paul Yorck von Wartenburg 1877–97* (Halle/Saale, 1923), p. 60), in that he viewed history in a totally detached manner, without becoming involved with it.

36 See William Baird, 'What is the Kerygma? A Study of I Corinthians 15.3–8 and Galatians 1.11–17', *Journal of Biblical Literature* 76 (1957), pp. 181–91.
37 See Berthold Klappert, *Die Auferweckung des Gekreuzigten: Der Ansatz der Christologie Karl Barths im Zusammenhang der Christologie der Gegenwart* (Neukirchen, 1971), pp. 3–5.
38 For example, see Richard Reitzenstein, *Poimandres* (Leipzig, 1904); Wilhelm Bousset, *Kyrios Christos* (Göttingen, 1913). Reitzenstein initially regarded gnosticism as arising from pre-Christian Egyptian sources, although from 1916 onwards he favoured pre-Christian Iranian sources. For an excellent general survey, see C. Colpe, *Die religionsgeschichtliche Schule: Darstellung und Kritik ihres Bildes vom gnostischen Erlösermythos* (Göttingen, 1961).
39 For example, see F. C. Burkitt, *Church and Gnosis: A Study of Christian Thought and Speculation in the Second Century* (Cambridge, 1932); Hans Jonas, *Gnosis und spätantiker Geist I: Die mythologische Gnosis* (Göttingen, 2nd edn, 1954); id., *The Gnostic Religion* (Boston, 1958); William Baird, 'The Problem of the Gnostic Redeemer and Bultmann's Programme of Demythologizing', in *Theologia Crucis – Signum Crucis: Festschrift für Erich Dinkler*, ed. Carl Andresen and Günter Klein (Tübingen, 1979), pp. 39–56.
40 One of the best discussions may be found in Helmut Thielicke, *Der evangelische Glaube I* (Göttingen, 1968), pp. 22–143; *The Evangelical Faith I* (Edinburgh, 1978), pp. 38–114.
41 See Adrian Thatcher, *The Ontology of Paul Tillich* (Oxford, 1978), pp. 2–7, and references therein.
42 *Systematic Theology* (3 vols: London, 1978), vol. 1, p. 21.
43 *Systematic Theology*, vol. 2, p. 152. Note also the similarity with Bultmann over the Fourth Gospel: p. 164.

For a discussion of Tillich's confusing concept of 'symbol', see H. McDonald, 'The Symbolic Theology of Paul Tillich', *Scottish Journal of Theology* 17 (1964), pp. 414–30; Klaus Rosenthal, 'Myth and Symbol', *Scottish Journal of Theology* 18 (1965), pp. 411–34; Thatcher, *Ontology of Paul Tillich*, pp. 33–52. Perhaps most useful is G. Weigel, 'Myth, Symbol and Analogy', in *Religion and Culture: Essays in Honour of Paul Tillich*, ed. W. Leibrecht (London, 1959), pp. 120–30.
44 *Systematic Theology*, vol. 2, p. 29.
45 Thatcher, *Ontology of Paul Tillich*, pp. 117–38.
46 *Systematic Theology*, vol. 2, pp. 55–8.
47 Thatcher is not among them: Thatcher, *Ontology of Paul Tillich*, pp. 137–8.
48 *Systematic Theology*, vol. 2, pp. 118–36; Thatcher, *Ontology of Paul Tillich*, pp. 139–57.
49 *Systematic Theology*, vol. 2, pp. 98–9.

50 *Systematic Theology*, vol. 2, p. 114.
51 *Systematic Theology*, vol. 2, p. 112.
52 *Systematic Theology*, vol. 2, p. 150.
53 *Systematic Theology*, vol. 2, p. 150.
54 See B. J. R. Cameron, 'The Historical Problem in Paul Tillich's Christology', *Scottish Journal of Theology* 18 (1965), pp. 257–72; Van A. Harvey, *The Historian and the Believer* (London, 1967), pp. 146–53, for a careful study of this deficiency. There are close parallels between Tillich and Hegel in this matter, despite Tillich's generally negative evaluation of the latter: see B. R. J. Cameron, 'The Hegelian Christology of Paul Tillich', *Scottish Journal of Theology* 29 (1976), pp. 27–48.
55 See René Marlé, 'Foi et parole: La théologie de Gerhard Ebeling', *Recherches de Sciences Religieuses* 49 (1962), pp. 5–31; pp. 5–6.
56 For example, see his *Evangelische Evangelienauslegung: Eine Untersuchung zu Luthers Hermeneutik* (Munich, 1942).
57 Ebeling, *Wort Gottes und Tradition: Studien zu einer Hermeneutik der Konfessionen* (Göttingen, 1964), pp. 9–27.
58 See Pietro Selvatico, *Glaubensgewissheit: Eine Untersuchung zur Theologie von Gerhard Ebeling* (Freiburg, 1977), pp. 61–74.
59 *Dogmatik des christlichen Glaubens* (3 vols: Tübingen, 1979). See his own comments on this work in 'Zu meiner "Dogmatik des christlichen Glaubens"', *Theologische Literaturzeitung* 105 (1980), 721–33.
60 Ebeling, *Wort und Glaube* (Tübingen, 1960), pp. 215–6.
61 *Dogmatik des christlichen Glaubens*, vol. 1, p. 348.
62 For example, see *Dogmatik des christlichen Glaubens*, vol. 3, p. 397.
63 Ebeling, *Einführung in theologische Sprachlehre* (Tübingen, 1971), pp. 11–12.
64 *Dogmatik des christlichen Glaubens*, vol. 2, pp. 296; 372; 395.
65 *Dogmatik des christlichen Glaubens*, vol. 2, p. 150.
66 The chief Christological titles are also to be regarded as mythical: *Dogmatik des christlichen Glaubens*, vol. 2, p. 394.
67 See his important essay, 'Die Bedeutung der historisch-kritischen Methode für die protestantische Theologie und Kirche', *Zeitschrift für Theologie und Kirche* 47 (1950), pp. 1–46; reprinted *Wort und Glaube*, pp. 1–49.
68 Ebeling, *Wort und Glaube III* (Tübingen, 1975), p. 277.
69 *Wort und Glaube*, pp. 208; 300–01 'Für die Christologie ist der Bezug auf Jesus konstitutiv. Sie muß, wenn sie sich recht versteht, den Anspruch erheben, nichts anderes auszusagen als: wer Jesus ist. Darum ist Jesus kriterium der Christologie. Wäre es zu erweisen, daß die Christologie keinen Anhalt habe am historischen Jesus, vielmehr eine Mißdeutung Jesu sei, so wäre die Christologie damit erledigt.'
70 Ebeling, *Theologie und Verkündigung: Ein Gespräch mit Rudolf Bultmann* (Tübingen, 1962), pp. 68–9, 115–16: 'Auch bei Bultmann ist zum

Verständnis des Offenbarung-Charakters der Erscheinung Jesu Christi in keiner Weise dessen geschichtliches Was und Wie, sondern nur dessen Daß von Bedeutung, an dem nun ausschließlich der Charakter göttlichen Handelns, des Heilsereignisses, haftet.' For a recent rejoinder from the Bultmann school, see Walter Schmithals, *Jesus Christus in der Verkündigung der Kirche* (Neukirchen, 1972), pp. 73–75, who asserts that the church has never been interested in the historical facts of the life of Jesus (*das Was und Wie des Lebens Jesu*).

71 *Theologie und Verkündigung*, pp. 89–90; 97; *Wort und Glaube III*, p. 244. It is significant that Ebeling regards the Pauline formula *pistis Iesou Christou* as analogous to *pistis Abraam*, so that the 'faith of Jesus' and the 'faith of Abraham' are generically the same – the difference lying in the situation of the respective believers, and the enhanced intensity of the faith of Jesus. See *Dogmatik des christlichen Glaubens*, vol. 2, pp. 521–3.

72 *Dogmatik des christlichen Glaubens*, vol. 2, p. 388.

73 See *Wort und Glaube*, p. 304 'Der Tod is die Grenze historischer Aussagen.' Ebeling bases his distinction between 'explicit' and 'implicit' Christology on this point.

74 For example, *Dogmatik des christlichen Glaubens*, vol. 2, pp. 300–1.

75 *Theologie und Verkündigung*, pp. 79–81.

76 *Dogmatik des christlichen Glaubens*, vol. 2, pp. 210; 219–20.

77 As pointed out by Jürgen Moltmann, 'Anfrage und Kritik: Zu Gerhard Ebelings "Theologie und Verkündigung"', *Evangelische Theologie* 24 (1964), pp. 25–34; Wolfgang Greive, 'Jesus und Glaube: Das Problem der Christologie Gerhard Ebelings', *Kerygma und Dogma* 22 (1976), pp. 163–80. The study of Jürgen Roloff, *Das Kerygma und der irdische Jesus: Historische Motive in den Erzählungen der Evangelien* (Göttingen, 1970), suggests that a significant distance has been preserved between the historical Jesus and the kerygmatic Christ in the New Testament, with important consequences, not merely for Ebeling, but for any kerygmatic Christology.

78 *Theologie und Verkündigung*, pp. 57; 64; 74–5.

79 See Wolfhart Pannenberg, *Grundzüge der Christologie* (Gütersloh, 6th edn, 1982), p. 18 n.14.

80 Ernst Fuchs, 'Die Frage nach dem historischen Jesus', in *Zur Frage nach dem historischen Jesus* (Tübingen, 1960), pp. 143–67; p. 157. See also the essays 'Jesus und der Glaube' (*Zur Frage nach dem historischen Jesus*, pp. 377–404; 'Die Theologie des Neuen Testaments und der historische Jesus' (*Zur Frage nach dem historischen Jesus*, pp. 238–57).

81 *Dogmatik des christlichen Glaubens*, vol. 2, p. 214.

82 *Dogmatik des christlichen Glaubens*, vol. 2, p. 315.

83 See James M. Robinson, *Kerygma und Historische Jesus* (Zurich, 1960), *passim*.

84 See the excellent essay of Joachim Jeremias, 'Der gegenwärtige Stand der Debatte um das Problem des historischen Jesus', in *Der historische Jesus und der kerygmatische Christus*, ed. H. Ristow and K. Matthiae (Berlin, 2nd edn, 1961), pp. 12–25; especially p. 12.

85 For example, Bultmann, *Kerygma und Mythos I*, p. 32; 'Geschichte und Eschatologie im Neuen Testament', in *Glauben und Verstehen III* (Tübingen, 3rd edn, 1965), pp. 91–106; especially pp. 105–06.

86 For example, Tillich, *Systematic Theology*, vol. 2, pp. 161–5.

87 For example, Ebeling's important statement: *Dogmatik des christlichen Glaubens*, vol. 3, pp. 398–9 'Die Zeit als solche ist eschatologisch: als befristete Zeit, die in unumkehrbarem Gefälle auf ein Ende zutreibt, das als Angst oder Hoffnung erweckende Zukunft existenzbestimmend ist, jede Zeit zur Entscheidungszeit, zum eschatologischen Augenblick qualifiziert und deshalb Einmaligkeit.' Note also his suggestion that Jesus did not preach apocalyptically on account of the *distance* of the God of apocalypticism: *Dogmatik des christlichen Glaubens*, vol. 2, p. 451.

88 Ernst Fuchs, *Glaube und Erfahrung: Zum christologischen Problem im Neuen Testament* (Tübingen, 1965), p. 359.

89 For example, see Fritz Buri, in *Kerygma und Mythos II*, pp. 85–101. The same point has been made more recently by Robert C. Roberts, *Rudolf Bultmann's Theology: A Critical Interpretation* (London, 1977), pp. 83–122, especially pp. 90–5.

90 Buri, *Kerygma und Mythos II*, p. 90. The study of Schubert M. Ogden, *Christ without Myth* (New York, 1961), is also useful.

91 See Herbert Braun, 'Der Sinn der neutestamentlichen Christologie', in *Gesammelte Studien zum Neuen Testament und seiner Umwelt* (Tübingen, 1962), pp. 243–82.

92 Braun, 'Sinn der neutestamentlichen Christologie', pp. 281–2.

93 Braun, 'Sinn der neutestamentlichen Christologie', p. 272.

94 For example, Helmut Gollwitzer, *Die Existenz Gottes im Bekenntnis des Glaubens* (Munich, 1963), *passim*.

95 The phrase may be found in John Macquarrie, *The Scope of Demythologizing*, *passim*.

7

The New Quest of the Historical Jesus: from Käsemann to Pannenberg

The original 'Quest of the historical Jesus', called into question by developments in the period 1890–1914, had finally been discredited and brought to an end by the rise of the 'kerygmatic' theology of Rudolf Bultmann and his school, discussed in the previous chapter. However, as we noted in concluding our survey of 'kerygmatic' Christologies, certain difficulties attending the relation of the historical Jesus and the Christ of the *kerygma* could not be ignored: how can it be shown that the *kerygma* is not a religious product of the primitive Christian church, but is firmly grounded in the history and destiny of Jesus of Nazareth? How may a *theological* account be given of the transition from the preaching of Jesus to the preaching about Jesus? How can it be shown that the Christian faith is not actually based upon a myth, rather than an historical (*historisch*) fact? It is of vital importance to establish that faith in Christ has its roots in the person and preaching of Jesus of Nazareth, and not simply in the faith and proclamation of the primitive Christian community. It is this concern, voiced by Gerhard Ebeling and others (such as Herbert Braun, Hans Conzelmann, and Ernst Fuchs), which has led to the development of a 'new quest' of the historical Jesus, distinguished from its discredited predecessor in terms of its presuppositions, methods and motives.[1] In the present chapter, we propose to discuss this important new development which has so direct a bearing on our subject, before considering its systematic development in one of the most significant works on Christology to emerge from the German tradition in recent years – Wolfhart Pannenberg's *Grundzüge der Christologie*, perhaps better known by its English title, *Jesus – God and Man*.

The 'new quest' is generally regarded as having been inaugurated with Ernst Käsemann's lecture of October 1953 on the problem of the historical Jesus,[2] delivered to the *alte Marburger* (that is, an audience of Bultmann's pupils). The full importance of this lecture can only be appreciated when it is set in the context of Bultmann's theological programme. Käsemann concedes that the synoptic gospels are primarily theological documents, and that their theological statements are frequently expressed in the form of the historical (a process of *Historisierung* perhaps best seen in the Matthaean infancy narratives). Nevertheless, Käsemann insisted that the evangelists believed that they had access to historical information concerning Jesus of Nazareth, and that this information was presented in some form in the synoptic gospels. The gospels contain not merely *kerygma*, but also narrative material, in that they present the *kerygma* in the context of the earthly life of Jesus. It must be emphasized that Käsemann was not suggesting that a new enquiry into the historical Jesus should be undertaken *in order to provide historical legitimation for the kerygma and hence for faith*; such an undertaking would, in his opinion, be absurd, or even blasphemous.[3] The fundamental question at issue is how continuity has been maintained in the evident *dis*continuity between the preaching *of* Jesus and the preaching *about* Jesus. The *theological* assertion of the identity of the earthly (*irdisch*) Jesus and the exalted Christ, of the Jesus of history and the Christ of the *kerygma*, is inextricably linked with, and dependent upon, the *historical* demonstration that the *kerygma* is already contained *in nuce* in the actions and preaching of Jesus of Nazareth. In so far as the *kerygma* speaks of Jesus *as an historical phenomenon*, it not merely legimates, but actually demands, an enquiry into the historical Jesus.

The growing realization of this point has led to intensive interest, from within the Bultmann school as well as outside it, in the question of the relation between the historical Jesus and the kerygmatic Christ. One extreme is represented by Joachim Jeremias, who appears to suggest that the basis of the Christian faith lies in what Jesus actually said and did, in so far as this can be established by historical enquiry.[4] The first part of his *Neutestamentliche Theologie* was thus devoted in its entirety to the 'proclamation of Jesus' *as an important aspect of New Testament theology*.[5] Käsemann himself identified the continuity between the historical Jesus and the kerygmatic Christ in their common declaration of the onset of the eschatological Kingdom of God: 'God has come close to man in his grace and with his demand'.[6]

Gerhard Ebeling, as we have already seen, locates the continuity in the 'faith of Jesus', which he understands to be analogous to the 'faith of Abraham' in Romans 4 – a prototypal faith, historically exemplified in the life of Jesus, and a present possibility for believers. Günther Bornkamm laid particular emphasis upon the note of authority evident in the ministry of Jesus: in Jesus, the actuality of God already faces men and calls them to decision.[7] Whereas Bultmann located the essence of Jesus' message in the future coming of the Kingdom of God, Bornkamm shifted the emphasis to the present confrontation of man with God in the person of Jesus of Nazareth.

By the year 1960, therefore, a new interest in the historical (*historisch*) Jesus had developed within German New Testament circles and the Bultmann school, without any significant alteration in the understanding of the sources or methods to be employed in the resulting historical investigation. The New Testament documents are not treated as 'historical' documents, nor are any new methods employed in their analysis: the difference between Bultmann and his pupils relates primarily to the conviction on the part of the latter that it is possible and legitimate to demonstrate continuity between the 'historical Jesus' and the 'kerygmatic Christ', and that it is possible to distinguish between the historicizing and kerygmatic tendencies within the New Testament tradition in relation to the essential features of the life of Jesus. Slenckza has summarised the two basic points upon which there was agreement as follows:[8] first, there was general agreement that it was both possisble and theologically necessary to go behind the *kerygma* to its historical foundations; second, the task of Christology was generally agreed to be not merely the 'unfolding' (*Entfaltung*) of the confession of Christ, but its establishment (*Begründung*) in the first place. On the basis of these presuppositions, the 'new quest' was able to demonstrate that the *kerygma* begins with Jesus of Nazareth, rather than the primitive Christian community, and that it has its foundations in the historical events of the life of Jesus (although we must emphasize that this most emphatically does not mean that the *kerygma* is reduced to the history of Jesus of Nazareth!). Our interest in this development relates primarily to the context which it established for a radical new development in Christology, heralded in 1959 with the publication of Wolfhart Pannenberg's essay on 'redemptive event and history'.[9] This important essay may be regarded as a manifesto for Pannenberg's basic theological programme, which finds its Christological culmination in the work noted above. Pannenberg's views appear to have developed within the context of the 'Pannenberg circle', an interdisciplinary group of graduate students at Heidelberg, who met weekly in the 1950s in an attempt to forge an integrated theological programme which would circumvent the impasse between biblical studies and systematic theology associated with Barth and Bultmann. Initially, the group consisted of Klaus Koch (Old Testament), Pannenberg (Systematic Theology), Rolf Rendtorff (Old Testament), Dietrich Rössler (New Testament) and Ulrich Wilckens (New Testament). As we shall see below, Rössler is of particular importance to our study. In view of the enormous importance of Pannenberg's Christological works to the present study, the remainder of the present chapter is given over to an exposition and critical analysis of Pannenberg's Christology, its presuppositions and methods.[10]

Pannenberg's essay of 1959 indicates a more significant break with the Bultmannian tradition than that envisaged by Bornkamm,[11] as may be judged from its opening statements:

> History (*Geschichte*) is the most comprehensive (*umfassendst*) horizon of Christian theology. All theological questions and answers have meaning only within the framework of the history which God has with mankind, and through mankind with the whole creation, directed towards a future which is hidden to the world, but which has already been revealed in Jesus Christ.[12]

These important opening sentences contain Pannenberg's theological programme *in nuce*, distinguishing him from the existential theology of Bultmann on the one hand, and the suprahistorical theology of Martin Kähler (which he detected as underlying Barth's *Urgeschichte*) on the other. There had been general agreement that revelation in the biblical sense of the term did not refer to the communication of direct revealed truths concerning God, but the self-disclosure of God himself. Pannenberg's attack on Barth on the one hand, and Bultmann on the other, was directed not so much against their notion of revelation as the self-disclosure of God, as against the idea of a *direct* self-disclosure of this type (as, for example, underlies theologies of the Word based upon dialogical personalism). Instead of establishing Christian theology on the basis of an analysis of *existence* or a kerygmatically mediated *suprahistory*, Pannenberg chose to base it upon an analysis of *universal history*, in which God was revealed *indirectly*. Barth and the *Heilsgeschichte* theologians took refuge from *Historie* in the diffuse realms of pre- or supra-history; Bultmann and the existentialists in the inwardness of existential historicity. For Pannenberg, revelation is essentially an historical event interpreted as an 'act of God'.[13]

The idea that history is the indirect self-disclosure of God can, of course, be traced back to Hegel. However, Hegel's followers had proved unable to maintain this concept of history as revelation without relativizing the Christ-event, in that Jesus of Nazareth was seen as but one stage in an essentially progressive development. Pannenberg, however, insisted that history in its totality can only be understood and interpreted as revelation when it is viewed from the standpoint of the end of history itself – and asserts that precisely this end of history is disclosed proleptically in the history of Jesus of Nazareth. This assertion that Jesus of Nazareth is the anticipation or proleptic disclosure of the end of history can only be justified, according to Pannenberg, in terms of the framework of apocalypticism. Whereas Bultmann was obliged to demythologize such apocalyptic elements in the New Testament, Pannenberg insists that they are essential if the eschatological character of the Christ-event is to be understood.

This point becomes clear when Pannenberg's seven 'dogmatic theses on the doctrine of revelation' are considered.

(1) The self-revelation of God in the biblical witnesses did not take place directly, after the fashion of a theophany, but indirectly, in the acts of God in history (*Gottes Geschichtstaten*).[14]
(2) Revelation is not completely apprehended at the beginning, but at the end of revelatory history (*am Ende der offenbarenden Geschichte*).[15]
(3) In contast to special divine manifestations, the revelation in history (*Geschichtsoffenbarung*) is open to anyone who has eyes to see it: it has a universal character.[16]
(4) The universal revelation of the divinity of God is not yet realized in the history of Israel (*Geschichte Israels*), but was first realized in the destiny (*Geschick*) of Jesus of Nazareth, in so far as the end of all events is anticipated in his destiny.[17]
(5) The Christ-event (*Christusgeschehen*) does not reveal the divinity of the God of Israel as an isolated event (*isoliertes Ereignis*), but in so far as it is an integral part of the history of God with Israel.[18]
(6) The universality of the eschatological self-demonstration of God in the destiny of Jesus comes to actual expression in the formulation

of non-Jewish conceptions of revelation in the gentile Christian church.[19]

(7) The Word relates itself to revelation as foretelling, forthtelling, and report.[20]

It is with the first six of these theses that we are particularly concerned in this study, in that they develop a general historical concept of revelation which finds its actual expression and concentration in the history and destiny of Jesus of Nazareth.

Pannenberg draws upon Gerhard von Rad's Old Testament interpretation in asserting that the origins of this understanding of revelation may be detected in the religion of ancient Israel: the Israelites experienced their own history as the self-disclosure of a God who was faithful to them. This opinion may be contrasted with the view, particularly associated with Bultmann, that a distinction must be drawn between historical events themselves, and the *interpretation* to be placed upon those historical events: the *kerygma* represents an essentially self-sufficient interpretation of the historical event of the history of Jesus of Nazareth, as we noted in the previous chapter. For Pannenberg, however, it is impossible to draw an absolute distinction between an event and its interpretation, in that the meaning of events inheres within them: it is only in the subsequent process of reflection and analysis that the distinction arises. Pannenberg thus asserts that:

> . . . [the] splitting up of historical consciousness into a detection of facts and an evaluation of them (or into history as known and history as experienced) is intolerable to Christian faith, not only because the message of the resurrection of Jesus and of God's revelation in him necessarily becomes merely subjective interpretation, but also because it is the reflection of an outmoded and questionable historical method . . . We must reinstate today the original unity of facts and their meaning.[21]

Events and their interpretations can only be considered in the unitary totality of their original historical context (*Geschehenszusammenhang*). It is therefore necessary in principle to undertake an historical investigation of the 'history and destiny' (*Geschichte und Geschick*) of Jesus of Nazareth in order to demonstrate that this event and its meaning as divine revelation may be verified, or at least demonstrated to be probable. As he states this principle in his main Christological work:

Christology is therefore concerned not only with *unfolding* the Christian community's confession of Christ, but above all with *grounding* it in the past activity and destiny of Jesus (*der Damals des Wirkes und Geschickes Jesu*)... Christology has to enquire concerning, and demonstrate, the extent to which the history (*Geschichte*) of Jesus substantiates faith in him. How else may the history of Jesus substantiate faith in him except by showing itself to be the revelation of God? Only when its revelatory character (*Offenbarungscharakter*) is not something additional to the events, but is rather something inherent within them, may these events constitute the basis of faith. Christology has to demonstrate precisely this.[22]

(It may be noted at this point that Pannenberg uses the phrase *Wirken Jesu* to refer to Jesus' activity, such as his preaching, and *Geschick Jesu* to refer to events in which he is passive, and God active, such as his crucifixion and resurrection). For Pannenberg, it is therefore legitimate, possible and necessary to go behind the *kerygma* to the history of Jesus.[23] In this sense, it is correct to refer to Pannenberg constructing a 'Christology from below'.[24] But how may this be done, given the substantial objections raised against the legitimacy and possibility of precisely such a procedure since the time of Martin Kähler? In order to answer this question, we must consider three important aspects of Pannenberg's thought: his understanding of the nature and significance of apocalypticism; his understanding of the limitations of the principle of analogy in historical analysis; and finally, his understanding of the significance of the resurrection of Jesus. We begin by considering his understanding of the Christological significance of apocalypticism.

Associated with the 'new quest of the historical Jesus' was a new interest in the problem of the relation between apocalyptic and early Christian theology.[25] Käsemann's assertion that 'apocalyptic was the mother of Christian theology' exemplified this new interest, as well as demonstrating the need to define more precisely what 'apocalyptic' was. In the fourth edition (1965) of his *Theologie des Alten Testaments*, Gerhard von Rad concluded his completely revised section on apocalypticism with the statement that the 'concept of apocalyptic urgently requires critical revision'.[26] By substituting an apocalyptic for an anthropological *Weltanschauung*, it was held by some scholars, such as Käsemann, to be possible to avoid the 'anthropological constriction' which many held to be implicit in Bultmann's existentialist approach to the *kerygma*. The pre-understanding (*Vorverständnis*) with which the history of Jesus of Nazareth should be approached was not the scientific and existential self-understanding of twentieth century man, but the first-century apocalyptic understanding of the world and history. The theological significance of this new interest on the part of New Testament scholars in apocalyptic will be evident.

In the midst of this renewed interest in the subject, the Pannenberg circle gave it a new significance by identifying apocalyptic as the context in which the early Christian understanding of revelation arose. This new understanding of the importance of apocalypticism, particularly evident in Ulrich Wilcken's essay on the understanding of revelation within primitive Christianity in *Offenbarung als Geschichte*,[27] appears to be based upon Dietrich Rössler's monograph on the theology of Jewish apocalyptic,[28] which argued that salvation-history was the central theme in apocalypticism as a whole. For Rössler, apocalypticism recognized that history was a universal process from its beginning to its end; the apocalyptic seer was granted a vision of the end of the historical process, in order that he might gain an understanding of both the meaning and the course of history *while the historical process was still continuing*. In other words, history was understood within apocalypticism as a divinely ordained process whose precise course and ultimate meaning could only be ascertained when it had ended; the characteristic of the apocalyptic seer or visionary was his divinely granted 'preview' of the end of the process, in order that he might interpret history to his contemporaries. Rössler's interpretation of apocalypticism is controversial,[29] and appears to be mistaken at several crucial points. For example, his assertion that apocalypticism grew out of the prophetic movement should be treated with a certain degree of scepticism.[30] Without wishing to engage in a detailed examination of the present state of scholarly opinion on apocalypticism, we wish to emphasize that the Pannenberg circle, and Pannenberg himself, appear to have based their views on revelation on a questionable set of theses concerning the understanding of world history associated with the apocalyptic movement at the time of Jesus of Nazareth. The new interest in apocalyptic had not been matched by substantial critical investigation of the movement at the time the Pannenberg circle were developing their views on the relation of history and revelation.

In his essay on the nature of revelation, Wilckens insisted that Jesus was an apocalypticist rather than a rabbi,[31] and interpreted his message and claims in terms of 'proleptic anticipation' similar to those of Rössler – to whom he refers with approval. Pannenberg himself is clearly influenced by Rössler at points: for example, his understanding of the relation between prophecy and apocalyptic,[32] and of the background to Jesus' relativization of the law.[33] Nevertheless, we must not permit these individual points to obscure the general point which must be emphasized: Pannenberg argues, with extensive (although at times questionable) documentation that the context of the action and destiny of Jesus of Nazareth is that of late Jewish apocalyptic expectation.[34] In so far as any event in history has meaning only in relation to the traditio-historical context within which it takes place, it necessarily follows that the meaning of the history and destiny of Jesus of Nazareth is determined by its apocalyptic context.

Pannenberg thus gives the apocalypticism of the New Testament a central place in his theology. Unlike Bultmann, Ebeling, Fuchs and Tillich, who treated the apocalyptic context and content of Jesus' activity and preaching as something of an embarrassment, from which it was necessary to extract (and thus detach) existential significance, Pannenberg treats it on its own terms, as essential to a correct understanding of the Christ-event. But how, it may be asked, is Pannenberg able to deal with so complex and such a poorly understood movement as late Jewish apocalyptic with the precision necessary for his purposes? Pannenberg argues that it is possible to identify three pervasive features of the movement:

(1) the full revelation of God is only to be found at the end of history, even though God does indeed disclose himself in the history of Israel;
(2) the end of history is of universal significance, embracing both Jew and Gentile, in that it discloses God as the God of all nations and all creation;
(3) the end of history entails a general resurrection of the dead.

While this is indeed a plausible generalization concerning the leading features of apocalypticism, it is impossible to avoid the suspicion that Pannenberg interprets the movement from a purely Christian perspective. (However, should Pannenberg choose to defend this point, it would be perfectly consistent with his general principle that the significance of an event or movement is only disclosed in its later outworking.) It is this apocalyptic context which determines the significance of the resurrection of Jesus from the dead – which Pannenberg insists to be an objective historical event, witnessed by all who had access to the evidence. Before we can consider Pannenberg's understanding of the *significance* of the resurrection, it is necessary to consider how he can treat it as *an historical event* in the first place. This brings us to Pannenberg's criticism of the principle of analogy, perhaps one of his most important contributions to the 'Jesus of history – Christ of faith' debate.

If the resurrection took place as an objective historical event, to be distinguished from mythical stories of the resuscitation of the dead heroes of mythology, it must be conceded that it was unique – and thus that there is no equivalent or analogous event in the present day. The problems raised for the historian by allegedly 'unique' events are well-established.[35] It was, however, Ernst Troeltsch who first fully articulated the consequences for theology of modern historical methods.[36] As we noted in chapter 4, Troeltsch enunciated three critical historical principles which were to be observed in this respect: the principles of *criticism*, *analogy* and *correlation*. Although Troeltsch insisted upon the necessity of *Gleichartigkeit* ('homogeneity') rather than *Gleichheit* ('absolute identity') in relation to historical events and their present day analogues, it was clear that this second principle posed serious difficulties for Christology. Traditional Christian beliefs, particularly the resurrection of Jesus, appeared to rest upon events without present-day analogies, with the result that Christian faith and historical enquiry seemed doomed to go their separate ways. As one observer has pointed out, 'without the principle of analogy, it seems impossible to understand the past; if, however, one employs the principle of analogy, it seems impossible to do justice to the alleged uniqueness of Christ.'[37] Precisely because the principle of analogy is already so important a component of the historian's methods, it would appear that certain events (by no means restricted to the history of Jesus of Nazareth, it may be added) cannot even be entertained as possible subjects for historical enquiry. Although the use of this principle had been called into question by Martin Kähler, it was Pannenberg who mounted the most sustained and penetrating criticism of the principle to date.

In his essay on 'redemptive event and history',[38] Pannenberg argued that the use of the principle of analogy in the manner suggested by Troeltsch represented the transformation of a method of enquiry into a view of reality as a whole. For Pannenberg, the *Weltanschauung* resulting from Troeltsch's unwarranted 'constriction of historico-critical enquiry' was 'biased' and 'anthropocentric', presupposing that the human viewpoint is the only valid viewpoint within history: fundamental to Pannenberg's programme is the recognition that it is God, rather than man, who is the ultimate bearer of history and its meaning. An analogy made from within the historical process is always an analogy *viewed from the standpoint of the human observer.* Pannenberg does not totally reject the use of the principle of analogy, but draws attention to what he regards as its serious abuse in defining a view of reality, rather than functioning as a tool of historical enquiry. Pannenberg draws a distinction between the *positive* and the *negative* use of the principle of analogy. An example of the former in the case of the history of Jesus of Nazareth is the crucifixion: in so far as contemporary analogues of condemnation to death and this specific mode of execution are known, this event may be deemed plausible (although it clearly requires further substantiating evidence before it may be considered proven). The negative use of analogy is based upon the Humean presupposition that if there are no other events subject to the experience of the historian which are analogous to the event under investigation, there is thereby sufficient reason to believe that the alleged 'event' did not, in fact, take place in the first instance. If there is no analogue to a past event in our present experience, that event may be deemed not to be historical (*historisch*). An obvious example from the history of Jesus of Nazareth is the resurrection, which is clearly without present-day analogues, and which must thence be deemed unhistorical. Pannenberg's point is simple, and may be stated thus: if the historian approached his work with the conviction that 'the dead do not rise', he has, in effect, already decided that Jesus did not rise, irrespective of whatever corroborating evidence may be brought forward to indicate otherwise. However:

> Historical enquiry always takes place within a predetermined context of meaning (*Bedeutungszusammenhang*), from a preunderstanding (*Vorverständnis*) of the object of enquiry, which is, however, modified and corrected in the process of investigation on the basis of the phenomenon. If history (*Historie*) does not begin in a dogmatic manner with a restricted concept of reality according to which 'dead men do not rise', it is not clear why history should not fundamentally be in a position to speak about the resurrection of Jesus as the best-established explanation of events such as the experiences of the disciples and the discovery of the empty tomb.[39]

Pannenberg's discussion of this whole question is an impassioned and impressive plea for a *neutral* approach to the whole question of the resurrection, to establish the most plausible solution to the riddle of Easter, without the dogmatic imposition of a *Weltanschauung* which excludes certain explanations on principle. Furthermore, Pannenberg argues that the resurrection took place within a cultural context (that of apocalypticism) where the idea of 'resurrection' was not merely plausible, but was actually an *expected* event. 'The expectation of resurrection must already be presupposed as a truth given by tradition.' Having established that it is not impossible to regard the resurrection as having taken place as an objective historical event – and thus thrown down the gauntlet to the Bultmann school – Pannenberg is able to proceed to enquire as to its significance within the apocalyptic context which determines its meaning.

For Pannenberg, Jesus' resurrection may be regarded as the 'pre-actualization' or 'pre-viewing' of the end of history, which derives its meaning from the apocalyptic *Weltanschauung* which Jesus shared with his contemporaries. Pannenberg summarizes the immediate significance of Jesus' resurrection in six theses,[40] of which the first four are of particular significance.

(1) If Jesus has been raised, then the end of the world has dawned.
(2) If Jesus has been raised, a Jew would recognize this as meaning that God himself had confirmed the pre-Easter activity of Jesus.
(3) Through his resurrection from the dead, Jesus moved so close to the apocalyptic figure of the 'Son of Man' that it was obvious that the 'Son of Man' was none other than the man Jesus who will come again.
(4) If Jesus, having been raised from the dead, is ascended to God, and if the end of the world has dawned as a result, then God is ultimately revealed in Jesus.

The apocalyptic tradition, in fact, recognized only the general resurrection of the dead at the end of time, so that Pannenberg is forced to interpret the *individual* resurrection of Jesus as a 'foretaste' of this general event. However, if the resurrection of Jesus did take place as an historical event, the inevitable question of the relation of the two resurrections can obviously be answered in this manner – with the result that Pannenberg is able to argue that, within the apocalyptic context of first century Palestine, the resurrection of Jesus must be understood as anticipating the final disclosure of the glory of God. It is on the basis of this insight that Pannenberg establishes the divinity of Christ.

For Pannenberg, God is disclosed indirectly through his actions in universal history. This disclosure, however, cannot be complete until the end of history, in that the future is always open to unpredictable and radical novelties which call present interpretations of the meaning of history into question. The apocalyptic movement regarded the end of history as including the general resurrection of the dead, so that it proves necessary, on account of the resurrection, to regard the divine self-disclosure as being complete in Jesus. This argument is somewhat subtle, perhaps reflecting the fact that Pannenberg's doctoral thesis concerned that most subtle of all medieval theologians, Duns Scotus, who here finds a worthy successor.[41] In that the end of history is disclosed in the resurrection of Jesus, and in that history discloses the acts of God which can only be fully interpreted as revelation from the standpoint of the *end* of history, Pannenberg is able to argue that the resurrection establishes Jesus as the final revelation of God.[42] In that the resurrection of Jesus is the actual event of revelation (in that it brings the end which stands before all men forward into history, before its time), one must be able to speak of God's self-revelation in Christ. Furthermore, this revelation must be unique and once-for-all, if it is to be a genuine self-disclosure of God, in that any future disclosure would imply the incompleteness of the first disclosure. Finally, Pannenberg argues that, as revelation is the *self*-disclosure of God, there must be a real identity of the person disclosed and the disclosing medium: therefore there must be a real identity between the disclosed God and the disclosing Christ. The *ordo cognoscendi* therefore establishes the resurrection as prior to the incarnation, in that the doctrine of the incarnation can only arise from the recognition of Jesus as the final revelation of God – a recognition which only arises through the acknowledgement of the historical nature of the resurrection, and its relation to the apocalyptic expectation of the future general resurrection of the dead at the end of the historical process itself. It is in this sense that Pannenberg refers to the 'retroactive significance' (*rückwirkende Bedeutung*) of the resurrection:[43] if Jesus had not been raised from the dead, his identity with God would have been unrecognized. However, the resurrection of Jesus has retroactive significance for his pre-Easter life, in that it confirms the claim to authority implicit in his activity. Although the argument is subtle and intensely compressed, it is sufficiently clear to command respect.

It will thus be clear that Pannenberg has developed a Christology 'from below' which is in no way a mere anthropological reduction.

The 'pre-understanding' implicit in any such Christology is not man's understanding of himself, but an understanding (specifically, that of late Jewish apocalyptic) of the significance of the resurrection which both creates an expectation of precisely such an event, and interprets its subsequent significance. The fact that the expectations and imagery of this apocalyptic context appear strange and unacceptable in the late twentieth century is of little significance, in that the *meaning* of the resurrection is 'given' by its traditio-historical context. It is therefore necessary for the modern enquirer to *understand* the context which determines the meaning of the resurrection, but not for him to *agree* with it in order to verify that 'given' meaning. A serious weakness nevertheless remains, in that Pannenberg appears to make his Christology dependent upon scholarly work in the area of late Jewish apocalyptic expectation. Pannenberg interprets the resurrection in terms of certain controversial present-day understandings of the poorly understood teachings of late Jewish apocalyptic expectations, and is therefore subject to correction or refutation in the light of developing scholarly research in this difficult area. In particular, it is open to question whether his interpretation of the apocalyptic understanding of the nature of universal history is tenable, and the suspicion has frequently been voiced that he has interpreted apocalypticism through a complex matrix of Christian and Hegelian presuppositions. Pannenberg is vulnerable in this area, and has not succeeded in creating an 'invulnerable zone' for faith.

It is clear that Pannenberg has undertaken a major new development within the development of modern German Christology, and that the subsequent decades will see more detailed critical analysis of his presuppositions and methods. It is, however, also clear that Pannenberg's presuppositions and methods are open to criticism at several points.[44] Of particular significance, it seems to us, is the weakness of his criticism of the soteriological approach to Christology, which prefaces his own approach in the *Grundzüge der Christologie*, and the apparent circularities implicit in his use of the New Testament material.[45] We propose to develop these points to indicate areas in which clarification and further justification of Pannenberg's position appears to be necessary.

In the *Grundzüge*, Pannenberg devotes an introductory chapter to a consideration of the relationship between Christology and soteriology.[46] After noting that it is impossible to separate the question of who Jesus Christ *is* from the related question of what Jesus

Christ *does*,[47] Pannenberg indicates how Christology has been heavily influenced by soteriological considerations in the course of the development of Christian thought.[48] The concept of 'salvation' has clearly been understood in a variety of manners in the course of the Christian era, varying from the realism of deification to the legalism of justification to the personalism of individual existence. How, he asks, given this variety in soteriologies, can we be sure that we are not merely attaching human desires, longings and expectations to the distant historical figure of Jesus of Nazareth, if the soteriological approach to Christology is adopted?[49] Pannenberg is, of course, too sophisticated a theologian to place much weight upon the Feuerbachian hypothesis that precisely this process underlies the Christian faith anyway: he is rather drawing attention to the Christological significance of the variety of manners in which the concept of 'salvation' has been understood. Of course, it must be pointed out in response to Pannenberg that the soteriological approach to Christology is actually based upon what 'salvation' is understood to *presuppose*, rather than how the concept of 'salvation' *is itself understood*: the variety of soteriological images and metaphors employed by the church over a period of two millenia is secondary to its underlying unity, which may be summarized in Athanasius' maxim that 'only God may save'. Salvation – however this is articulated or portrayed – can only come from God: the idea of 'salvation *in Christ*' thus raises the Christological question, in that at least a *functional*, and possibly an *ontological*, identity of God and Christ is suggested. Pannenberg does not appear to appreciate this point.

A further point which might be made at this stage relates to the changing understanding of the nature of history itself, which parallels, although to a lesser degree, the variety of manners in which salvation has been understood within the Christian community. Pannenberg appears to suggest that the inherently destructive variation in soteriological images and concerns poses a serious threat to the soteriological approach to Christology, in that it raises the possibility that 'salvation' is conceived in an anthropologically or culturally conditioned manner, which *may* (although Pannenberg is careful not to state that it *does*) reflect man's needs, aspirations or self-understanding. The appeal to the history of Jesus is thus presented as a means of establishing a more reliable foundation for Christology than man's changing concerns or self-understanding. But, it might reasonably be asked, does not man's changing understanding of the nature of *history* itself – which, at least in part, reflects his changing understanding of himself – open this approach to precisely the same difficulty? Pannenberg himself is aware of the changing understandings of history within the German consciousness over the period 1750–1960, and in the previous chapter we pointed out the considerable impact of the rise of the existentialist understanding of history upon German theology. The changing understandings of the nature of history and the role of the historian in the present day[50] must serve to call the objectivity and stability of Pannenberg's approach into question, or at least to greatly diminish, if not eliminate, its perceived advantages over the soteriological approach.

It must, however, be emphasized that Pannenberg's theological programme represents a new and more positive approach to the vexed question of the relation between faith and history than has been seen for some time. For Lessing, the accidental truths of history could never become the basis of the necessary truths of reason; however, as we indicated in chapter 1, this assertion rested upon an essentially rational and static view of reality, owing much to Spinoza and Descartes, which led to the despising of the study of history in general; the modern period has not chosen to endorse this negative attitude to history, and Pannenberg's understanding of truth may be regarded as a reversion to a more Hebraic understanding of the concept ('truth as event'), which necessarily entails historical enquiry. Where Bultmann and Barth retreated from history (the latter taking refuge in eternity), Pannenberg engaged directly with it, and with all the critical problems raised by the assertion that Christianity ultimately rests upon an *event*, rather than an *idea*.

Pannenberg's concern is essentially that of Käsemann and others engaged in the 'new quest of the historical Jesus' – to account for, and indicate the probable legitimacy of, the crucial transition from the preaching *of* Jesus to the preaching *about* Jesus. For Pannenberg, this necessarily entails the enquiry into the 'historical reality of Jesus of Nazareth'. The difficulty is that Pannenberg is obliged, along with everyone else, to base his analysis upon the New Testament documents themselves – which are universally recognized to be unsuitable as historical sources. Furthermore, in so far as the soteriological convictions of the first generation(s) of Christians are inextricably linked with the form and content of these sources, Pannenberg, by using them, is inevitably obliged to base his conclusions, at least in part, if not upon his own soteriological convinctions, then upon those of an earlier generation. The essential difficulty, which Pannenberg does not appear to have resolved, is that of determining the extent of the influence of these convictions upon the New Testament passages which Pannenberg employs in his analysis of the significance of the resurrection of Jesus. The resurrection of Jesus is treated by New Testament writers such as Paul as part of the *kerygma*, with the inevitable result that its soteriological significance has become enmeshed with the event itself. Every testimony which we possess to the historical and existential significance of Jesus of Nazareth is an expression of, and a consequence of, faith in him, and cannot be isolated from this faith. It is thus necessary to draw attention to what appears to be a certain degree of ambiguity in Pannenberg's discussion of faith and reason.

Pannenberg's theological programme appears to be based upon the assumption that it is possible to move from understanding to faith, based upon the rational analysis of covert universal history. Knowledge of the history of Jesus of Nazareth appears to be treated as prior to, and independent of, faith. Yet, as has been demonstrated beyond reasonable doubt, the New Testament sources present historical facts as they are perceived by faith – faith operates in the perception and interpretation of historical fact in the *kerygma*. Pannenberg may well insist that knowledge is *logically* prior to faith – yet his use of sources suggests that this logical point is confounded on theological grounds, through the irreversible intermingling of faith and history in his sources. Just as a soteriological approach to Christology is latent in Pannenberg's alleged 'historical' approach, so faith is latent within the 'reason' he employs. Indeed, it is possible to argue that Pannenberg's fundamental assumption (that God reveals himself in history) is a presupposition of faith, which thus gives *faith* logical priority over knowledge.[51]

This point is of particular importance, as it gives added weight to the conservative Lutheran Paul Althaus's criticisms of Pannenberg's concept of 'revelation as history'.[52] Taking up Pannenberg's assertion in he 'seven dogmatic theses on the doctrine of revelation' (especially the third thesis), Althaus argues that Pannenberg's concept of the 'universal openness' of revelation in history fails to adequately explain why 'everyone who has eyes to see' does not recognize history as revelation in the first place. For Althaus, revelation must be understood to be *hidden* in history, requiring divine assistance, through the gift of the Holy Spirit, *if it is to be recognized as such by faith*, in that history is not recognized *as revelation* without the divine gift of faith. This important point may be related to our observation that Pannenberg is actually obliged to presuppose, apparently on the basis of faith, that history is, in fact, the revelation of God, a pre-understanding of history which would most emphatically not command universal assent outside Christian circles. In his reply to Althaus, Pannenberg pointedly excluded any 'knowledge' other than *natural* knowledge - that is, universally open and reasonable knowledge.[54] Nevertheless, it is clear that this response is not satisfactory: the question concerning why some recognize history as revelation, and others do not, raises crucial points relating to the alleged 'openness' of revelation which merit further consideration on Pannenberg's part.[55]

Pannenberg's approach necessitates beginning with the history of Jesus of Nazareth, interpreting his *Wirken* (such as his preaching) in terms of his *Geschick* (particularly his resurrection). Whereas the soteriological approach, exemplified by the kerygmatic Christology of Bultmann, begins directly from the *kerygma* (either in its apostolic or present-day form), and proceeds from that point to consider the significance of Jesus of Nazareth, Pannenberg's approach necessitates beginning from the *kerygma* and reconstructing the history of Jesus of Nazareth on its basis, in order that this history may be interpreted. Pannenberg himself is obliged to begin from the *kerygma*, precisely because he is obliged to use the New Testament sources, thus moving backwards before he may move forwards. The Christian *kerygma* must be recognized as having had a far greater effect upon both the context and the content of the New Testament material than Pannenberg appears willing to concede. It is quite simply impossible to begin Christological speculation from the history of Jesus of Nazareth, precisely because the primitive Christian kerygma has influenced the interpretation placed upon that history, and hence upon the presentation of that history within the New Testament, by the first Christians. Furthermore, if the history of Jesus of Nazareth were to be objectively reconstructed by universally accepted means, the question of the manner in which it is interpreted thus comes to be acutely pressing. Can a late twentieth century mind really be expected to come to the same interpretation of every aspect of that history as a contemporary mind? The experienced meaning of that history is inextricably linked to, and 'given' with, that history itself (as Pannenberg himself emphasizes). Only by being born again as a first century Palestinian, by being immersed in the matrix of the messianic and apocalyptic hopes, expectations and beliefs of the period (and perhaps even only within one specific section of a complex movement), and by interpreting that history at first hand, can Pannenberg hope to reconstruct Christology with the precision which he appears to demand. As Dilthey emphasises, the experienced meaning of a situation is trapped wthin the historicality of that situation – and although the 'experienced meaning' is transmitted to us in the *kerygma*, the historical situation itself is lost for ever. The *event* of the resurrection of Jesus is clearly and inextricably linked with the *interpretation* of the meaning of that event in the New Testament kerygma – upon which we are ultimately dependent for our Christological reflections. Unless Pannenberg destroys this synthesis of event and interpretation, characteristic of the New Testament 'histories' and *kerygmata* alike, he cannot hope to interpret the resurrection (or, indeed, *any* aspect of the history of Jesus) in terms significantly different from those already 'given' to him – and hence the most he can reasonably expect to do is confirm the internal consistency of the *kerygma*, and indicate its probable legitimation in terms of its (poorly-understood) historical context. What Pannenberg appears to be doing, however, is attempting to find a basis for faith in historical fact[56] – a procedure dismissed by Käsemann as absurd.

Pannenberg is unquestionably correct in suggesting that the analysis of the history of Jesus of Nazareth is the most appropriate and desirable method of reconstructing a Christology: that method is, however, no longer open to us today. We are primarily concerned with the question of how a Christology may be constructed, or an existing Christology or range of Christologies verified, here and now, twenty centuries after the history of Jesus of Nazareth has taken place. The only persons in a position to undertake such an analysis were the apostles, and their conclusions – as both event and interpretation, inextricably linked – are encapsulated in the *kerygma*. Pannenberg's method need only – and, in fact, does little more than – demonstrate that the content of that *kerygma* is inherently plausible.

It will, however, be clear that Pannenberg's critique of the soteriological approach to Christology has considerable force under two circumstances:

(1) The actual historical reality of Jesus of Nazareth is ignored, so that the proclamation of the community of faith is not grounded in the history and destiny of Jesus of Nazareth. This is a real possibility within the context of the theologies of A. E. Biedermann or Paul

Tillich – but it is not an inevitable consequence of the soteriological approach to Christology!

(2) A discontinuity is suggested between the proclamation concerning Christ and the historical person of Jesus of Nazareth – in other words, that the Christian proclamation is either an *inaccurate* or an *inadequate* representation of the historical and existential significance of Jesus of Nazareth. This suggestion lay at the heart of the quest for the historical Jesus initiated during the *Aufklärung*, although it receives scant critical support today. It most emphatically does not underlie the soteriological approach to Christology!

For Pannenberg, the signficance of an event is only to be fully discerned at the end of the historical process: similarly, the significance of a Christological development may only be fully discerned when the effect of its stimulus upon a tradition is fully developed and worked out. It is thus difficult to assess Pannenberg's significance, in that it is too soon to determine whether he has initiated a new and significant line of enquiry in modern German Christology, or whether he has merely sidetracked the debate into what may prove to be a theological cul-de-sac. All the indications, however, are that a new line of enquiry has been mapped out which will exercise considerable influence over subsequent Christological reflection within the German Christological tradition. A similar judgement may be passed upon the Christology of Jürgen Moltmann and Eberhard Jüngel, to which we now turn.

NOTES

1 See Raymond E. Brown, 'After Bultmann, What? – An Introduction to the Post-Bultmannians', *Catholic Biblical Quarterly* 26 (1964), pp. 1–30. The outstanding study in English remains James M. Robinson, *A New Quest of the Historical Jesus* (London, 1959), especially pp. 48–125. The reader who has yet to work his way through this important essay is recommended to do so at the earliest opportunity. Robinson has been criticized at several points of importance: see Van A. Harvey and S. M. Ogden, 'How New is the 'New Quest of the Historical Jesus'?', in *The Historical Jesus and the Kerygmatic Christ*, ed. C. E. Braaten and R. A. Harrisville (New York, 1964), pp. 197–242. For Robinson's response, see his *Kerygma und historischer Jesus* (Zurich, 2nd edn, 1967).

2 'Das Problem des historischen Jesus', reprinted in *Exegetische Versuche und*

Besinnungen I (Göttingen, 2nd edn, 1960), pp. 187–214; English translation in *Essays on New Testament Themes* (London, 1964), pp. 15–47 (note that this translation renders *Historie* as 'mere history', and *Geschichte* as 'history' – an interpretative, and potentially confusing, practice).

3 See his later essay 'Sackgassen im Streit um den historischen Jesus', in *Exegetische Versuche und Besinnungen II* (Göttingen, 2nd edn, 1965), pp. 31–68; p. 53; English translation in *New Testament Questions of Today* (London, 1969), pp. 23–66; p. 47.

4 See his important essay 'Der gegewärtige Stand der Debatte um das Problem des historischen Jesus', in *Der historische Jesus und der kerygmatische Christus*, ed. H. Ristow and K. Matthiae (Berlin, 2nd edn, 1961), pp. 12–25. For criticism, see Käsemann, 'Sackgassen', pp. 32–41 (English translation, pp. 24–35). A shortened English version of this essay may be found in *Expository Times* 69 (1958), pp. 333–9. The approach he suggests is developed with some brilliance in *Die Gleichnisse Jesu* (Göttingen, 8th edn, 1970); English translation from the sixth German edition: *The Parables of Jesus* (London, 3rd edn, 1976).

5 *Neutestamentliche Theologie. 1. Teil. Die Verkündigung Jesu* (Gütersloh, 1971); *New Testament Theology I* (London, 1975).

6 'Das Problem des historischen Jesus', pp. 206–12; 'The Problem of the Historical Jesus', pp. 37–45.

7 *Jesus von Nazareth* (Stuttgart, 6th edn, 1963); *Jesus of Nazareth* (London, 1960).

8 Reinhard Slenckza, *Geschichtlichkeit und Personsein Jesu Christi: Studien zur christologischen Problematik der historischen Jesus-Frage* (Göttingen, 1967), p. 311.

9 Wolfhart Pannenberg, 'Heilsgeschehen und Geschichte', *Kerygma und Dogma* 5 (1959), pp. 218–37; 259–88; English translation in *Basic Questions in Theology I* (London, 1970), pp. 15–80.

10 Two useful introductions to Pannenberg's theology in English may be noted: E. Frank Tupper, *The Theology of Wolfhart Pannenberg* (London, 1974); Allan D. Galloway, *Wolfhart Pannenberg* (Contemporary Religious Thinkers Series: London, 1973). For a biographical profile of Pannenberg, see the introductory essay by Richard John Neuhas, 'Wolfhart Pannenberg: Portrait of a Theologian', in Pannenberg, *Theology and the Kingdom of God* (Philadelphia, 1969), pp. 9–50.

11 See Tupper, *Theology of Wolfhart Pannenberg*, pp. 21–5.

12 'Heilsgeschehen und Geschichte', p. 218; 'Redemptive Event and History', p. 15.

13 See the seven 'Dogmatic Theses on the Doctrine of Revelation', in *Offenbarung als Geschichte*, ed. Wolfhart Pannenberg (Kerygma und Dogma Beiheft 1: Göttingen, 1961), pp. 91–114; English translation in *Revelation*

as History, ed. W. Pannenberg (London, 1969), pp. 123–58. For the initial reaction to this work, see Paul Althaus, 'Offenbarung als Geschichte und Glaube: Bemerkungen zu W. Pannenbergs Begriff der Offenbarung', *Theologische Literaturzeitung* 87 (1962), 321–30; Lothar Steiger, 'Offenbarungsgeschichte und theologische Vernunft: Zur Theologie W. Pannenbergs', *Zeitschrift für Theologie und Kirche* 59 (1962), pp. 88–113. For Pannenberg's response to Althaus, see Pannenberg, 'Einsicht und Glaube: Antwort an Paul Althaus', *Theologische Literaturzeitung* 88 (1963), pp. 81–92.

14 *Offenbarung als Geschichte*, pp. 91–5; *Revelation as History*, pp. 125–31. With all of these theses, the reader is referred to Pannenberg's remarkably lucid discussion for further details. A more detailed analysis may be found in Ignace Berten, *Histoire, révélation et foi: dialogue avec Wolfhart Pannenberg* (Brussels/Paris, 1969), pp. 17–45; Maurizio Pagano, *Storia ed escatologia nel pensiero di W. Pannenberg* (Milan, 1973), pp. 64–134; Mauro Pedrazzoli, *Intellectus quaerens fidem: fede-ragione in W. Pannenberg* (Rome, 1981), pp. 55–98; Pierre Warin, *Le chemin de la théologie chez Wolfhart Pannenberg* (Rome, 1981), pp. 75–117. The reader restricted to the English language will find Tupper, *Theology of Wolfhart Pannenberg*, pp. 79–128, reliable. Warin and Pedrazzoli, of course, are able to draw upon more recent secondary studies, as well as Pannenberg's later writings on the subject. Harvey, *The Historian and the Believer*, refers only once to Pannenberg, in passing (p. 205): the absence of any discussion of *Offenbarung als Geschichte* in this work is difficult to understand.

15 *Offenbarung als Geschichte*, pp. 95–8; *Revelation as History*, pp. 131–5.

16 *Offenbarung als Geschichte*, pp. 98–102; *Revelation as History*, pp. 135–9.

17 *Offenbarung als Geschichte*, pp. 103–6; *Revelation as History*, pp. 139–45.

18 *Offenbarung als Geschichte*, pp. 107–9; *Revelation as History*, pp. 145–8.

19 *Offenbarung als Geschichte*, pp. 109–11; *Revelation as History*, pp. 149–52.

20 *Offenbarung als Geschichte*, pp. 112–4; *Revelation as History*, pp. 152–5.

21 Pannenberg, 'The Revelation of God in Jesus of Nazareth', in *Theology as History*, ed. James M. Robinson and John B. Cobb (New Frontiers in Theology 3: New York, 1967), pp. 101–33; pp. 126–7. See further Iain G. Nicol, 'Facts and Meanings: Wolfhart Pannenberg's Theology as History and the Role of the Critical-Historical Method', *Religious Studies* 12 (1976), pp. 129–39.

22 Pannenberg, *Grundzüge der Christologie* (Gütersloh, 6th edn, 1982), pp. 22–3; *Jesus – God and Man* (London, 1970), pp. 28–30. Note p. 23 (English translation, p. 30) 'Die Aufgabe der Christologie ist es also, aus der Geschichte Jesu die wahre Erkenntnis seiner Bedeutung zu begründen.'

23 For example, see *Grundzüge der Christologie*, pp. 15–24, especially p. 17; *Jesus – God and Man*, pp. 21–30, especially p. 23.

24 In an important postscript to the fifth and subsequent editions of the

Grundzüge, Pannenberg concedes the difficulties of the 'from above – from below' dichotomy: *Grundzüge der Christologie*, pp. 421–3; *Jesus – God and Man*, pp. 405–7. These difficulties are not, however, of material significance to his theological programme. See further Nicholas Lash, 'Up and Down in Christology', in *New Studies in Theology I*, ed. Stephen Sykes and Derek Holmes (London, 1980), pp. 31–46.

25 For example, see Ernst Käsemann, 'Die Anfänge christlicher Theologie', *Zeitschrift für Theologie und Kirche* 57 (1960), pp. 162–85, especially the assertion that 'apocalyptic – since the preaching of Jesus cannot really be described as theology – was the mother of all Christian theology' (p. 180); Gerhard Ebeling, 'Der Grund christlicher Theologie', *Zeitschrift für Theologie und Kirche* 58 (1961), pp. 227–44; Ernst Fuchs, 'Über die Aufgabe einer christlichen Theologie', *Zeitschrift für Theologie und Kirche* 58 (1961), pp. 245–67; Käsemann, 'Zum Thema der urchristlichen Apokalyptik', *Zeitschrift für Theologie und Kirche* 59 (1962), pp. 257–84. The papers by Ebeling and Fuchs, originally delivered to the editorial conference of *Zeitschrift für Theologie und Kirche* on 30 April 1961, are responses to Käsemann's 1960 essay. Käsemann's second essay responds to these papers.

26 *Theologie des Alten Testaments* (2 vols: Munich, 4th edn, 1965), vol. 2, pp. 315–30; p. 330; as pointed out by Hans Dieter Benz, 'Zum Problem des religionsgeschichtlichen Verständnisses der Apokalyptik', *Zeitschrift für Theologie und Kirche* 63 (1966), pp. 391–409; p. 392. The English translation (*Old Testament Theology* (2 vols: London, 1965)) follows the third German edition at this point.

27 Ulrich Wilckens, 'Das Offenbarungsverständnis in der Geschichte des Urchristentums', in *Offenbarung als Geschichte*, pp. 42–90; *Revelation as History*, pp. 55–121.

28 Dietrich Rössler, *Gesetz und Geschichte: Untersuchungen zur Theologie der jüdischen Apokalyptik und der pharisäischen Orthodoxie* (Neukirchen, 1960).

29 For example, A. Nissen, 'Tora und Geschichte im Spätjudentum', *Novum Testamentum* 9 (1967), pp. 241–77. It should also be noted that Klaus Koch – a member of the 'Pannenberg circle' – based his analysis of the apocalyptic understanding of history on the book of Daniel: K. Koch, 'Spätisraelitisches Geschichtsdenken am Beispiel des Buches Daniel', *Historische Zeitschrift* 193 (1961), pp. 1–32. However, the Book of Daniel can hardly be taken as typical of the apocalyptic understanding of history, in that there is a virtual absence of the cosmological speculation typical of the apocalyptic literature: see L. Ginzberg, 'Some Observations on the Attitude of the Synagogue towards the Apocalyptic-Eschatological Writings', *Journal of Biblical Literature* 41 (1922), pp. 115–36; W. Murdoch, 'History and Revelation in Jewish Apocalypticism', *Interpretation* 21 (1967), pp. 167–87.

30 For example, see von Rad, *Theologie des Alten Testaments*, vol. 2, pp. 317–20; 322, who locates its origins in the wisdom tradition.
31 *Offenbarung als Geschichte*, p. 50; *Revelation as History*, p. 66.
32 See Pannenberg, 'Revelation of God in Jesus of Nazareth', especially p. 122; *Grundzüge der Christologie*, pp. 222–3; *Jesus – God and Man*, pp. 216–7. The reference to Koch's study of the understanding of history in Daniel (p. 222 n.16; English translation, p. 217 n.17) should be noted: see the critical comments made above at note 29.
33 See Pannenberg, 'Revelation of God in Jesus of Nazareth', pp. 111–2, where Wilckens's essay in *Offenbarung als Geschichte* (which, as we have noted, is heavily dependent upon Rössler) is cited in support.
34 See Pagano, *Storia ed escatologia*, pp. 143–71.
35 See Carey B. Joynt and Nicholas Rescher, 'The Problem of Uniqueness in History', *History and Theory* 1 (1960–1), pp. 150–62. The same authors' earlier paper is also relevant here: 'On Explanation in History', *Mind* 68 (1959), pp. 383–8.
36 Ernst Troeltsch, 'Über historische und dogmatische Methode in der Theologie', *Gesammelte Schriften* (4 vols: Tübingen, 1912–25), vol. 2, pp. 729–53. See chapter four of the present study for a full discussion.
37 Van A. Harvey, *The Historian and the Believer* (London, 1967), p. 32.
38 'Heilsgeschehen und Geschichte'; 'Redemptive Event and History', *passim*. Two useful studies in English are: Ted Peters, 'The Use of Analogy in Historical Method', *Catholic Biblical Quarterly* 35 (1973), pp. 474–82 (which deals specifically with Pannenberg, despite the generality of the title); Herbert Burhenn, 'Pannenberg's Argument for the Historicity of the Resurrection', *Journal of the American Academy of Religion* 40 (1972), pp. 368–79. G. E. Michalson, 'Pannenberg on the Resurrection and Historical Method', *Scottish Journal of Theology* 33 (1980), pp. 345–59, appears to become confused over precisely what Pannenberg means by the resurrection (pp. 355–7), and his conclusion that 'Pannenberg's conception of the resurrection turns out to be as vague, indeterminate and unhelpful as the Bultmannian notion of the "rise of faith in the disciples" (p. 358) represents a serious misunderstanding of what Pannenberg was trying to do (and may well have succeeded in doing).
39 *Grundzüge der Christologie*, p. 107; *Jesus – God and Man*, p. 109. The whole section dealing with 'the resurrection of Jesus as an historical problem', pp. 85–103 (English translation, pp. 88–106) should be read.
40 *Grundzüge der Christologie*, pp. 62–9; *Jesus – God and Man*, pp. 67–73.
41 Pannenberg, *Die Prädestinationslehre des Duns Skotus* (Göttingen, 1954).
42 See *Grundzüge der Christologie*, pp. 113–89, especially pp. 127–31. *Jesus – God and Man*, pp. 115–90, especially pp. 129–33.
43 For example, *Grundzüge der Christologie*, pp. 134–5: *Jesus – God and Man*, pp. 136–7. Pannenberg's use of Walter Künneth, *Theologie der Auferstehung*

(Munich, 4th edn, 1951), is significant.

44 See Steiger, 'Offenbarungsgeschichte und theologische Vernunft', for penetrating criticisms. Pannenberg responds to some earlier criticisms in an important *Nachwort* to the fifth and subsequent German editions: *Grundzüge der Christologie*, pp. 415–26; *Jesus – God and Man*, pp. 399–410. For further references and discussion, see Tupper, *Theology of Wolfhart Pannenberg*, pp. 253–302. Pannenberg's later essay 'Christologie und Soteriologie', *Kerygma und Dogma* 21 (1975), pp. 159–75, should also be consulted in connection with such criticisms.

45 Alister E. McGrath, 'Christologie und Soteriologie: Eine Entgegnung zu Wolfhart Pannenbergs Kritik des soteriologischen Ansatzes in der Christologie', *Theologische Zeitschrift* 42 (1986), forthcoming.

46 *Grundzüge der Christologie*, pp. 32–44; *Jesus – God and Man*, pp. 38–49.

47 *Grundzüge der Christologie*, pp. 32–3; *Jesus – God and Man*, pp. 38–9.

48 *Grundzüge der Christologie*, pp. 33–41; *Jesus – God and Man*, pp. 39–47.

49 *Grundzüge der Christologie*, p. 41; *Jesus – God and Man*, p. 47.

50 The following studies dating from Pannenberg's formative period may be noted with care: Gerhard Ritter, 'Gegenwärtige Lage und Zukunftsaufgaben deutscher Geschichtswissenschaft', *Historische Zeitschrift* 170 (1950), pp. 1–22; O. F. Anderle, 'Theoretische Geschichte', *Historische Zeitschrift* 185 (1958), pp. 1–54; H. Heimpel, 'Geschichte und Geschichtswissenschaft', *Vierteljahreshefte für Zeitgeschichte* 5 (1957), pp. 1–17. Pannenberg appears to be influenced by Collingwood: more recent hermeneutics of history adopt a somewhat different approach – see A. C. Danto, *Analytical Philosophy of History* (Cambridge, 1965).

51 See the thoughtful study of Helmut G. Harder and W. Taylor Stevenson, 'The Continuity of Faith and History in the Theology of Wolfhart Pannenberg: Toward an Erotics of History', *Journal of Religion* 51 (1971), pp. 34–56.

52 Althaus, 'Offenbarung als Geschichte und Glaube'.

53 Althaus, 'Offenbarung als Geschichte und Glaube', 328.

54 Pannenberg, 'Einsicht und Glaube'. In this essay, Pannenberg develops an unusual doctrine of the Holy Spirit, which clearly requires elaboration, particularly in terms of its relation to the *kerygma*. In view of Pannenberg's programme of developing a Christology 'from below' *within a Trinitarian context*, it is clearly of considerable importance that this aspect of his theology be developed, and its relation to more traditional understandings of the Holy Spirit analysed.

55 See Pedrazzoli, *Intellectus quaerens fidem*, for a useful discussion of the points raised.

56 See the critical comments of Hans Conzelmann, 'Randbemerkungen zur Lage im Neuen Testament', *Evangelische Theologie* 22 (1962), p. 228.

8

The Crucified God: Moltmann and Jüngel

The new interest in apocalyptic which we noted in connection with the 'new quest of the historical Jesus' led to a new emphasis in the early 1960s upon the eschatological dimension of the Christian faith. The work which is widely held to be the best example of this new interest in eschatology is Jürgen Moltmann's *Theologie der Hoffnung* ('Theology of Hope'), which appeared in 1964.[1] In this work, Moltmann develops the consequences of regarding eschatology as the 'universal horizon of all theology in general'.[2] Taking up Barth's famous prophetic statement in the second edition of the *Römerbrief* concerning the radically eschatological nature of Christianity, Moltmann insists that Christianity is *totally* eschatological.[3] By thus transferring eschatology from the appendices to the prolegomena of Christian dogmatics, Moltmann is able to characterize Christianity as a 'religion of expectation', orientated towards the future and the promised fulfilment of the promises of God. All theological statements are thus 'statements of hope', and all theological concepts are 'anticipations' (*Vorgriffe*). The strong parallels between Moltmann and Marxism on this point has served to intensify awareness of the importance of the theme of *liberation* in the Christian tradition. As Moltmann puts it: 'The theologian is not concerned with *interpreting* the world, history and human nature, but with their *transformation*, in the expectation of a divine transformation (*sondern sie in der Erwartung göttlicher Veränderung zu verändern*).'[4] Moltmann grounds his 'theology of hope' upon the *theologia crucis*, the 'theology of the cross', in that the 'theology of hope' is grounded in the crucifixion and resurrection of Christ. The sombre scene at Calvary, and the present suffering of the Christian community, give the 'theology of hope' a perspective and a foundation which prevent it ever becoming mere utopianism or a flight from reality into the realms of futurist fantasy. Thus Moltmann prefaces his Christological classic *Der gekreuzigte Gott* ('The Crucified God') with the assertion that:

...the theology of the cross is nothing other than the reverse side of the Christian theology of hope, if this has its point of departure in the resurrection of *the one who was crucified*. The 'theology of hope' itself was, as may be seen therein, already being developed into an *eschatologia crucis*...The 'theology of hope' is set up by the *resurrection* of the one who was crucified, and I am now turning to examine the *cross* of the one who is risen. I was then concerned with the remembrance of Christ in the form of the *hope* of his future, and I am now concerned with hope in the form of the remembrance of his death.[5]

This important statement indicates that Moltmann's major Christological work is a continuation, and an important qualification, of the 'theology of hope'. It is to an examination of this work that we now turn.

It is essential to appreciate that *Der gekreuzigte Gott* derives not merely its title, but also a significant amount of its theological substance, from the *theologia crucis* of Martin Luther.[6] In the preface, Moltmann indicates the high importance which he came to attach to this theology, which spoke of abandonment by God, in the immediate aftermath of the Second World War, as he – and a generation of theologians with him – returned to the lecture theatres and seminar rooms from the prisoner of war camps.[7] For Luther, everything in Christian theology – from the doctrine of God downwards – was established by, and was subject to criticism on the basis of, the cross of Christ: *crux probat omnia*.[8] For Moltmann, the cross is either the end of all theology, or else the beginning of all specifically *Christian* theology:

'My God, why have you forsaken me'? Every Christian theology and every Christian existence fundamentally respond to this question of the dying Jesus. Both protest-atheism and the metaphysical revolt against God also respond to this question. Either the Jesus who was abandoned by God is the end of all theology, or the beginning of a specifically Christian, and therefore critical and liberating, theology and existence.[9]

As such, for Moltmann as for Luther, the cross of Christ is the decisive epistemological criterion for our knowledge of God: if there is no more to the end of Jesus than his abandonment and death upon the cross, then atheism is the only authentic response to the suffering of the world; Jesus' message perishes with his person, so intimate is the link between his person and his gospel. Equally, Jesus, both God and man, suffered and died on the cross; if it is impossible for God to suffer or die – as an exponent of classical theism would insist to be the case – the event of the cross loses its significance. Moltmann is therefore obliged to challenge protest-atheism on the one hand, and classical theism on the other, in order to demonstrate the possibility and the nature of an authentically *Christian* theology. We begin our analysis by considering the significance of the question of whether God can be said to suffer, and the importance of Moltmann's answer to this question.

As is well known, the development of Christian doctrine in the first five centuries was subject to considerable influence from the Greek philosophical milieu (a complex matrix of various types of Platonism and Stoicism).[10] One particular element of the concept of God associated with this milieu was the concept of divine *apatheia* ('impassibility'),[11] which plays a particularly significant role in the theology of the Hellenistic Jewish theologian Philo,[12] as well as in the Christian tradition of the first two centuries up to Clement of Alexandria.[13] The biblical portrayal of God, however, raised difficulties for this doctrine: the Old Testament prophetic tradition portrayed God as suffering[14] – which caused considerable discomfort to the Hellenistic translators of the Septuagint![15] – and the New Testament accounts of Christ's suffering, when linked with the Alexandrian Logos-Christology, clearly raised the possibility of a suffering God.[16] As a result, there has been a permanent tension between two elements within the Christian conception of God. The recognition of the *dogmatic* dimension of the problem dates from the nineteenth century;[17] the full recognition of the *apologetic* dimension of the problem, however, dates from the present century,[18] in the aftermath of two world wars of unparalleled viciousness, which raised once more the vexed problem of theodicy. It is to this *political* aspect of the theodicy question that Moltmann addresses himself in *Der gekreuzigte Gott*. Where an earlier generation of apologists grappled somewhat ineffectively with the problem of natural suffering – and the Lisbon earthquake of 1755 probably stimulated more theological reflection on this matter than any event before or after – Moltmann is concerned with the suffering inflicted by man upon man. For Moltmann, Auschwitz symbolizes the dreadful question which Christian theology is forced to answer if it is to have any continuing relevance and integrity in the modern period: where is God in such suffering? Christian theology is obliged to meet the objections of protest-atheism against a God who permits such atrocities to take place. For Moltmann, protest-atheism is effective against a monotheistic understanding of God, such as that of classical theism, whose omnipotence and goodness are called into question by the presence of human evil and suffering in the world. Arguing that the foundation of any serious atheism is the problem of suffering, Moltmann insists that the specifically *Christian* idea of God must be established and evaluated on the basis of the experience of the suffering of God in the cross of Christ:

> God was not reduced to silence, nor was he inactive in the cross of Jesus. Nor was he absent in the God-forsakenness of Jesus. He acted in Jesus, the Son of God; in that men betrayed him, handed him over and delivered him up to death, God himself delivered him up (*hat Gott selbst ihn dahingegeben*). In the passion of the Son, the Father himself suffers the pain of abandonment. In the death of the Son, death comes upon God himself (*kommt der Tod auf Gott selbst*), and the Father suffers the death of the Son in his love for sinful man.[19]

The central concept employed by Moltmann in his analysis of the event of the cross is that of *Dahingabe*, 'delivering up' corresponding to the Greek verb *paradidonai*. Drawing heavily – perhaps too heavily – upon the Zurich dissertation of Wiard Popkes,[20] Moltmann identifies a double *Dahingabe* in the event of the cross: the Father 'delivers up' his Son to the fate of death; the Son 'delivers himself up' for sinful man.[21] There is a 'deep conformity' or 'community' of will between the Father and the Son, which is expressed most powerfully at the moment at which it appears to be absent – in the godforsaken and accursed death of Jesus on the cross. Moltmann thus views what happened upon the cross as an event (*Geschehen*) between God and the Son of God – an event which calls into question the interpretations which the atheist and classical theist provide of the cross in favour of a trinitarian theology of the cross.[22] On this basis, Moltmann is able to argue that the criticisms of protest-atheism are misguided, in that they are directed against a God (that is, the presently omnipotent and sovereign Lord of classical theism) who does not actually exist.

Moltmann criticizes classical theism for its uncritical adoption of the axiom of the divine *apatheia*,[23] as well as H. Richard Niebuhr's often-repeated (and much less frequently justified) assertion that Christianity is ultimately radical monotheism.[24] In this sense, Moltmann has often playfully suggested that he considers himself to be an *a*-theist.[25] Faith in the one who was crucified points to the identity and nature of the God who is really God for us, providing the criterion necessary to reject the superstitions which arise within Christianity itself, as well as the secular ideologies of legitimation. Thus for Moltmann, the essence of Christianity is not belief in God *per se*, but faith in Jesus, the one who was crucified and who is risen again. In this sense, Moltmann appears to develop a 'revelational fundamentalism', in that his emphasis upon the event of the cross is interpreted as the event in which God makes himself known.[26] 'God is revealed in the cross of the God-forsaken Christ.'[27] Moltmann thus makes *theology* posterior to *Christology*, in that it is our understanding of the event of the cross which shapes and determines our understanding of God, and forces us to re-evaluate inadequate (which, for Moltmann, means non-Trinitarian) concepts of God. This assertion has had considerable impact upon Moltmann's contemporaries (such as Eberhard Jüngel and the Roman Catholic theologian Walter Kasper), and has led to growing emphasis upon the necessity to resolve the Christological question before a resolution of the theological question is possible.

This new recognition of the *importance* of Christology is related to Moltmann's insistence that the 'death of Jesus' must be seen as a statement about God. Moltmann observes shrewdly that earlier Protestant theology tended to regard the cross primarily as a means of expiating human sin, but failed to ask the crucial question: 'What does the cross of Jesus mean for God himself?' It is this point which Moltmann detects as lying behind Paul Althaus' somewhat delphic remark: 'Jesus died for God before he died for us.' Liberal Protestantism was even worse in this respect, developing a 'Jesuology' which saw the death of Jesus as faithfulness of his 'calling' (*Beruf*), and an example of obedience in suffering.[28] For Moltmann, the cross of Christ demonstrates that human suffering is incorporated into, and transformed within, the history of God. Although the spectres of patripassianism and theopaschitism are raised by such assertions, Moltmann is able to avoid these ancient heresies by insisting that the Father and the Son experience the crucifixion in different manners: the Father suffers the grief of the loss of his Son, and the Son suffers the agony of God-forsakenness.[29] The Father delivers up his Son on the cross in order that he may be the Father of all those who are delivered up; the Son is delivered up to this death in order to become the Lord of both the dead and the living. In making the assertion that God suffers, Moltmann broke new – and apparently perilous – ground in modern theology, taking a position not previously acknowledged even by Karl Barth, who had little hesitation in breaking with classical theism at other points. If the event of the cross has *any* meaning for God himself, it can only mean that he suffers the death of his Son. Turning theory into praxis, Moltmann argues that the *historical* event of the crucifixion gives solace and strength to those presently suffering, and the *eschatological* event of the resurrection of the one who was crucified points to the final eschatological resolution of human suffering. The theological foundation thus laid for 'liberation theology' will be evident. It will also be evident that Moltmann has raised an intriguing question which cannot be ignored: can one speak of the '*death* of God'? Moltmann replies in the negative, recognizing death *in* God[30] – by which he appears to mean *death in the history of God*.[31] 'When God becomes man in Jesus of Nazareth, he not only enters into the finitude of man, but, in his death on the cross, also enters into the situation of man's God-forsakenness'.[32] The following passage perhaps summarizes Moltmann's position most succinctly, as well as raising a question which we shall pursue in the following paragraph:

> A trinitarian theology of the cross recognises God in the negative [element of the world] (*im Negativen*), and therefore the negative [element of the world] in God, and in this dialectical way is panentheistic. For in the hidden way of humiliation to the point of the cross, all that is (*alles Seiende*) and all that annihilates (*alles Vernichtendes*) have already been taken up (*aufgehoben*) in God, and God begins to become 'all in all'. To recognise God in the cross of Christ, conversely, means to recognise the cross, inescapable suffering, death and hopeless rejection in God.[33]

The strongly Hegelian overtones to this passage – and to Moltmann's understanding of the relationship between God and history in general[34] – render its translation difficult, particularly the statement that the contradictory elements have been 'taken up in God': the German term *Aufhebung* is often used in the Hegelian sense of 'sublimation', in the sense of resolving a dialectical tension, and it is possible that Moltmann may wish to convey the idea of the resolution of the seemingly irresolvable dialectic between 'being' and 'non-being' in the resurrection of the one who was crucified. The above cited passage is of particular importance in that it illustrates the 'dialectical principle of knowledge', to which we now turn.

Moltmann contrasts the 'analogical principle of knowledge' ('like is known from like') with the dialectical principle ('like is known from unlike'):

> As applied to Christian theology, this means that God is only revealed as 'God' in his opposite, in his Godlessness and God-forsakenness. In concrete terms: God is revealed in the cross of the God-forsaken Christ. His grace is revealed in sinners. His righteousness is revealed in the unrighteousness and those without rights, and his election of grace in the damned. The epistemological principle of the theology of the cross can only be this dialectical principle: the divinity of God is revealed in the paradox of the cross.[35]

This principle has been heavily criticized,[36] in that it appears to call into question the actuality of revelation in the first place. It is, however, clear that Moltmann is simply developing a major theme of Luther's *theologia crucis* – namely, the *indirectness* or *hiddenness* of God's revelation.[37] For Luther, as for Moltmann, man has preconceptions of the form which God's self-revelation should take (expressed in the 'principle of analogy'), which inhibit him from recognizing that revelation when it actually takes place. Although it is a genuine revelation of God, it is not immediately recognizable as such a revelation. The biblical revelation of God must be permitted to develop its own ontology, rather than be interpreted in the light of predetermined philosophical presuppositions or onotological conceptions which hinder, rather than assist, the recognition and interpretation of the divine self-revelation. If the cross is indeed the criterion of our knowledge of God, as Luther and Moltmann alike insist it to be, preconceptions of the form of that revelation must be abandoned. It is this radical critical principle which Luther encapsulated in his concept of *abscondita sub contrariis*.[38] Furthermore, Moltmann, like Luther, finds no difficulty in accomodating the idea of natural knowledge of God;[39] both concede the reality and yet the inadequacy of this knowledge, and insist that it be modified in the light of the cross of Christ. Moltmann thus paraphrases the crucial theses of Luther's Heidelberg Disputation of 1519 – in which the *theologia crucis* is clearly stated – as follows:

God is not known through his works in reality, but through his suffering in the passivity of faith, which allows God to work on it; killing in order to make alive, judging in order to set free. So knowledge of him is not achieved through the guide of analogies from earth to heaven, but *sub contrario*, through contradiction, anguish and suffering. . . Christ the crucified alone is 'man's true theology and the knowledge of God'. This presupposes that while indirect knowledge of God is possible through his works, God's being can be seen and known directly only in the cross of Christ.[40]

Man's natural knowledge of God may thus serve as a point of contact between the revelation of God and the one to whom it is revealed, but the 'true theology and the knowledge of God' – to use Luther's phrase here appropriated by Moltmann – only comes about through recognizing the event of the cross as an event between the Father and the Son, in which God is hidden, and yet revealed, for those who care to find him.

Moltmann's achievement in *Der gekreuzigte Gott* is thus a *tour de force* which draws upon the Hegelian panentheism of history and the contemporary preoccupation with apocalyptic to reinterpret and thus to re-establish Luther's 'theology of the cross' in the modern period. Although, like Barth, Moltmann tends to ignore many of the critical questions raised by the contemporary Christological debate, he has emphasized and justified the priority of Christology over theology by his brilliant critique of classical theism. Where Moltmann appears to be inadequate is in his failure to establish the foundation of his theology, and to undertake its systematic analysis. It is for this reason that we now turn to consider perhaps the most brilliant theologian currently working within the German theological tradition – Eberhard Jüngel.

Jüngel's theological programme relates fundamentally to the question concerning how it is possible to speak responsibly about God in a world in which man lives, to use Bonhoeffer's famous phrase, *etsi Deus non daretur*.[41] In an age apparently dominated by anthropocentrism, and even anthropotheism, Jüngel may be regarded as having developed a theological programme whose fundamental theme is that of distinguishing between God and man.[42] Jüngel's programme involves the engagement with and development of the Christological concerns of post-war Germany, and as such engages directly with a number of important themes and problems.

In his doctoral dissertation on the relation between Jesus of Nazareth and the primitive Christian proclamation, Jüngel developed Ernst

Fuch's contribution to the 'new quest of the historical Jesus' by emphasizing the unity of the person and proclamation of Jesus in the synoptic parables.[43] However, whereas Fuchs and the existentially orientated 'new hermeneutics' tended to regard eschatology as an essentially *anthropological* concept, Jüngel had no hesitation in asserting that it was an authentically *theological* concept,[44] and thus placed himself close to the new line of interpreting the New Testament apocalptic being developed by the Pannenberg circle. Like Pannenberg, Jüngel insisted that 'fact' and 'meaning' were inextricably linked in their historical context.[45] Whilst legimitating critical historical enquiry, Jüngel was thus able to reject the old, and by now discredited, approach, which saw the brute facts of history as the primary concern of theological speculation.

Jüngel's distinctive approach to the historical dimension of Christology is outlined succinctly in his *Thesen zur Grundlegung der Christologie*, given in the course of his Tübingen Christology lectures for the academic year 1969–70.[46] We may begin by considering his attitude to the resurrection. For Jüngel, the proclamation of the resurrection of Jesus (which is peculiar to the Christian faith) must be investigated in two manners: first, on the basis of the historical (*historisch*) origins of the tradition of the resurrection; second, on the basis of the *religionsgeschichtlich* context of the representation of the resurrection.[47] On the historical side, Jüngel indicates that there are excellent reasons for supposing that, shortly after Jesus' death, analogous events were experienced by various individuals (such as Peter and subsequently Paul) and interpreted as meaning that Jesus was alive, thus permitting and obliging them to witness to Jesus Christ.[48] Jüngel regards it as being historically significant that the tradition does not refer to any of these individuals doubting this event.[49] On the *religionsgeschichtlich* side, Jüngel suggests that the apocalyptic context was suggestive, but not of decisive significance, in establishing the interpretation of the appearances of Jesus after his death as his *resurrection from the dead*.[50] The apocalyptic understanding of the world (*Vorstellungswelt*) and its expectations were, in fact, at odds with the present resurrection of a *single* individual, in that the future resurrection of all the dead was envisaged. Furthermore, the fact that *proclamation* of the resurrection was required to generate faith – linked with the fact that the appearance of the Messiah or Son of Man was invisible to the world at large – further differentiated the Christian account of the resurrection from that of apocalypticism.[51] Jüngel thus suggests that the event (*Ereignis*) of the resurrection of Jesus must be regarded as *sui generis*, possessing a 'once-for-all' character (*Einmaligkeit*) which cannot be verified by analogy, partly on account of the interpretation placed upon it by the *kerygma* as the eschatological act of God – which immediately raises critical questions concerning the unity of Jesus with God, and the purity of faith in God.[52] For Jüngel, the resurrection of Jesus is the example *par excellence* of the interpenetration of event and meaning in the narrative tradition underlying the Christian proclamation. Christological language in general is language which refuses to isolate event and interpretation.[53] The New Testament accounts of the resurrection of Jesus thus represent a complex and irreducible mixture of historical and dogmatic truth-affirmations (*Verwechslung und Vermischung historischer und dogmatischer Wahrnehmung*),[54] in which the Easter faith has resulted in the revision of the significance of the formative events of the narrative tradition underlying the *kerygma*. Jüngel thus affirms the general estimate of the New Testament, and particularly the gospels, as *theological* documents, containing a complex mixture of dogmatic and historical affirmations which legitimates historical enquiry as a means of stimulating dogmatic reflection upon the present significance of Christ.[55] Jüngel thus lays a complex historical and dogmatic framework for his Christological affirmations, by which historical enquiry is allocated a genuine and significant role in dogmatic theology, without thereby permitting theology to be reduced to history.

Why is the resurrection important? For Pannenberg, the importance of the resurrection, as we noted in the previous chapter, lay in its significance as revelation. Jüngel, however, develops a position closer to that of Moltmann. The resurrection discloses the relation of the death of Jesus to God, in that God is disclosed as identifying himself with the crucified Christ.[56] Faith recognizes the crucified man Jesus of Nazareth as identical with God. Jüngel thus follows Pannenberg's insistence that the dogmatic problem of the incarnation follows in the *ordo cognoscendi* from the death and resurrection of Christ, as opposed to those who regard the incarnation as establishing the significance of Christ's death and resurrection:[57] like Moltmann, however Jüngel links the death and resurrection of Jesus in a manner which differentiates him from Pannenberg. Although it is not clear, at points, whether Jüngel is suggesting that God is *identical* with, or that God *identifies himself* with, the crucified Jesus, it is clear that we are dealing with a theology of the 'crucified God'.

In his major study *Gott als Geheimnis der Welt*, Jüngel deals with the crucial question of how it is possible and meaningful to speak of God in a world from which he has been displaced.[58] Like Moltmann, Jüngel firmly anchors the Christian understanding of God in the crucified Christ. A member of a church theological committee considering the relation between the *theologia crucis* and the proclamation of the church,[59] and himself an able Luther scholar,[60] the contemporary importance of Luther's *theologia crucis* had not escaped him. For Jüngel, faith in the crucified Jesus Christ leads to the heart of Christian belief. Christian theology is thus essentially *theologia crucifixi*. As with Moltmann, the cross is established as the criterion of a correct understanding of God:

> The mode of speaking of the Christian tradition (*die christliche Sprachüberlieferung*) insists that *we must be told* what we are to *think* of the word 'God'. It is thus presupposed that only the God who speaks (*der redende Gott*) himself can finally tell us what we are to understand by the word 'God'. Theology expresses this fact with the category of revelation...When we attempt to think of God as the one who communicates and expresses himself in the man Jesus, it must be remembered that, in fact, this man was *crucified*, that he was killed in the name of the law of God. The one who was crucified is thus precisely the concrete definition (*Realdefinition*) of what is meant by the word 'God', for responsible Christian use of the word. Christian theology is thus fundamentally a 'theology of the one who was crucified' (*Theologie des Gekreuzigten*).[61]

(The German term *Realdefinition* conveys the idea of *tangibility*, which is difficult to express in English – the translation 'concrete definition' represents our attempt to convey the nuances of the German.) Christian theology is therefore *theologia crucifixi*. It is significant that Jüngel locates the origins of all heresy in the refusal or reluctance to recognise God in Jesus Christ.[62] Theology is therefore concerned with the unfolding of the knowledge of God which is to be had from the crucified Christ. An excellent example of the application of this epistemological programme may be found in his discussion of the foundations of the doctrine of the Trinity.[63]

For Jüngel, the resurrection of Jesus Christ is the revelation of the Lordship of the one who was crucified (*die Offenbarung der Herrschaft des Gekreuzigten*).[64] Moving away from Pannenberg's interpretation of the nature of the resurrection as revelation, Jüngel develops the theological significance of the historical link between the one who was crucified and the one who is risen again. With Moltmann, Jüngel insists that that resurrection only attains its full meaning if it is understood *as the resurrection of the one who was crucified*. In the case of Pannenberg, of course, the resurrection has an epistemological function essentially independent of the crucifixion, and the critical reader of his *Grundzüge der Christologie* is left with the impression that the death of Jesus is purely incidental, being merely the necessary precondition of resurrection. Jüngel and Moltmann alike re-establish the historical and theological continuity between the crucifixion and resurrection, which Pannenberg must be regarded as weakening, by their frequent repetition of formulae such as 'the resurrection of the one who was crucified' (*die Auferstehung des Gekreuzigten*). This is not to say that Jüngel does not regard the resurrection as revelation in its own right: rather, he insists that this 'revelation' cannot adequately be understood in terms such as the ultimate meaning of history, but only in terms relating to the nature of God himself. The resurrection is the event in which God demonstrates his unity with Jesus,[65] identifying himself with the dead Jesus.[66] The resurrection thus permits the crucifixion to be viewed in a new light, in that God's self-differentiated nature is revealed in the event (*Ereignis*) of his self-identification with the one who was crucified. This identification of God with the dead Jesus raises a number of questions (the 'death of God' himself being one to which which shall sortly return) – particularly the question of the new distinction it is necessary to acknowledge, on the basis of this self-identification of God with the one who was crucified, between 'God' and 'God'. As Jüngel states: 'The knowledge of the identification of God with Jesus necessitates the distinction of God from God.'[67] The New Testament itself makes such a distinction, when it distinguishes God the Son (the crucified Jesus) from God the Father (who raised him from the dead).[68] This 'self-differentiation' (*Selbstdifferenzierung* or *Selbstunterscheidung*) within God, recognized on the basis of the relation between the resurrection and the crucifixion, not merely constitutes the basis of the doctrine of the Trinity, but forms the basis of the Christian critique of monotheism, metaphysical theism, and the atheism which corresponds to these concepts of God.[69] The third 'person' of the Trinity, the Holy Spirit, is regarded as the bond of unity between these apparently irreconcilable aspects of God – the God who gives life and the God who dies; the God who loves, and the God who is loved. The foundation of the doctrine of the Holy Spirit lies in the recognition that, even with this most dreadful tension within the Godhead, God does not cease to be *one* and *living*.[70] This assertion, however, brings us immediately to the question of the 'death of God', one of the more intriguing questions to have been thrown up by the post-war Christological debate.

The idea of the 'death of God' attracted considerable attention during the 1960s,[71] frequent reference being made to its poetical expression in the dreadful *Predigt des toten Christus vom Weltgebäude herab, dass kein Gott sei* of the nineteenth century visionary Jean Paul (Johann Paul Friedrich Richter), in which the dead Christ proclaims that there is no God. The origins of the modern use of the phrase may be traced to Hegel.[72] Sometime around 1641, Johannes Rist composed a hymn whose second verse runs thus:

> O grosse Not!
> Gott selbst liegt tot.
> Am Kreuz ist er gestorben;
> hat dadurch das Himmelreich
> uns aus Lieb erworben.[73]

The second line of this hymn – 'God himself lies dead' – is quite striking, to say the least (so much so, in fact, that the modern version amends it to read *Gotts Sohn liegt tot*, 'the Son of God lies dead').[74] This remarkable hymn attracted the attention of Hegel: anxious not to be classed an atheist at a time when political circumstances made this inopportune, he was able to develop his speculative theology of the 'death of God' without undue criticism by reminding his audience that he was simply quoting a 'Lutheran hymn'. Hegel transforms this theological affirmation into the philosophical idea of the 'truth and harshness of God-forsakenness' – that is, the basic atheistic feeling of the modern period, to which Hegel's philosophy of the Absolute was addressed.[75] It must, however, be understood that the place of the concept of the 'death of God' in Hegel's dialectical system relates to the dialectical presupposition that the Absolute posits itself only as it opposes itself. The Absolute opposes itself, thus negating itself (and at this moment may be said to 'die') – but this negation is then itself negated in the dialectical process. The 'death of God' is thus conceived by Hegel as a 'moment' in which God confirms himself, denoting a transition in which God may be said to come to be himself. This 'death' is essentially a transition in which the counterpart of the finite within the dialectical process reaches its greatest depth – a 'speculative Good Friday' (*spekulative Karfreitag*) – as an extreme of antithetical finitude, prior to its negation within the dialectical process of becoming. Thus Hegel argues that the 'feeling that God is dead' (*das Gefühl: Gott selbst ist tot* – note the allusion to the 'Lutheran hymn'!) is 'a moment, *but only a moment*, of pure idea'.[76] It is therefore seriously misleading to treat Hegel as a theological atheist, or even as a precursor of one: the 'death of God' is merely a negative transitional stage in the process of the development of the concept of 'God', totally consistent with his dialectical presuppositions, and linked to the *Zeitgeist* in a remarkably shrewd manner. Similarly, Jean Paul's concept of the 'death of God' was essentially a heuristic presupposition or premise, rather than a conclusion, in his quest for meaning. It was through the exploration of the *possibility* that God was dead that insights were to be had.

The same conclusion is not, of course, applicable to Nietzsche. Adopting Feuerbach's theory of *Vergegenständigung*[77] (discussed in chapter two), Nietzsche argued that God was seen as the correlate of human weakness, either as an objectification of this weakness, or else as an unscrupulous device by which the human race might be weakened and tamed.[78] The idea of 'God' is a monstrous and decadent perversion, obstructing man's own autonomy, will and power. For Nietzsche, the history of man is essentially the history of his gods; 'all gods must die', including the God of Christianity. The 'death of God' is thus, according to Nietzsche, the most important recent event.[79] While Nietzsche, like his madman, ran around shouting 'God is dead! we have killed him!', the gradual process of secularization was achieving something similar to this deicidal programme, although in a much less spectacular manner. The full theological significance of this was recognized by the incarcerated Dietrich Bonhoeffer, who took the opportunity afforded by the increasing trend towards communal atheism to reinvestigate the Christian understanding of God.[80] It was Bonhoeffer's affirmation of the autonomy of the world which did much to prepare the way for the 'death of God' theologies which sprang up in the 1960s, and which Jüngel addresses with considerable insight.

Jüngel insists that it is the Christian faith itself which gives the phrase 'the death of God' its meaning and significance.[81] Yet the Christian faith is based upon the unquestionable presupposition that God is very much alive.[82] How, then, may the phrase 'the death of God' be given a proper *theological* – as opposed to a purely cultural or metaphysical

– interpretation? For Jüngel, it is necessary for theology to reclaim as its own this treasured possession, which has been so devalued and abused since the time of Hegel. To understand *das dunkle Wort vom Tode Gottes*, it is necessary to trace the 'dark word' back to its origins[83] – a theme proclaimed by Goethe:

> Jedem Worte klingt
> der Ursprung nach,
> wo es sich herbedingt.

The origins of theological discussion of the 'death of God' are Christological, as Jüngel demonstrates with particular reference to Martin Luther's theology of the cross,[84] and he thus argues that the contemporary exposition of this theme must also be explicitly and unashamedly Christological. Thus Jüngel points out that talk of the 'death of God' cannot be permitted to refer merely to an episode or experience in intellectual or cultural history, in which man ceases to believe in God: rather, it refers to the specific attempt to ascertain the *nature* of God with reference to the historical event of the death of Jesus on the cross.

This may be illustrated with reference to Jüngel's discussion of the nature of the divine presence at the death of Christ. Drawing heavily on Luther's *theologia crucis*, particularly the dialectic between the *deus revelatus* and *deus absconditus*, Jüngel asserts that God is present, although hidden, at the cross to the eye of faith: faith allows the absence of God to be interpreted as his presence; faith recognizes that God is present as the one who is absent.[85] Like Luther before him, Jüngel is not suggesting that two distinct realms of existence may be discerned by faith and unbelief; rather, he is making a fundamental statement concerning the mode of God's *activity* in the world. God acts in such a way that he appears to be hidden to those who expect him to act in a different manner. Faith, however, learns to recognize the presence of God in the apparent God-forsakenness of the death of Jesus on the cross. Jüngel expresses this difficult idea thus:

> His omnipresence must now be understood on the basis of the actual presence of God in the cross of Jesus, and thus not without a Christologically grounded (*christologisch begründet*) withdrawal of God. The idea of the omnipresence of God must therefore pass through the eye of the needle of the properly-understood idea of the death of God.[86]

Jüngel makes this opaque affirmation in the context of his discussion of Bonhoeffer, in which he comments on the latter's concept of God as the one who allows himself to be 'pushed out of the world' – an idea which Bonhoeffer develops with specific reference to the cross:

God allows himself to be pushed out of the world onto the cross (*Gott läßt sich aus der Welt herausdrängen ans Kreuz*); God is impotent and weak in the world, and in precisely that way, and that way alone, is he present among us and assists us. It is clear from Matthew 8.17, that Christ helps us, not through his omnipotence, but through his weakness and his suffering.[87]

For Bonhoeffer, only the suffering God can help. Jüngel, taking up this Christologically focussed notion of the hidden presence of God upon the cross, and linking it with the ideas developed by Luther in the *theologia crucis*, expounds the concept of the hidden presence of God upon the cross – the mystery of God in the world – as a paradigm for theological hermeneutics which forces the theologian to re-evaluate his concept of God and the manner in which he is present in, and acts within, his world. For Jüngel, this involves the rejection of theism, and the espousal of a profoundly Trinitarian concept of God, shaped by the event of the cross.

On the basis of such Christologically derived insights, Jüngel mounts a sustained and passionate attack upon the 'metaphysical concept of God' (*der metaphysische Gottesgedanke*).[88] It is precisely this concept of God which he detects as underlying both classical theism, and its antithetically conceived atheisms – which Jüngel identifies as *anti-theisms*. In an important essay of 1972, Jüngel pointed out how the atheism of both Feuerbach and Nietzsche appeared to be based upon precisely such a metaphysically conceived God:[89] their critique of Christianity was thus, in Jüngel's opinion, based upon an unwarranted (and apparently implicit) identification of the divinity of philosophical theism with that of Christianity. Jüngel therefore feels able to take the slogan 'the death of God', and employ it against precisely this God - the metaphysically conceived God of theism, who is now 'dead':

The dark word of the death of God, at any rate by forcing theology to make an unequivocal decision, achieves the clarity of an alterative: *either* the unity of God with temporality (*Vergänglichkeit*) is conceived in such a manner that God and faith are things of the past, and atheism is the destiny of the spirit; *or* the unity of God with temporality is conceived in such a manner that previous conceptions of both God and temporality are recognised to have been inadequate, and the way of the spirit can be opened up through the (dubious) alternative of theism and atheism into a situation in which God may once more be conceived in the presence of the Spirit.[90]

Jüngel emphasizes that the metaphysically conceived God 'dies' precisely because his deity is compromised by temporality. The metaphysical expression 'the death of God' thus signifies nothing more than an image or a cipher, expressing the fact that it is no longer permissible, legitimate or possible to think of such a 'God'. It does not mean that God *encounters* death – yet it is precisely this astonishing idea that is expressed in the Christologically-constituted sense of the phrase, 'the death of God'.[91] The Christian theologian is forced to identify God with the concrete existence of the crucified man Jesus of Nazareth,[92] and thus to develop a *theologia crucifixi* – a theology in which the essence of God is both conceived and articulated in terms of the identification of God with the crucified Jesus. As with Moltmann, the cross puts everything to the test, functioning as the foundation and the criterion of responsible Christian discourse concerning God.

In the present chapter, we have considered the new emphasis upon the importance of Christology in relation to Christian theology. There has been a growing recognition on the part of theologians such as Moltmann, Jüngel and others (such as Walter Kasper)[93] that it is necessary to develop an authentically *Trinitarian* theology as a viable alternative to both theism and atheism. That attempt has been concentrated and focused upon the nature of the involvement of God with the death of Jesus upon the cross, and represents an attempt to answer the question: who is the God of Jesus Christ? The growing recognition that Christology is prior to theology in the *ordo cognoscendi* (whatever their relation may be in the *ordo essendi*, and whether the *ordo essendi* has any bearing upon such discussion or not) has led to the identification of Christology and its associated themes and problems as the major area of theological enquiry in the years which lie ahead. As one observer has commented: 'Whatever trinitarian or binitarian claims we now construct, we must above all recognise that it is in essence Christology, as in essence all such theologies have always been.'[94] Even more significantly, the question of whether Christianity can be considered as a form of *theism*, with the enormous ramifications a negative response would have in the fields of apologetics and philosophical theology, has now been firmly placed upon the agenda of contemporary theological debate, and has been identified as inextricably linked with the mystery of the death of Jesus upon the cross. *Crux probat omnia!*

NOTES

1 Jürgen Moltmann, *Theologie der Hoffnung: Untersuchungen zur Begründung und zu den Konsequenzen einer christlichen Eschatologie* (Munich, 11th edn, 1980); English translation from the fifth German edition: *Theology of Hope: On the Ground and the Implications of a Christian Eschatology* (London, 1967). For comments, see *Diskussion über die 'Theologie der Hoffnung' von Jürgen Moltmann*, ed. Wolf-Dieter Marsch (Munich, 1967). The following studies in English are important: Francis P. Fiorenza, 'Dialectical Theology and Hope', *Heythrop Journal* 9 (1968), pp. 143–63; 10 (1969), pp. 26–42; Walter H. Capps, *Time Invades the Cathedral: Tensions in the School of Hope* (Philadelphia, 1972); M. Douglas Meeks, *Origins of the Theology of Hope* (Philadephia, 1974); Christopher Morse, *The Logic of Promise in Moltmann's Theology* (Philadelphia, 1979); John J. O'Donnell, *Trinity and Temporality: The Christian Doctrine of God in the Light of Process Thought and the Theology of Hope* (Oxford, 1983), pp. 108–58.

2 *Theologie der Hoffnung*, p. 124; *Theology of Hope*, p. 137.

3 *Theologie der Hoffnung*, p. 12; *Theology of Hope*, p. 16 'Das Christentum ist ganz und gar und nicht nur in Anhang Eschatologie.' Cf. Barth, *Der Römerbrief* (Zurich, 8th end, 1947), p. 298 'Christentum, das nicht ganz und gar und restlos Eschatologie ist, hat mit Christus ganz und gar und restlos nichts zu tun.' It is reasonable to regard Moltmann's Christology as a development of Barth's: see Hermann Dembowski, *Einführung in der Christologie* (Darmstadt, 1976), pp. 168–9.

4 *Theologie der Hoffnung*, p. 74; *Theology of Hope*, p. 84. Cf. *Diskussion über die 'Theologie der Hoffnung'*, p. 230.

5 Moltmann, *Der gekreuzigte Gott: Das Kreuz Christi als Grund und Kritik christlicher Theologie* (Munich, 4th edn, 1981), p. 10; English translation of the second German edition: *The Crucified God: The Cross of Christ as the Foundation and Criticism of Christian Theology* (London, 1974), p. 5. The Japanese theologian Peter Fumiaka Momose, *Kreuzestheologie: Eine Auseinandersetzung mit Jürgen Moltmann*, (Freiburg, 1978), pp. 40–1, emphasizes the continuity between the 'theology of hope' and the 'theology of the cross'.

The title of Moltmann's book derives from several important phrases of Martin Luther, and the sense of the title would be better conveyed if *Kritik* were translated as *Criterion*, rather than the somewhat clumsy literal equivalent as present. It is recommended that the English translation of this work be checked against the German original before drawing any conclusions of substance.

On the sense of the phrase *eschatologia crucis*, see *Theologie der Hoffnung*, pp. 144–5; *Theology of Hope*, p. 160. The useful study of Richard Bauckham, 'Moltmann's Eschatology of the Cross', *Scottish Journal of Theology* 30 (1977), pp. 301–11, should be consulted.

6 See Alister E. McGrath, *Luther's Theology of the Cross: Martin Luther's Theological Breakthrough* (Oxford, 1985), for a discussion of the origins and development of this concept. The earlier German study of Walther von Loewenich, *Luthers Theologia Crucis* (Munich, 4th edn, 1954) is still useful, although now recognized to be inaccurate. The English translation of this work (*Luther's Theology of the Cross* (Belfast, 1976)) is seriously inaccurate, and should not be used. For the phrase *Deus crucifixus*, see Luther, *Resolutiones disputationum de indulgentiarum virtute*, WA 1.613.23–8; cited McGrath, *Luther's Theology of the Cross*, p. 147 n.168.

For the use made of Luther's *theologia crucis* in nineteenth century German philosophy of religion, see Fritz Buri, *Kreuz und Ring: Die Kreuzestheologie des jungen Luthers und die Lehre von der ewigen Wiederkunft in Nietzsches Zarathustra* (Berne, 1947); W. Schulz, 'Die Transformierung der theologia crucis bei Hegel und Schleiermacher', *Neue Zeitschrift für systematische Theologie und Religionsphilosophie* 6 (1964), pp. 290–317.

7 *Der gekreuzigte Gott*, p. 7; *The Crucified God*, p. 1.

8 WA 5.179.31; cited by Moltmann as 'Luthers lapidare Satz': *Der gekreuzigte Gott*, p. 12; *The Crucified God*, p. 7.

9 *Der gekreuzigte Gott*, p. 10; *The Crucified God*, p. 4.

10 See Wolfhart Pannenberg, 'Die Aufnahme des philosophischen Gottesbegriffs als dogmatisches Problem der frühchristlichen Theologie', *Zeitschrift für Kirchengeschichte* 70 (1959), pp. 1–45.

11 See R. B. Edwards, 'The Pagan Doctrine of the Absolute Unchangeableness of God', *Religious Studies* 14 (1978), pp. 305–13.

12 See J. C. McLelland, *God the Anonymous: A Study in Alexandrian Philosophical Theology* (Cambridge, Mass., 1976), pp. 37–40.

13 See T. Rüther, *Die sittliche Forderung der Apatheia in den beiden ersten christlichen Jahrhunderten und bei Clemens von Alexandrien* (Freiburg, 1949); McLelland, *God the Anonymous*, pp. 78–92.

14 See T. E. Pollard, 'The Impassibility of God', *Scottish Journal of Theology* 8 (1955), pp. 353–64; L. J. Kuyper, 'The Suffering and Repentance of God', *Scottish Journal of Theology* 22 (1969), pp. 257–77; E. Jacob, 'Le Dieu souffrante, un thème théologique véterotestamentaire', *Zeitschrift für die alttestamentliche Wissenschaft* 95 (1983), pp. 1–8.

15 See H. M. Orlinksy, 'The Treatment of Anthropomorphisms and

Anthropopathisms in the Septuagint of Isaiah', *Hebrew Union College Annual* 27 (1956), pp. 193–200.

16 On this in general, see J. K. Mozley, *The Impassibility of God: A Survey of Christian Thought* (Cambridge, 1926), particularly his discussion of Gregory Thaumaturgus on the theme (pp. 63–72). More specifically, see T. Rüther, 'Die Leiblichkeit Christi nach Clemens von Alexandrien', *Theologische Quartalschrift* 107 (1926), pp. 231–54.

17 See the important essay of Isaak August Dorner, 'Über die richtige Fassung des dogmatischen Begriffs der Unveränderlichkeit Gottes', in *Gesammelte Schriften* (Berlin, 1883), pp. 188–377. Dorner, of course, understands the divine immutability to be ethical, rather than physical: see Robert R. Williams, 'Dorner's Concept of Divine Immutability', in *Papers of the Nineteenth Century Working Group*, ed. Walter E. Wyman (Berkeley, 1983), pp. 94–105; Robert F. Brown, 'Schelling and Dorner on Divine Immutability', *Journal of the American Academy of Religion* 53 (1985), 237–49.

18 For example, see Heribert Mühlen, *Die Veränderlichkeit Gottes als Horizont einer zukünftigen Christologie: Auf dem Wege zu einer Kreuzestheologie in Auseinandersetzung mit der altkirchlichen Christologie* (Münster, 1969); Jung Young Lee, *God suffers for us: A Systematic Inquiry into a Concept of Divine Passibility* (The Hague, 1974); Jean Galot, *Dieu souffre-t-il?* (Paris, 1976); Warren McWilliams, 'Divine Suffering in Contemporary Theology', *Scottish Journal of Theology* 33 (1980), pp. 35–54. Momose, *Kreuzestheologie*, pp. 17–9, emphasises the importance of theodicy for Moltmann.

19 *Der gekreuzigte Gott*, p. 179; *The Crucified God*, p. 192.

20 Wiard Popkes, *Christus Traditus: Eine Untersuchung zum Begriff der Dahingabe im Neuen Testament* (Zurich, 1967) especially pp. 286–7; cited Moltmann, *Der gekreuzigte Gott*, p. 228; *The Crucified God*, p. 241. In this work, Popkes draws attention to the parallelism between the Johannine concept of 'self-surrender' and 'sending'. See further Mühlen, *Veränderlichkeit Gottes*, pp. 31–3.

21 See *Der gekreuzigte Gott*, pp. 229–31; *The Crucified God*, pp. 242–4. Note especially his assertion: 'Eine radikale Umkehrung des Sinnes von 'dahingeben' bringt Paulus, wenn er die Gottverlassenheit Jesu nicht im historischen Kontext seines Lebens, sondern im eschatologischen Kontext seiner Auferweckung erkennt und verkündet'; p. 229 (English translation, p. 242).

22 See Carl E. Braaten, 'A Trinitarian Theology of the Cross', *Journal of Religion* 56 (1976), pp. 113–21, for a useful description of this theme.

23 *Der gekreuzigte Gott*, pp. 214–6; 256–63; *The Crucified God*, pp. 228–9; 267–74.

24 *Der gekreuzigte Gott*, p. 201; *The Crucified God*, p. 215. See H. R. Niebuhr, *Radical Monotheism and Western Culture* (London, 1961).

25 For example, *Der gekreuzigte Gott*, p. 182; *The Crucified God*, p. 195.
26 See O'Donnell, *Trinity and Temporality*, p. 147.
27 *Der gekreuzigte Gott*, p. 32; *The Crucified God*, p. 27.
28 *Der gekreuzigte Gott*, p. 185; *The Crucified God*, p. 201.
29 *Der gekreuzigte Gott*, pp. 229–30; *The Crucified God*, p. 243.
30 For example, see *Der gekreuzigte Gott*, p. 266; *The Crucified God*, p. 277.
31 See the useful discussion of whether Moltmann actually dissolves God into history, in O'Donnell, *Trinity and Temporality*, pp. 147–9.
32 *Der gekreuzigte Gott*, p. 265; *The Crucified God*, p. 276.
33 *Der gekreuzigte Gott*, p. 266; *The Crucified God*, p. 277.
34 The reader is referred to the difficult study of Rolf Ahlers, 'Hegel's Theological Atheism', *Heythrop Journal* 25 (1984), pp. 158–77, for a discussion; for further discussion, see Christian Link, *Hegels Wort, 'Gott selbst ist tot'* (Zurich, 1974).
35 *Der gekreuzigte Gott*, p. 32; *The Crucified God*, p. 27.
36 For example, see Bauckham, 'Moltmann's Eschatology of the Cross', pp. 305–8; O'Donnell, *Trinity and Temporality*, pp. 114–5.
37 See H. Bandt, *Luthers Lehre vom verborgenen Gott: Eine Untersuchung zu dem offenbarungsgeschichtlichen Ansatz seiner Theologie* (Berlin, 1958); McGrath, *Luther's Theology of the Cross*, pp. 149–50; 155–69.
38 See McGrath, *Luther's Theology of the Cross*, pp. 158–9. The present writer, having recently worked extensively on Luther's *theologia crucis*, recognized immediately in Moltmann's 'dialectical principle' both substantial and verbal allusions to Luther's concept of the *Deus absconditus* (as expounded over the period 1514–19) which it is impossible to document here, in the very limited space available.
39 See Momose, *Kreuzestheologie*, p. 179.
40 *Der gekreuzigte Gott*, p. 197; *The Crucified God*, p. 212. Cf. Luther's Heidelberg Disputation, Theses 19 and 20: McGrath, *Luther's Theology of the Cross*, pp. 148–9. Moltmann's section at pp. 193–9 (English translation, pp. 207–14) is simply a brilliant contemporary exposition of Luther's *theologia crucis*.

The politicization of Luther's *theologia crucis* has been subjected to a penetrating examination by Pierre Bühler, *Kreuz und Eschatologie: Eine Auseinandersetzung mit der politischen Theologie, im Anschluß an Luthers theologia crucis* (Tübingen, 1981), pp. 292–330.
41 Dietrich Bonhoeffer, *Widerstand und Ergebung* (Munich, 1962), p. 241. The relationship between Christianity, atheism, and 'modern emancipated man' is explored by Walter Kern, 'Atheismus – Christentum – emanzipierte Gesellschaft', *Zeitschrift für katholische Theologie* 91 (1969), pp. 289–321.
42 This theme is developed and analysed in the best study of Jüngel currently available in the English language: J. C. Webster, *Eberhard Jüngel: An*

Introduction to His Theology (Cambridge, 1986). His earlier study (based on extracts from this work) is also valuable: id., 'Eberhard Jüngel on the Language of Faith', *Modern Theology* 1 (1985), pp. 253–76.

43 Jüngel, *Paulus und Jesus: Eine Untersuchung zur Präzisierung der Frage nach dem Ursprung der Christologie* (Tübingen, 1962), p. 87. Note also p. 81, where he identifies the continuity between the preaching *of* Jesus and the preaching *about* Jesus.

44 *Paulus und Jesus*, p. 265.

45 *Paulus und Jesus*, pp. 2–4. For a fuller development of the position outlined here, see Jüngel, 'Die Wirksamkeit des Entzogenen: Zum Vorgang geschichtlichen Verstehens als Einführung in die Christologie', in *Gnosis: Festschrift für Hans Jonas*, ed. B. Aland (Göttingen, 1978), pp. 15–32. In this essay, Jüngel makes the point, already associated with Kähler and Pannenberg, that the meaning of an historical event is inextricably linked with its subsequent out-working in history.

46 'Thesen zur Grundlegung der Christologie', in *Unterwegs zur Sache: Theologische Bemerkungen* (Munich, 1972), pp. 274–95. These theses are referred to initially by *section* (A or B), then the number of the *thesis*, and subsequently by the number of the *page*. Thus 'A 2.117; p. 275' refers to the thesis from section 'A' ('Das dogmatische Problem der Christologie') numbered '2.117', to be found on page 275 of the collection.

47 *Thesen* B 2.23; B 2.231; B 2.32; p. 286.

48 *Thesen* B 2.24; p. 286. Elsewhere, Jüngel makes it clear that the resurrection should not be regarded as *reversal* of the events of Good Friday: 'Vom Tod des lebendigen Gottes: Ein Plakat', in *Unterwegs zur Sache*, pp. 105–25; pp. 121–2 'Wer in der Kraft der Auferstehung Jesu von den Toten das Kreuz Jesu reden, wirklich ausreden läßt, nicht so naiv sein und meinen, Auferstehung bedeute Rückgängigmachung des Todes. Sie bedeutet vielmehr, daß Gottes Leben zum Tode fähig ist und sich nun um unsertwillen den Tod gefällen läßt – mit allen Konsequenzen, die das für Gott im Blick auf den als Weltphänomen ja noch selbstständig redenden Tod hat. Die Auferstehungsbotschaft macht den *logos tou staurou* nicht rückgängig, sondern bringt ihn zur Geltung.'

49 *Thesen* B 2.241; p. 286.

50 *Thesen* B 2.242; pp. 286–7; cf. B 2.244; p. 287.

51 *Thesen* B 2.243; B 2.2431; B 2.2432; B 2.2433; p. 287.

52 *Theses* B 2.25; B 2.251; B 2.252; B 2.255; B 2.2551; B 2.2552; p. 288.

53 See the intensely compressed statements in *Thesen* B 2.215; B 2.216; B 2.217; p. 285.

54 *Thesen* B 2.221; p. 286. Cf. *Thesen* B 2.22; p. 286.

55 *Thesen* B 2.217; p. 285.

56 For example, *Thesen* A 6.1; p. 278. See also the important essay 'Das Sein Jesu Christi als Ereignis der Versöhnung Gottes mit einer gottlosen

Welt: Die Hingabe der Gekreuzigten', *Evangelische Theologie* 38 (1978), pp. 510–7.

57 *Thesen* A 5.1; p. 277.

58 Jüngel, *Gott als Geheimnis der Welt: Zur Begründung der Theologie des Gekreuzigten im Streit zwischen Theismus und Atheismus* (Tübingen, 4th edn, 1982), pp. 1–16; English translation of third German edition: *God as the Mystery of the World: On the Foundation of the Theology of the Crucified One in the Dispute between Theism and Atheism* (Edinburgh, 1983), pp. 3–14. See further P. Lønning, 'Zur Denkbarkeit Gottes: Ein Gesprach mit Wolfhart Pannenberg und Eberhard Jüngel', *Studia Theologica* 34 (1980), pp. 37–71; J. Seim, 'Wovon sprechen wir, wenn wir 'Gott' sagen?', *Evangelische Theologie* 38 (1978), pp. 269–79; Webster, *Eberhard Jüngel*, pp. 39–51.

59 The EKU (*Evangelische Kirche der Union*) committee published two documents of relevance to our study: *Zur Bedeutung des Todes Jesu*, ed. Fritz Viering (Gütersloh, 1967), and *Das Kreuz Jesu als Grund des Heils*, ed. Fritz Viering (Gütersloh, 1967). For the background to this committee, see Fritz Viering, *Der Kreuzetod Jesu: Interpretation eines theologischen Gutachtens* (Gütersloh, 1969). See the collection of articles from these works translated in *Interpretation* 25 (1970), pp. 139–242. For the members of the committee, see *Interpretation* 25 (1970), 132 n.2.

60 For an outstanding piece of Luther research, see 'Die Welt als Möglichkeit und Wirklichkeit: Zum ontologischen Ansatz der Rechtfertigungslehre', in *Unterwegs zur Sache*, pp. 206–33; on his appreciation of the contemporary significance of the Reformer, see 'Zur Bedeutung Luthers für die gegenwärtige Theologie', in *Luther und die Theologie der Gegenwart: Referate und Berichte des 5. Internationalen Kongresses für Lutherforschung*, ed. L. Grane and B. Lohse (Göttingen, 1980), pp. 17–79. Jüngel, of course, is no uncritical admirer of Luther: his comments on certain Lutheran Christological theses are significant: *Thesen* A 5.311; p. 277; A 5.321; p. 278.

61 *Gott als Geheimnis der Welt*, pp. 14–15; *God as the Mystery of the World*, p. 13.Cf. 'Das Sein Jesu Christi', 2.5.

62 *Thesen* B 1.45; p. 283 'Die Ursache aller Häresien ist die Unfähigkeit (die Unlust), Gott in Jesus Christus ausreden zu lassen.'

63 The reader is reminded of Jüngel's 'Barth-paraphrase', in which he developed important insights into this doctrine: *Gottes Sein ist im Werden: Verantwortliche Rede vom Sein Gottes bei Karl Barth* (Tübingen, 1964). For an analysis of this work, see Webster, *Eberhard Jüngel*, pp. 16–24.

64 *Thesen* B 3; p. 290.

65 *Thesen* B 3.4; p. 290.

66 *Thesen* B 3.41; B 3.42; B 3.43; p. 291.

67 *Thesen* B 5.2; p. 293 'Zur Unterscheidung von Gott und Gott nötigt die Erkenntnis der Identifikation Gottes mit Jesus.'

68 *Thesen* B 5.21; p. 293.
69 *Thesen* B 5.5; p. 294.
70 For the full argument, see *Gott als Geheimnis der Welt*, pp. 446–53; *God as the Mystery of the World*, pp. 326–30. Cf. *Thesen* B 5.22; B 5.221; B 5.222; B 5.223; B 5.224; B 5.226; p. 293.
71 For example, see *The Meaning of the Death of God: Protestant, Jewish and Catholic Scholars Explore Atheistic Theology*, ed. Bernard Murchland (New York, 1967).
72 See Rolf Ahlers, 'Hegel's Theological Atheism'; Christian Link, *Hegels Wort, 'Gott selbst ist tot'.*
73 Published in Johann Porst, *Geistliche und liebliche Lieder* (Berlin, 1796), no. 114. For its modern version, see *Evangelisches Kirchengesangbuch* (Hamburg, 1959), no. 73. The alteration to line 2 of verse 2 appears to date from 1915.
74 The controversy over the *Hohensteinisches Gesangbuch*, culminating in the Rostock disputation of 1703, is one of the more diverting episodes in the history of the period. Rist could always have appealed to Tertullian: 'bene autem, quod Christianorum est etiam mortuum deum credere et tamen viventem in aeva aevorum' (*adv. Marcion.* 2, 16; CSEL 47.356.20–2).
75 See Ahlers, 'Hegel's Theological Atheism'. For the modern transformation of this sentiment, see William Hamilton, 'The Death of God Theology', *The Christian Scholar* 48 (1965), pp. 27–48; especially pp. 31, 41, 45 'We are not talking about the absence of the experience of God, but about the experience of the absence of God'.
76 For example, see Hegel, *Glauben und Wissen*, in *Sämtliche Werke: Jubiläumausgabe*, ed. H. Glockner (20 vols: Stuttgart, 1927-30), vol. 1, p. 433.
77 See Henri de Lubac, *Die Tragödie des Humanismus ohne Gott: Feuerbach, Nietzsche, Comte und Dostojewsky als Prophet* (Salzburg, 1950), pp. 39–41. (We have been unable to consult the French original.) For an excellent introduction to Nietzsche, see Carl Heinz Ratschow, 'Friedrich Nietzsche', in *Nineteenth Century Religious Thought in the West*, ed. Ninian Smart, John Clayton, Patrick Sherry and Steven T. Katz (3 vols: Cambridge, 1985), vol. 3, pp. 37–69.
78 For a valuable recent study, see Dieter Henke, *Gott und Grammatik: Nietzsches Kritik der Religion* (Pfullingen, 1981), pp. 39–136.
79 Nietzsche, *Die fröhliche Wissenschaft*, no. 343; in *Werke: Kritische Gesamtausgabe*, ed. Giorgio Colli and Mazzino Montinari (Berlin, 1967–), vol. 5/2, p. 255. See further Eugen Biser, *'Gott ist tot': Nietzsches Destruktion des christlichen Bewußtseins* (Munich, 1962).
80 Published as *Widerstand und Ergebung* (see note 41). For Jüngel's assessment of the significance of the phenomenon of secularization, see his

essay 'Säkularisierung: Theologische Anmerkungen zum Begriff einer weltlichen Welt', in *Christliche Freiheit im Dienst am Menschen: Deutungen der kirchlichen Aufgabe heute*, ed. K. Herbert (Frankfurt, 1972), pp. 163–8. A familar assessment of the situation in English is Harvey Cox, *The Secular City: Secularization and Urbanization in Theological Perspective* (New York, 1965).

81 This is brought out in his careful analysis of Bonhoeffer and Hegel: *Gott als Geheimnis der Welt*, pp. 74–132; *God as the Mystery of the World*, pp. 57–100.

82 See Jüngel, 'Das dunkle Wort vom Tode Gottes', *Evangelische Kommentare* 2 (1969), pp. 133–8; 198–202; id., 'Vom Tod des lebendigen Gottes: Ein Plakat', in *Unterwegs zur Sache*, pp. 105–25. The essay of H. G. Meyer, 'Atheismus und Christentum', *Evangelische Theologie* 30 (1970), pp. 255–74, should be noted in this discussion.

83 See the section 'Die Heimkehr der Rede vom Tode Gottes in der Theologie', in 'Vom Tod des lebendigen Gottes', pp. 106–11.

84 'Vom Tod des lebendigen Gottes', pp. 111–6. The important study of Reinhard Schwarz, 'Gott ist Mensch: Zur Lehre von der Person Christi bei den Ockhamisten und bei Luther', *Zeitschrift für Theologie und Kirche* 63 (1966), pp. 289–351, should be noted here.

85 *Gott als Geheimnis der Welt*, pp. 246; 410; *God as the Mystery of the World*, pp. 182; 300.

86 *Gott als Geheimnis der Welt*, p. 82; *God as the Mystery of the World*, p. 63.

87 Bonhoeffer, *Widerstand und Ergebung*; cited Jüngel, *Gott als Geheimnis der Welt*, p. 79; *God as the Mystery of the World*, p. 60.

88 *Gott als Geheimnis der Welt*, pp. 167–203; *God as the Mystery of the World*, pp. 126–52.

89 Jüngel, '"Deus qualem Paulus creavit, Dei negatio": Zur Denkbarkeit Gottes bei Ludwig Feuerbach und Friedrich Nietzsche. Eine Beobachtung', *Nietzsche-Studien* 1 (1972), pp. 286–96. The observations made concerning Feuerbach and Nietzsche in the section of *Gott als Geheimnis der Welt* indicated in note 88 will be clearer if this essay is read as background material.

90 *Gott als Geheimnis der Welt*, p. 274; *God as the Mystery of the World*, p. 202. The German original is very difficult to translate, and should be consulted.

91 *Gott als Geheimnis der Welt*, pp. 277–8; *God as the Mystery of the World*, p. 205.

92 *Gott als Geheimnis der Welt*, p. 276; *God as the Mystery of the World*, p. 203. Cf. 'Deus qualem Paulus creavit', pp. 289–90; *Thesen* A 6.43; p. 278 'Es ist unverantwortbar, das (auch nach traditioneller Gotteslehre mit der Existenz Gottes identische) Wesen Gottes *nicht* von der Identifizierung Gottes mit Jesus her zu begreifen und zu bestimmen.'

93 Walter Kasper, *Der Gott Jesu Christi* (Mainz, 1982).

94 James P. Mackey, *The Christian Experience of God as Trinity* (London, 1983), p. 247.

Conclusion

In the present study, we have attempted to identify and analyse the main problems, themes and personalities underlying the development of the Christology of modern German-speaking Protestantism from the *Aufklärung* to the present day. The danger underlying any such attempt is that it will either represent an uncritical paraphrase of given individuals' contributions to that development, or the imposition of the present writer's views concerning the nature and task of Christology upon his source material. We have attempted to minimize these dangers by treating the development of German Christology over the period as a unitary process, within which previous opinions are subjected to continuing criticism and evaluation, thus permitting that tradition itself to establish the main lines of criticism of both individual personalities and themes within it. This approach is clearly at its least effective when dealing with developments within the last 25 years, in that the tradition itself has not yet had sufficient time to respond definitively to these developments: in these cases, some provisional assessment is provided, although it must be recognized that the significance of these developments remains an open question at present. A further difficulty is that the severely limited space available inevitably means that the reader has frequently had to be referred elsewhere within the literature for further comment and analysis. It is hoped that this will not prove infuriating to the reader without access to library facilities.

It is clear that the development of modern German Christology illustrates the broad features of the development of theology in general over the period. Reason and rationality, 'humanity' and human nature, history and 'historicism' – these themes which, in various ways, have dominated the development of theology in the modern period are of importance to our study. The rise, and subsequent decline, of liberalism and the dialectical theology are as evident in the development of Christology as they are elsewhere. The present study may therefore be regarded as a 'case-study' in the development of modern theology in general. It is, however, also clear that there are certain themes which are peculiar to, or of particular importance in relation to, the development of modern German Christology. In this concluding chapter, we propose to indicate briefly three main themes and problems which have dominated the development of the Christology of German-speaking Protestantism since 1750, and which have been discussed in this work. These are the understandings of:

(1) history;
(2) the nature of the New Testament sources for Christology;
(3) the apocalyptic orientation of the New Testament sources.

We shall note these three points individually.

(1) *The understanding of history.* The early representatives of the *Aufklärung* regarded history with distaste, in that it was regarded as an inadequate basis for the truths of reason. The strongly rationalist concept of 'truth', inherited from Descartes and Spinoza, predisposed the early *Aufklärer* to exclude history from serious consideration in the search for truth. It is this negative attitude to history in general, rather than the specific case of the history of Jesus of Nazareth, which underlies Lessing's famous statement: 'The accidental truths of history can never become a proof for the necessary truths of reason.' This attitude to history was called into question by the rise of empiricism, which held that truth could be arrived at from the contingent natural order.[1] One result of this tension between rationalism and empiricism within the later *Aufklärung* was an increasing interest in history *as a source of knowledge*. The force of Lessing's *dictum*, which rested upon an essentially static view of reality, was therefore greatly reduced, possibly to the point of near-insignificance,[2] not by any *theological* development, but simply through the rise of a different understanding of the nature of reality.

Interest in the historical aspects of Christology (in other words, the historical significance of the history of Jesus of Nazareth) was further stimulated in the nineteenth century through the rise of an understanding of reality which differed from that of late eighteenth century empiricism – that of historicism. The historicizing of the human consciousness is one of the more significant developments in our survey. Its origins are not clear, and it is possible that they may lie with the distaste of the Romantics for the concept of history they found in the *philosophes* and *Weltweiser*: the term *Historismus* is found in the writings of Friedrich Schlegel for the year 1797.[3] There was a general tendency to suppose that it was possible to reconstruct the past *wie es eigentlich gewesen*, a supposition which lay behind some of the attempts to reconstruct the 'Jesus of history' (as opposed to the dogmatic 'Christ of faith'). The full Christological significance of the historicization of reality was first indicated by Ernst Troeltsch: the history of Jesus of Nazareth could not be regarded as exempt from the critical historical method, and as such, could be examined on the basis of the normal methods of critical history. Of particular importance was Troeltsch's enunciation of the principle of analogy, which called into question, not merely the resurrection of Jesus (in so far as this was without present-day analogues), but also any claim to uniqueness upon the part of Jesus.

This challenge was met in two manners in the twentieth century. First, a school of thought arose which held that it was possible and necessary to distinguish *event* and *meaning* in history. Martin Kähler, and subsequently Rudolf Bultmann, argued that Christology was primarily concerned with the perceived meaning of the history of Jesus of Nazareth, rather than the history itself. Developed into the 'theology of the kerygma', this led to the detachment of the *historical event* (the history of Jesus of Nazareth) from its *perceived meaning* (transmitted in the *kerygma*), and the recognition that Christian theology was based upon the latter, rather than the former. The parallel rise of the existentialist understanding of history, and its appropriation by theologians such as Bultmann, further diminished the force of historicism in this respect. Second, the school of thought, of which Wolfhart Pannenberg is an excellent example, which recognized that meaning and event were interconnected in history, argued that Troeltsch's principle of analogy represented the unwarranted extension of an historical method into a view of reality. It was possible, and even necessary, for the undogmatic observer to conclude that the resurrection of Jesus was an historical event. One result of this renewed interest in history is a concomitant interest in the philosophy of Hegel, one of the few philosophers to construct a philosophy of history. It may well be that the years ahead will witness the re-emergence of Hegel as *the* philosopher to whom theologians appeal, for precisely this reason.

(2) *The understanding of the nature of the sources.* The early *Aufklärung* was characterized by its tendency to regard the four gospels as historical sources. The early 'quest of the historical Jesus' was based upon the assumption that all four gospels could be treated as sources for a biography of Jesus. This view is no longer held, with important consequences for Christology. The first major development was the recognition, through the work of Ferdinand Christian Baur and others, that the Fourth Gospel could not be treated as an historical source. Although an embarrassment for Schleiermacher, who relied extensively upon that gospel for his *Jesusbild*, this still appeared to leave three gospels available as reliable historical sources. The increasing recognition (on *literary* grounds) that Mark was the earliest gospel appeared to indicate that it was the most reliable *historically*, with the result that it became increasingly attractive to the biographers of Jesus.

This view became untenable during the period 1890–1901. The work of Martin Kähler suggested that the gospels were actually *theological*, rather than *historical* documents, and thus quite unsuitable as historical sources. William Wrede demonstrated that Mark used history as a framework for his theological statements, thus engendering a strongly sceptical approach to his historical statements. The rise in interest in the *kerygma*, associated with Rudolf Bultmann, led to the development of *Formgeschichte*. It was recognized that the gospels reflected the *kerygma* of the primitive Christian community, so that, although they were unquestionably based upon history, they were not concerned with the transmission of historical details. Although the work of Käsemann and his circle have caused this judgement to be revised slightly, modern Christology is obliged to proceed upon the assumption that the gospels contain a mixture of history and theology which it is impossible to untangle. Among the casualties of this contemporary understanding of the nature of the gospels were the old 'quest of the historical Jesus', and the view that it was possible to reconstruct a non-theological, presuppositionless account of the history of Jesus.

(3) *The understanding of the apocalyptic orientation of the New Testament sources.* The strongly apocalyptic colouring of the synoptic accounts of the history of Jesus had long been recognized, and is of particular importance in relation to Reimarus. The nineteenth century, however, found this aspect of the gospel accounts of Jesus very difficult to deal with. The liberal school preferred to ignore them, in order

to develop the idea of the Kingdom of God as a realm of ethical values. Although this idea persisted into the twentieth century, the work of Weiss and Schweitzer called its foundations into question. Both the preaching and the actions of Jesus were to be recognized as arising from the apocalyptic expectation of the end of the world, and it was impossible to isolate aspects of his preaching or actions which were not thus coloured. The first decade of the twentieth century was thus presented with an apocalyptic view of Christ which it did not really know what to do with. For the young Barth, it demonstrated the total futility of liberal Christologies – but that was a purely negative function. It was not at all clear that anything positive could be done with it. Both Weiss and Schweitzer drew back from the full implications of their 'consistent eschatology'.

The later twentieth century has seen two major lines of interpretation developing, by which this impasse has been overcome. First, Rudolf Bultmann developed the programme of demythologization, by which the apocalyptic framework of the first century was translated into the existential framework of the twentieth. It was argued that apocalypticism was merely the pre-understanding of one age, which required translation into that of another. Second, the Pannenberg school argued that apocalypticism provided the context which gave the Christ-event its meaning, in that it permitted his resurrection to be understood in terms of the dawning of the end of time, and hence as the revelation of God. Although this view has been modified in recent years, it is clear that it is still highly significant. In effect, it is argued that the connection between an historical event and its meaning is such that the meaning of the resurrection of Jesus can only be interpreted in terms of late Jewish apocalyptic expectation – without the interpreter being obliged to share the presuppositions of an apocalyptic *Weltanschauung*. Apocalyptic, which was once an embarrassment, is now regarded as of central importance to the correct interpretation of the history of Jesus of Nazareth.

Anyone who approaches the Christology of the modern period after that of the first 17 centuries of Christological speculation must find himself seriously disorientated. Where, he may ask, is there to be found discussion of the nature of the hypostatic union, so crucial in the formative periods of Christian doctrine, and embedded in the creeds of Christendom? And what of the doctrine of the two natures? And what of the concept of incarnation? As in so many other areas of human knowledge, Christology has undergone a radical change in the last two centuries, perhaps even greater than at any previous period in the history of the Christian church. The questions which so troubled the fathers and the schoolmen, and the Reformers and Protestant scholasticism after them, are not the questions of today. By disregarding the critical questions considered in the present study, others – and the Church of England exemplifies this folly[4] – have failed to address themselves to the spirit of the age, and thus evaded the responsibility of proclaiming Christ in the contemporary world. All too often, English-speaking theologians still present the results of the nineteenth and early twentieth centuries as if the debate ended there and then, with Strauss, Marx, Darwin, Schweitzer, Troeltsch and Freud collectively heralding the end of any attempt to find God in Jesus of Nazareth – but the debate has gone on, and the results have indicated that it is legitimate, possible and necessary to rediscover the identity of Christianity in the crucified God, the mystery of the world. The late twentieth century theologian cannot ignore the crucial Christological developments of the last half-century! Critical historical research does not cause us to abandon, and, as recent developments indicate, even goes some considerable way towards strengthening, faith in the resurrection of Jesus, and the mysterious crucified God. Although the present study is intended to introduce an important subject, it may perhaps be permitted to serve a second purpose – to inform, and bring up to date, the Christological debate within English-speaking circles. In particular, the Christological consequences of the critical historical method appear to have been seriously misunderstood by a generation of English theologians. Modern German Christology since 1960 provides an outstanding illustration of how a correct understanding of this method can lead to a Christological positivism, so that, for the moment, the debate has perhaps brought us closer than ever before to the recognition of God in Jesus of Nazareth.

NOTES

1 There is, of course, a closer connection between 'rationalism' and 'empiricism' than might be expected: see Peter A. Schouls, *The Imposition of Method: A Study of Descartes and Locke* (Oxford, 1980), pp. 1–30.

2 We here disagree with the estimate of Lessing's significance to be found in the study of Gordon E. Michalson, 'Faith and History: The Shape of the Problem', *Modern Theology* 1 (1985), pp. 277–90.

3 See Peter Hünermann, *Der Durchbruch des geschichtlichen Denkens im 19. Jahrhundert* (Freiburg/Basel/Vienna, 1967).

4 See Robert Morgan, 'Non Angli sed Angeli: Some Anglican Reactions to German Gospel Criticism', *New Studies in Theology I*, eds. Stephen Sykes and Derek Holmes (London, 1980), pp. 1–30. Perhaps it would be more accurate to suggest that the developments Morgan documents so well consolidate the dogma of the resurrection, rather than the incarnation (pp. 24–5) – but this is a minor quibble over a fine study.

Bibliography

For the sake of convenience, English translations have been noted in the case of works of major importance.

Rolf Ahlers, 'Hegel's Theological Atheism', *Heythrop Journal* 25 (1984), pp. 158–77.

Paul Althaus, 'Theologie und Geschichte: Zur Auseinandersetzung mit der dialektischen Theologie', *Zeitschrift für systematische Theologie* 1 (1923), pp. 763–76.

— 'Offenbarung als Geschichte und Glaube: Bemerkungen zu W. Pannenbergs Begriff der Offenbarung', *Theologische Literaturzeitung* 87 (1962), 321–30.

Ernst-Heinz Amberg, *Christologie und Dogmatik: Untersuchung ihres Verhältnisses in der evangelischen Theologie der Gegenwart* (Göttingen, 1966).

Karl Aner, *Die Theologie des Lessingzeit* (Halle/Saale, 1929).

Karl-Ernst Apfelbacher, *Frömmigkeit und Wissenschaft: Ernst Troeltsch und sein theologisches Programm* (Munich/Paderborn/Vienna, 1978).

Hans Urs von Balthasar, *Karl Barth: Darstellung und Deutung seiner Theologie* (Köln, 1962).

Karl Barth, *Der Römerbrief* (Zurich, 8th edn, 1947) (English translation of sixth German edition: *The Epistle to the Romans* (Oxford, 1933)).

— 'Die dogmatische Prinzipienlehre bei Wilhelm Herrmann', *Zwischen den Zeiten* 3 (1925), pp. 246–75.

— *Das Wort Gottes und die Theologie* (Munich, 1925).

— *Die protestantische Theologie im 19. Jahrhundert: Ihre Vorgeschichte und ihre Geschichte* (Zurich, 1952).

— *Kirchliche Dogmatik* (Zurich, 1932–70) (English translation: *Church Dogmatics* (Edinburgh, 1936–74)).

— *Fides quaerens intellectum: Anselms Beweis der Existenz Gottes im Zusammenhang seines theologischen Programms* (Zurich, 1981).

Joerg Bauer, *Salus Christiana: Die Rechtfertigungslehre in der Geschichte des christlichen Heilsverständnisses* (Gütersloh, 1968).

Manfred Baumotte (ed.), *Die Frage nach dem historischen Jesus: Texte aus drei Jahrhunderten* (Gütersloh, 1984).

F. C. Baur, 'Das christlich des Platonismus oder Sokrates und Christus', *Tübinger Zeitschrift für Theologie* 10 (1837), pp. 1–154.

— *Die christliche Gnosis* (Tübingen, 1835).

— 'Über die Composition und den Charakter der johanneïschen Evangeliums', *Theologische Jahrbücher* 3 (1844), pp. 1–191; 397–475; 615–700.

— *Vorlesungen über die christlichen Dogmengeschichte* (3 vols: Leipzig, 1865–67).

F. Beisser, *Schleiermachers Lehre von Gott* (Göttingen, 1970).

Ignace Berten, *Histoire, révélation et foi: dialogue avec Wolfhart Pannenberg* (Brussels/Paris, 1969).

Hans-Dieter Betz, 'Zum Problem des religionsgeschichtlichen Verständnisses der Apokalyptik', *Zeitschrift für Theologie und Kirche* 63 (1966), pp. 391–409.

A. E. Biedermann, *Christliche Dogmatik* (2 vols: Zurich, 2nd edn, 1884–85).

— *Ausgewählte Vorträge und Aufsätze*, ed. J. Kradolfer (Berlin, 1885).

Eugen Biser, *'Gott ist tot': Nietzsches Destruktion des christlichen Bewußtseins* (Munich, 1962).

Walter Bodenstein, *Neige des Historismus: Ernst Troeltschs Entwicklungsgang* (Gütersloh, 1959).

T. Bohlin, 'Die Reich-Gottes-Idee im letzten halben Jahrhundert', *Zeitschrift für Theologie und Kirche* 10 (1929), pp. 1–27.

Dietrich Bonhoeffer, *Widerstand und Ergebung* (Munich, 1962).

Wilhelm Bousset, 'Die Bedeutung der Person Jesu für den Glauben: Historische und rationale Grundlagen des Glaubens', in *Fünfter Weltkongress für freies Christentum*, eds. Max Fischer and Michael Schiele (Berlin, 1911), pp. 291–305.

Maurice Boutin, *Relationalität als Verstehenprinzips bei Rudolf Bultmann* (Munich, 1974).

Carl E. Braaten, 'Martin Kähler on the Historic, Biblical Christ' in *The Historical Jesus and the Kerygmatic Christ*, eds. C. E. Braaten and R. A. Harrisville (Nashville, 1964), pp. 79–105.

— 'A Trinitarian Theology of the Cross', *Journal of Religion* 56 (1976), pp. 113–21.

E. Brinkschmidt, *Sören Kierkegaard und Karl Barth* (Neukirchen, 1971).

Emil Brunner, *Erlebnis, Erkenntnis und Glaube* (Tübingen, 1921).

— *Der Mittler: Zur Besinnung über den Christusglauben* (Tübingen, 1927) (English translation of first German edition: *The Mediator: A Study of the Central Doctrine of the Christian Faith* (London, 1934)).

— *Gott und Mensch: Vier Untersuchungen über das personhafte Sein* (Tübingen, 1920).

— 'Das Einmalige und der Existenzcharakter', *Blätter für deutsche Philosophie* 3 (1929), pp. 265–82.

— *Wahrheit als Begegnung: Sechs Vorlesungen über das christliche Wahrheitsverständnis* (Zurich, 2nd edn, 1963).
— *Ein offenes Wort: Vorträge und Aufsätze 1917–1962* (2 vols: Zurich, 1981).
Martin Buber, *Werke* (3 vols: Munich/Heidelberg, 1962–64).
Pierre Bühler, *Kreuz und Eschatologie: Eine Auseinandersetzung mit der politischen Theologie, im Anschluß an Luthers theologia crucis* (Tübingen, 1981).
Rudolf Bultmann, 'Neues Testament und Mythologie', in *Kerygma und Mythos I*, ed. H. W. Barthsch (Hamburg, 2nd edn, 1951) (English translation in *Keryma and Myth* (London, 1953), pp. 1–44).
— *Das Verhältnis der urchristlichen Christusbotschaft zum historischen Jesus* (Heidelberg, 3rd edn, 1962).
— *Jesus Christus und die Mythologie* (Hamburg, 1964).
— *Glaube und Verstehen* (4 vols: Tübingen, 1964–65) (partial English translation of sixth German edition of vol. 1 as *Faith and Understanding* (London, 1969)).
Fritz Buri, *Kreuz und Ring: Die Kreuzestheologie des jungen Luthers und die Lehre von der ewigen Wiederkunft in Nietzsches Zarathustra* (Berne, 1947).
B. R. J. Cameron, 'The Historical Problem in Paul Tillich's Christology', *Scottish Journal of Theology* 18 (1965), pp. 257–72.
Stephen Crites, *In the Twilight of Christendom: Hegel vs. Kierkegaard on Faith and History* (Chambersburg, Pa., 1972).
Wilhelm Dantine, *Jesus von Nazareth in der gegenwärtigen Diskussion* (Gütersloh, 1974).
Daniel L. Deegan, 'Albrecht Ritschl on the Historical Jesus', *Scottish Journal of Theology* 15 (1962), pp. 133–50.
Hermann Dembowski, *Einführung in die Christologie, mit einem Beitrag von Wilhelm Breuning* (Darmstadt, 1976).
Bernhard Dieckmann, *'Welt' und 'Entweltlichung' in der Theologie Rudolf Bultmanns* (Munich/Paderborn/Vienna, 1977).
I. A. Dorner, *System der christlichen Glaubenslehre* (2 vols: Berlin, 1879–81).
Anthony O. Dyson, 'Theological Legacies of the Enlightenment: England and Germany', in *England and Germany: Studies in Theological Diplomacy*, ed. S. W. Sykes (Frankfurt, 1982), pp. 45–62.
Gerhard Ebeling, *Wort und Glaube* (Tübingen, 1960) (English translation: *Word and Faith* (Philadelphia, 1963)).
— *Theologie und Verkündigung: Ein Gespräch mit Rudolf Bultmann* (Tübingen, 1962).
— *Wort Gottes und Tradition: Studien zu einer Hermeneutik der Konfessionen* (Göttingen, 1964).
— *Wort und Glaube III* (Tübingen, 1975).
— *Dogmatik des christlichen Glaubens* (3 vols: Tübingen, 1979).
Ferdinand Ebner, *Schriften* (2 vols: Munich, 1963).
Gustav Ecke, *Die theologische Schule Albrecht Ritschls* (Berlin, 1897).

Ludwig Feuerbach, *Das Wesen des Christenthums*, ed. W. Schuffenhauer (2 vols: Berlin, 1956).

Felix Flückiger, *Existenz und Glaube: Kritische Betrachtungen zur existentialen Interpretation* (Wuppertal, 1966).

H. Jackson Forstman, *A Romantic Triangle: Schleiermacher and Early German Romanticism* (Missoula, Mont., 1977).

Hans Frei, *The Eclipse of Biblical Narrative: A Study in Eighteenth and Nineteenth Century Hermeneutics* (New Haven/London, 1977).

— 'David Friedrich Strauss', in *Nineteenth Century Religious Thought in the West*, eds. Ninian Smart, John Clayton, Steven Katz and Patrick Sherry (3 vols: Cambridge, 1985), vol. 1, pp. 215–60.

E. H. Friedmann, *Christologie und Anthropologie: Methode und Bedeutung des Lehre vom Menschen in der Theologie Karl Barths* (Münsterschwarzach, 1972).

Ernst Fuchs, *Zur Frage nach dem historischen Jesus* (Tübingen, 1960).

— *Glaube und Erfahrung: Zum christologischen Problem im Neuen Testament* (Tübingen, 1965).

Michael von Gagern, *Ludwig Feuerbach: Philosophie- und Religionskritik* (Munich/Salzburg, 1970).

Allan D. Galloway, *Wolfhart Pannenberg* (London, 1973).

Hayo Gerdes, *Das Christusbild Sören Kierkegaards: Vergleichen mit der Christologie Hegels und Schleiermachers* (Düsseldorf, 1960).

Brian A. Gerrish, 'The Possibility of an Historical Theology: An Appraisal of Troeltsch', in id., *The Old Protestantism and the New: Essays on the Reformation Heritage* (Edinburgh, 1982), pp. 208–29.

— 'Jesus, Myth and History: Troeltsch's Stand in the Christ-Myth Debate', in *The Old Protestantism and the New*, pp. 230–47.

— 'Friedrich Schleiermacher', in *Nineteenth Century Religious Thought in the West*, eds. Ninian Smart, John Clayton, Steven Katz and Patrick Sherry (3 vols: Cambridge, 1985), vol. 1, pp. 123–56.

John Glasse, 'Barth on Feuerbach', *Harvard Theological Review* 57 (1964), pp. 69–96.

F. W. Graf, 'Ursprüngliches Gefühl unmittelbarer Koinzidenz des Differenten: Zur Modifikation des Religionsbegriffs in der verschiedenen Auflagen von Schleiermachers Reden über die Religion', *Zeitschrift für Theologie und Kirche* 75 (1978), pp. 147–86.

Wolfgang Greive, *Der Grund unseres Glaubens: Die Christologie Wilhelm Herrmanns* (Göttingen, 1976).

— 'Jesus und Glaube: Das Problem der Christologie Gerhard Ebelings', *Kerygma und Dogma* 22 (1976), pp. 163–80.

Aloys Grillmeier, 'Hellenisierung-Judaisierung des Christentums als Deuteprinzipien der Geschichte des kirchlichen Dogmas', *Scholastik* 33 (1958), pp. 321–55; 528–58.

Wilfried Groll, *Ernst Troeltsch und Karl Barth: Kontinuität im Widerspruch* (Munich, 1978).

Ernst Guenther, *Die Entwicklung der Lehre von der Person Christi im 19. Jahrhundert* (Tübingen, 1911).

Helmut G. Harder and W. Taylor Stevenson, 'The Continuity of Faith and History in the Theology of Wolfhart Pannenberg: Toward an Erotics of History', *Journal of Religion* 51 (1971), pp. 34–56.

Adolf von Harnack, *Das Wesen des Christentums* (Leipzig, 1906).

Horton Harris, *The Tübingen School* (Oxford, 1975).

Van A. Harvey, *The Historian and the Believer: The Morality of Historical Knowledge and Christian Belief* (London, 1967).

Paul Hazard, *La crise de la conscience européene (1680–1715)* (3 vols: Paris, 1935).

— *La pensée européene au XVIIIe siècle de Montesquieu à Lessing* (3 vols: Paris, 1946).

G. W. F. Hegel, *Werke* (18 vols: Berlin, 1832–45).

Ian Henderson, 'Der Historiker und der Theologe', in *Der historische Jesus und der kerygmatische Christus*, eds. H. Ristow and K. Matthiae (Berlin, 2nd edn, 1961), pp. 93-101.

Dieter Henke, *Gott und Grammatik: Nietzsches Kritik der Religion* (Pfullingen, 1981).

Wilhelm Herrmann, 'Der geschichtlichen Christus, der Grund unseres Glaubens', *Zeitschrift für Theologie und Kirche* 2 (1892), pp. 232–73.

Peter C. Hodgson, *The Formation of Historical Theology: A Study of Ferdinand Christian Baur* (New York, 1966).

— 'Georg Wilhelm Friedrich Hegel', in *Nineteenth Century Religious Thought in the West*, eds. Ninian Smart, John Clayton, Steven Katz and Patrick Sherry (3 vols: Cambridge, 1985), vol. 1, pp. 81–121.

Gösta Hök, *Die elliptische Theologie Albrecht Ritschls* (Uppsala, 1942).

D. L. Holland, 'History, Theology and the Kingdom of God: A Contribution of Johannes Weiss to Twentieth Century Theology', *Biblical Research* 13 (1968), pp. 54–66.

G. W. Ittel, 'Die Hauptgedanken der religionsgeschichtliche Schule', *Zeitschrift für Religions- und Geistesgeschichte* 10 (1958), pp. 61–78.

Joachim Jeremias, 'Der gegenwärtige Stand der Debatte um das Problem des historischen Jesus', in *Der historische Jesus und der kerygmatische Christus*, eds. H. Ristow and K. Matthiae (Berlin, 2nd edn, 1961), pp. 12–25.

Carey B. Joynt and Nicholas Rescher, 'The Problem of Uniqueness in History', *History and Theory* 1 (1960–61), pp. 150–62.

Eberhard Jüngel, 'Das dunkle Wort vom Tode Gottes', *Evangelische Kommentare* 2 (1969), pp. 133–8.

— *Unterwegs zur Sache: Theologische Bemerkungen* (Munich, 1972).

— '"Deus quem Paulus creavit, Dei negatio": Zur Denkbarkeit Gottes bei

Ludwig Feuerbach und Friedrich Nietzsche. Eine Beobachtung', *Nietzsche-Studien* 1 (1972), pp. 286–96.
— 'Das Sein Jesu Christi als Ereignis der Versöhnung Gottes mit einer gottlosen Welt: Die Hingabe der Gekreuzigten', *Evangelische Theologie* 38 (1978), pp. 510–7.
— 'Die Wirksamkeit des Entzogenen: Zum Vorgang geschichtlichen Verstehens als Einführung in die Christologie', in *Gnosis: Festschrift für Hans Jonas*, ed. B. Aland (Göttingen, 1978), pp. 15–32.
— *Gott als Geheimnis der Welt: Zur Begründung der Theologie des Gekreuzigten im Streit zwischen Theismus und Atheismus* (Tübingen, 4th edn, 1982) (English translation of third German edition: *God as the Mystery of the World: On the Foundation of the Theology of the Crucified One in the Dispute between Theism and Atheism* (Edinburgh, 1983)).
— *Barth-Studien* (Zurich/Cologne/Gütersloh, 1982).
Martin Kähler, *Der sogenannte historische Jesus und der geschichtliche, biblische Christus* (Leipzig, 1892) (English translation of first German edition: *The so-called Historical Jesus and the Historic, Biblical Christ* (Philadelphia, 1964)).
Julius Kaftan, 'Die Selbständigkeit des Christentums', *Zeitschrift für Theologie und Kirche* 6 (1896), pp. 373–94.
F. W. Kantzenbach, *Protestantisches Christenheit im Zeitalter des Rationalismus* (Gütersloh, 1965).
Berthold Klappert, *Die Auferweckung des Gekreuzigten: Der Ansatz der Christologie Karl Barths im Zusammenhang der Christologie der Gegenwart* (Neukirchen, 1971).
Gerhard Kuhlmann, 'Zum theologischen Problem der Existenz: Fragen an Rudolf Bultmann', *Zeitschrift für Theologie und Kirche* 10 (1929), pp. 28–58.
W. G. Kümmel, *Das Neue Testament: Geschichte der Erforschung seiner Probleme* (Munich, 1958).
— 'Das Problem des geschichtlichen Jesus in der gegenwärtigen Forschungslage', in *Der historische Jesus und der kerygmatische Christus*, eds. H. Ristow and K. Matthiae (Berlin, 2nd edn, 1961), pp. 39–53.
Hans Küng, *Menschwerdung Gottes: Eine Einführung in Hegels theologisches Denken als Prolegomena zu einer künftigen Christologie* (Freiburg, 1970).
D. Lange, *Historischer Jesus oder mythischer Christus: Untersuchungen zu dem Gegensatz zwischen Friedrich Schleiermacher und David Friedrich Strauss* (Gütersloh, 1975).
Peter Lange, *Konkrete Theologie? Karl Barth und Friedrich Gogarten 'Zwischen den Zeiten' (1922–1933)* (Zurich, 1972).
Nicholas Lash, 'Up and Down in Christology', in *New Studies in Theology I*, eds. Stephen Sykes and Derek Holmes (London, 1980), pp. 31–46.
Eckardt Lessing, *Die Geschichtsphilosophie Ernst Troeltschs* (Hamburg, 1965).
G. E. Lessing, *Theologische Schriften*, ed. Leopold Zscharnack (4 vols: Berlin, 1929).

Christian Link, *Hegels Wort, Gott selbst ist tot* (Zurich, 1974).
Hans-Georg Link, *Geschichte Jesu und Bild Christi: Die Entwicklung der Christologie Martin Kählers in Auseinandersetzung mit der Leben-Jesu-Theologie und der Ritschl-Schule* (Neukirchen, 1975).
Karl Löwich, *Von Hegel zu Nietszche* (Stuttgart, 4th edn, 1958).
Alister E. McGrath, 'Justification and Christology: The Axiomatic Correlation between the Historical Jesus and the Proclaimed Christ', *Modern Theology* 1 (1984–85), pp. 45–54.
— 'Karl Barth als Aufklärer? Der Zusammenhang seiner Lehre vom Werke Christi mit der Erwählungslehre', *Kerygma und Dogma* 30 (1984), pp. 273–83.
— 'The Moral Theory of the Atonement: An Historical and Theological Critique', *Scottish Journal of Theology* 38 (1985), pp. 205–20.
— 'Christologie und Soteriologie: Eine Entgegnung zu Wolfhart Pannenbergs Kritik des soteriologischen Ansatzes in der Christologie', *Theologische Zeitschrift* 42 (1986), forthcoming.
John Macquarrie, *The Scope of Demythologizing* (London, 1960).
— *An Existentialist Theology: A Comparison of Heidegger and Bultmann* (London, 1973).
L. Malevez, *Le message chrétien: la théologie de Rudolf Bultmann* (Brussels/Bruges/Paris, 1954).
E. Mechels, *Analogie bei Erich Przywara und Karl Barth: Das Verhältnis von Offenbarungstheologie und Metaphysik* (Neukirchen, 1974).
Gordon E. Michalson, 'Faith and History: The Shape of the Problem', *Modern Theology* 1 (1985), pp. 277–90.
Jürgen Moltmann, *Theologie der Hoffnung: Untersuchungen zur Begründung und zu den Konsequenzen einer christlichen Eschatologie* (Munich, 11th edn, 1980) (English translation of fifth German edition: *Theology of Hope: On the Ground and Implications of a Christian Eschatology* (London, 1967)).
— *Der gekreuzigte Gott: Das Kreuz Christi als Grund und Kritik christlicher Theologie* (Munich, 4th edn, 1981) (English translation of second German edition: *The Crucified God: The Cross of Christ as the Foundation and Criticism of Christian Theology* (London, 1974)).
Peter F. Momose, *Kreuzestheologie: Eine Auseinandersetzung mit Jürgen Moltmann* (Freiburg, 1978).
Robert Morgan, *The Nature of New Testament Theology: The Contribution of William Wrede and Adolf Schlatter* (London, 1973).
— 'Ernst Troeltsch and the Dialectical Theology', in *Ernst Troeltsch and the Future of Theology*, ed. J. P. Clayton (Cambridge, 1976), pp. 33–77.
— 'Non Angeli sed Angli: Some Anglican Reactions to German Gospel Criticism', in *New Studies in Theology I*, ed. Stephen Sykes and Derek Holmes (London, 1980), pp. 1–30.
— 'Historical Criticism and Christology: England and Germany', in

England and Germany: Studies in Theological Diplomacy, ed. S. W. Sykes (Frankfurt, 1982), pp. 80–112.

— 'Ferdinand Christian Baur', in *Nineteenth Century Religious Thought in the West*, ed. Ninian Smart, John Clayton, Steven Katz and Patrick Sherry (3 vols: Cambridge, 1985), vol. 1, pp. 261–89.

Iain D. Nichol, 'Facts and Meanings: Wolfhart Pannenberg's Theology as History and the Role of the Critical Historical Method', *Religious Studies* 12 (1976), pp. 129–39.

Richard R. Niebuhr, *Schleiermacher on Christ and Religion* (London, 1965).

D. Offermann, *Schleiermachers Einleitung in die Glaubenslehre* (Berlin, 1969).

Maurizio Pagano, *Storia ed escatologia del pensiero di W. Pannenberg* (Milano, 1973).

Wolfhart Pannenberg, 'Heilsgeschehen und Geschichte', *Kerygma und Dogma* 5 (1959), pp. 218–37; 259–88. (English translation in Pannenberg, *Basic Questions in Theology I* (London, 1970), pp. 15–80).

— *Offenbarung als Geschichte* (Göttingen, 1961) (English translation: *Revelation as History* (London, 1969)).

— 'The Revelation of God in Jesus of Nazareth', in *Theology as History*, ed. James M. Robinson and John B. Cobb (New York, 1967), pp. 101-33.

— *Grundzüge der Christologie* (Gütersloh, 6th edn, 1982) (English translation of second German edition, with appended postscript from fifth German edition: *Jesus – God and Man* (London, 1968)).

— 'Christologie und Theologie', *Kerygma und Dogma* 21 (1975), pp. 159–75.

Mauro Pedrazzoli, *Intellectus quaerens fidem: fede-ragione in W. Pannenberg* (Roma, 1981).

H. G. Pohlmann, *Analogia Entis oder Analogia Fidei? Die Frage nach Analogie bei Karl Barth* (Göttingen, 1965).

Regin Prenter, 'Karl Barths Umbildung der traditionellen Zweinaturlehre in lutherischer Beleuchtung', *Studia Theologica* 11 (1957), pp. 1–88.

Martin Redeker, *Schleiermacher: Life and Thought* (Philadelphia, 1973).

Alan Richardson, *History Sacred and Profane* (London, 1964).

James Richmond, *Ritschl: A Reappraisal* (London, 1978).

A. B. Ritschl, *Die christliche Lehre von der Rechtfertigung und Versöhnung* (3 vols: 3rd edn, 1888–89) (English translation of the third volume of this edition: *The Christian Doctrine of Justification and Reconciliation* (Edinburgh, 1900)).

Otto Ritschl, 'Der historische Christus, der christliche Glaube und die theologische Wissenschaft', *Zeitschrift für Theologie und Kirche* 3 (1893), pp. 371–426.

J. M. Robinson, *A New Quest of the Historical Jesus* (London, 1959).

Roman Roessler, *Person und Glaube: Der Personalismus der Gottesbeziehung bei Emil Brunner* (Munich, 1965).

H. M. Rumscheid, *Revelation and Theology: An Analysis of the Barth-Harnack Correspondence of 1923* (Cambridge, 1972).

Y. Salakka, *Person und Offenbarung in der Theologie Emil Brunners während der Jahre 1914-1937* (Helsinki, 1960).
Gerhard Sauter, 'Fragestellungen der Christologie', *Verkündigung und Forschung* 11 (1966), pp. 37–68.
— 'Christologie in geschichtlicher Perspektive', *Verkündigung und Forschung* 21 (1976), pp. 2–31.
— 'Fragestellungen der Christologie II', *Verkündigung und Forschung* 23 (1978), pp. 21–41.
Rolf Schäfer, 'Das Reich Gottes bei Albrecht Ritschl und Johannes Weiß', *Zeitschrift für Theologie und Kirche* 61 (1964), pp. 68–88.
Stephan Scheld, *Die Christologie Emil Brunners: Beitrag zur Überwindung liberaler Jesuologie und dialektisch-doketisch Christologie in Zuge geschichtlich-dialogische Denken* (Wiesbaden, 1981).
F. D. E. Schleiermacher, *Der christliche Glaube* (2 vols: Berlin, 4th edn, 1842) (English translation of third German edition: *The Christian Faith* (Edinburgh, 1928)).
— *Die Weihnachtsfeier: Ein Gespräch*, ed. Hermann Mulert (Philosophische Bibliothek 117: Leipzig, 1908).
E. Schneider, *Die Theologie und Feuerbachs Religionskritik: Die Reaktion des 19. Jahrhunderts auf Ludwig Feuerbachs Religionskritik* (Göttingen, 1972).
W. Schulze, 'Schleiermachers Theorie des Gefühls und ihre religiöse Bedeutung', *Zeitschrift für Theologie und Kirche* 53 (1956), pp. 75–105.
Albert Schweitzer, *Geschichte der Leben-Jesu-Forschung* (2 vols: Munich/ Hamburg, 3rd edn, 1966) (English translation of the first German edition: *The Quest of the Historical Jesus* (London, 3rd edn, 1954)).
P. Seifert, *Die Theologie des jungen Schleiermachers* (Gütersloh, 1960).
Christoph Seiler, *Die theologische Entwicklung Martin Kählers bis 1869* (Göttingen, 1966).
Jacques de Senarclens, 'La concentration christologique', in *Antwort: Karl Barth zum siebzigsten Geburtstag* (Zurich, 1956), pp. 190–207.
F. Seven, *Die Ewigkeit Gottes und die Zeitlichkeit des Menschen: Eine Untersuchung der hermeneutischen Funktion der Zeit in Karl Barths Theologie der Krisis und im Seinsdenken Martin Heideggers* (Göttingen, 1979).
Reinhard Slenczka, *Geschichtlichkeit und Personsein Jesu Christi: Studien zur christologischen Problematik der historischen Jesus-Frage* (Göttingen, 1967).
Lothar Steiger, 'Offenbarungsgeschichte und theologische Vernunft: Zur Theologie W. Pannenbergs', *Zeitschrift für Theologie und Kirche* 59 (1962), pp. 88–113.
G. S. Steinbart, *System der reinen Philosophie oder Glückseligkeitslehre des Christenthums* (Züllichau, 1778).
Hans Stickelberger, *Ipsa assumptione creatur: Karl Barths Rückgriff auf die klassische Christologie und die Frage nach der Selbstständigkeit des Menschen* (Berne, 1979).
D. F. Strauss, *Das Leben Jesu, kritisch bearbeitet* (2 vols: Tübingen, 3rd edn,

1838) (English translation of fourth German edition: *The Life of Jesus Critically Examined*, ed. P C. Hodgson (London, 1972)).
Adrian Thatcher, *The Ontology of Paul Tillich* (Oxford, 1978).
John Thompson, *Christ in Perspective: Christological Perspectives in the Theology of Karl Barth* (Edinburgh, 1978).
Paul Tillich, *Systematic Theology* (3 vols: London, 1978).
Ernst Troeltsch, *Vernunft und Offenbarung bei Johann Gerhard und Melanchthon: Untersuchungen zur Geschichte der altprotestantischen Theologie* (Göttingen, 1891).
— *Die Absolutheit des Christenthums* (Tübingen, 1902).
— *Gesammelte Schriften* (4 vols: Tübingen, 1912–25).
— *Writings on Theology and Religion*, ed. and trans. Robert Morgan and Michael Pye (London, 1977).
E. Frank Tupper, *The Theology of Wolfhart Pannenberg* (London, 1974).
M. H. Vogel, 'The Barth-Feuerbach Confrontation', *Harvard Theological Review* 59 (1966), pp. 27–52.
Hermann Volk, 'Die Christologie bei Emil Brunner und Karl Barth', in *Das Konzil von Chalcedon: Geschichte und Gegenwart* ed. Aloys Grillmeier (3 vols: Würzburg, 1951-54), vol. 3, pp. 644–73.
Pierre Warin, *Le chemin de la théologie chez Wolfhart Pannenberg* (Rome, 1981).
Max Wartofsky, *Feuerbach* (Cambridge, 1982).
J. B. Webster, 'Eberhard Jüngel on the Language of Faith', *Modern Theology* 1 (1985), pp. 253–76.
— *Eberhard Jüngel: An Introduction to His Theology* (Cambridge, 1986).
G. Weigel, 'Myth, Symbol and Analogy', in *Religion and Culture: Essays in Honour of Paul Tillich*, ed. W. Leibrecht (London, 1959), pp. 120–30.
Michael Weinrich, *Der Wirklichkeit begegnen. . .Studien zu Buber, Grisebach, Gogarten, Bonhoeffer und Hirsch* (Neukirchen, 1980).
Johannes Weiss, *Die Predigt Jesu vom Reich Gottes* (Göttingen, 2nd edn, 1900) (English translation of first German edition: *Jesus' Proclamation of the Kingdom of God* (London, 1971)).
Michael Welker (ed.), *Diskussion über Jürgen Moltmanns Buch 'Der gekreuzigte Gott'* (Munich, 1979).
Robert R. Williams, *Schleiermacher the Theologian: The Construction of the Doctrine of God* (Philadelphia, 1978).
William Wrede, *Das Messiasgeheimnis in den Evangelien* (Göttingen, 1901) (English translation: *The Messianic Secret* (Cambridge/London, 1971)).
Marcel Xhaufflaire, *Feuerbach et la théologie de la sécularisation* (Paris, 1972).
James Yerkes, *The Christology of Hegel* (Albany, N.Y., 1983).
Agnes von Zahn-Harnack, *Adolf von Harnack* (Berlin, 2nd edn, 1951).

Index